"In the age of super-fast communication, the art of letter writing is a reminder of earlier, slower, and more nurturing times. Diane Charney in her new book *Letters to Men of Letters* gives us a refreshing opportunity to reconnect with important literary and artistic figures. This book is part detailed scholarly research; part entertaining memoir; part sensitive, personal reflection on a myriad of topics.

Beautifully written and artfully crafted, this is a book to be savored, placed lovingly on a bedside table and read slowly on sleepless nights. The author guides us on a journey of ongoing learning and discovery—not only of these selected literary figures but also of her own fascinating and full life. Her willingness to reveal her inner world can inspire readers to reflect on the fine line between imagination and reality, between the ordinary and the extraordinary that gives color and depth to each of us. Readers of all ages can find renewed energy 'to cultivate' a unique garden."

—Susan Roe Gravina

* * *

"I can't think of anyone more interested, interesting or empathetic than Diane Charney with whom to have an exchange of letters. What she has done in this book is to turn dreams into reality. She has the writing, language and educational skills, and dexterity to get inside the heads and works of her authors. We all might wish to have had the intimacy of communication with this collection of greats that only private letters can achieve. Through Diane Charney's work we are able to experience exactly that."

—Ian Morley, Author, Journalist, Founder of Wentworth Hall Family Office

* * *

D1352699

"*Letters to Men of Letters* is fun, thoughtful, clever, and serious all at once, and has made me want to return to old favorite texts and think about what I might say to some of the authors that Diane Charney and I both admire. I was delighted to read about Professor Charney's approach to teaching Proust in jewel-like bites that feel 'like little marvels.' Her Yale office was a place of learning, conviviality, and curiosity, from which we always emerged with a smile and something new to read. These letters share the very same qualities, and have the same effect."

—Benjamin Mappin-Kasirer, Rhodes Scholar, winner of the James T. King Prize at Yale for his thesis on science and the weather in Proust, organizer of Yale University's Proust Marathon

* * *

"Diane Charney's inimitable style and heartfelt immersion in her relationships with her men of letters show how what one reads can be inseparable from the person one becomes."

—Erika Pauli Bizzarri, Author of *Orvieto As It Was And Is*

* * *

"Diane Charney knows more about French men of letters than I, who am French from head to toe. What I take away from her romantic correspondence is the love she has for writers, a love that resembles an endless Russian river, a love that sweeps away everything in its path and commands our admiration."

—Jacqueline Raoul-Duval, Author of *Kafka in Love*

* * *

"With a talent for personal narration and the epistolary form, Diane Joy Charney invites us into her literary salon to reveal the writers and artists who most informed her sensibilities and made her who she is today. In a remarkable labor of love, Charney addresses her subjects directly through letters, giving us a spirited and intimate account of those writers and revealing a deep knowledge of their work and immortal influence."

—Constance Sherak, Yale University Dept. of French

LETTERS TO MEN OF LETTERS

Diane Joy Charney

WE READERS ARE MARKED FOREVER BY GREAT
AUTHORS—THEY ARE NEVER REALLY DEAD.
WE CARRY THEM AROUND WITH US.
I WRITE THEM LETTERS.

LETTERS TO MEN OF LETTERS

Published by Ology Books

ISBN: 978-1-7360206-1-6

Cover design, interior design and layout by Urška Charney

Portrait Drawings by Mirella Daniell
mirelladaniell.it

TABLE OF CONTENTS

About the Author

Diane Joy Charney has taught at Yale University for thirty-three years as a Lecturer in French, in Creative Writing, and as Writing Tutor-in-Residence. She studied at University of Rochester, La Sorbonne in Paris from which she was awarded the Diplôme Supérieur d'Études Françaises and received her PhD from Duke University.

A lifelong musician (piano, flute, viola), Diane studied at Juilliard and the Eastman School of Music. An enthusiastic chamber musician, she enjoys playing in Yale student orchestras where she tries to hide behind the better players and *never* play any unintended solos. Among her other passions are yoga, growing her own food, and tap dance.

She has been president of the Center for Independent Study and directed Yale's Mellon Senior Forum for 25 years. In addition to academic writing, Diane's writing background includes restaurant and book reviews, and poetry. As a student in Paris, she lived in Jean-Paul Sartre's childhood apartment. Her PhD thesis was on André Pieyre de Mandiargues, long suspected as the author of *The Story of O,* whom she met during return teaching stints in Paris.

Her Italian alter-ego, Donatella de Poitiers, authors the blog, "In Love with France, At Home in Italy" (franceoritaly.blogspot.com). She divides her time between Umbria and New Haven.

Dear Reader,

Despite being married to the same man for decades, I confess to having some unusual pen-pals with whom I am quite in love. Among them are Franz Kafka, Gustave Flaubert, and Vladimir Nabokov. Not to mention Albert Camus and Marcel Proust, with whom I am in constant communication by letter. And lest you think I only fall for long-dead guys, I'll add the already-married André Aciman, who had me from the first line of his essay, "Lavender." Further, let's not forget Christo, who gifted me with an enormous, well-wrapped tube of signed posters, in thanks for the poem I wrote about him, "Willing to Take the Wrap: Christo Comes to Tea."

I'm old enough to have met some of the great authors of the previous century. I've often kicked myself, because there were some I was too dumb to realize that I could have met; others I did meet during the formative year that I lived in Jean-Paul Sartre's childhood apartment. An advantage to being an old dinosaur is that I remember the excitement of receiving an actual letter, and in my teaching I am constantly reminded that literature is full of examples of everything hinging on a letter.

Writers like Franz Kafka and Flaubert express and reveal themselves differently in their letters. In pre-email days, I had always been a dedicated letter writer, and a friend who liked what I wrote, regularly threatened to send my letters to *The New Yorker*. I'm not sure what they would have made of them, but I have decided to "out" my own letters to men of letters.

This book features letters, both real and imaginary, that I have written to literary figures with whom I have an intense relationship. Although always passionate about these authors, I was shy about approaching them. And to do so would, in several cases, have required time travel, as most of them are no longer physically with us.

Because I teach French Literature, many of the writers are French. Each letter is part memoir, part intellectual coming-of-age, part reaction to having read, loved, studied, and taught the work of these timeless writers. Libraries are full of essays and literary studies about these authors, but a letter is more personal and intimate. These letters reflect my own relationship with the authors—what they have taught me about myself, but also what they can offer the reader.

We are marked forever by great authors—they are never dead. We readers carry them around with us. I write them letters. It may sound odd to be writing a letter to a dead person, but it isn't really, because they are still with me. The "conversations" I have with them have made me who I am. I can put a flower on the grave of Camus, but he's not dead to me.

In this era, when the humanities so often come under attack, dismissed as off-putting and irrelevant, my book of *Letters to Men of Letters* aims to be accessible, and to prove that truly great writers do not have to be intimidating. They can be approached and reconsidered at any age.

Letters bear witness to how one can have lived multiple lives within a lifetime. And not just in terms of chronology or different phases of life, because a deep epistolary connection transcends time and place, permeating everything, via memory. It can be easy to delude oneself that things may have been as we remember. But letters hold a truth of their own.

I felt this when going through a cache of my own youthful letters, from a seven-year relationship with someone who later became a public figure. This was in service to the current writing project of my friend, a historian, who is trying to piece together and make sense of a complicated life that took more than one strange turn. It feels a bit uncanny to be simultaneously the recipient of a letter and to stand outside it.

Maybe letters remind us that we are all like a puzzle composed of many pieces that may never actually reconnect to become a whole. Some will have gone missing. Others may have worn away here or there, and no longer seem to fit.

Perhaps after reading the above, you will understand why I have found it difficult to use a chronological through-line—what the French call *un fil conducteur*—to embrace my letters to men of letters. Although I can pinpoint a first contact with an author, they regularly reappear. Or to put it more precisely, once having appeared, they are always with me. In fact, I seem to have known them even prior to their official appearance. It's as if author André Aciman, with whom I continue to share many "*correspondances*" (here I am using the French spelling and meaning of the word) read my mind when he said, "Great books...always let us find things we think are only in us, and couldn't possibly belong elsewhere, but that turn out to be broadcast everywhere we look. Great artists are those who give us what we think was already ours."

I've reached an age when it's time to consider more closely the Big Questions—whether to go gently into the night, having poured my soul into painstakingly-crafted emails to friends, or to aim for something in another form. In my field of French literature, I find sobering the image of bookstore remainder tables filled with hard-won works of scholarship by my famous colleagues, who have (as a dear friend who died the week I wrote this essay, put it) "cast their lot with the profession." In using that phrase, she had been referring to a particularly ambitious and briefly successful (before they burned out) wing of the independent scholarship movement. What does it mean that our own little New Haven Independent Scholars' Group, of which I was once president, which has always had more modest aspirations, is still going, even if my friend is not?

*

It's been tricky to try to explain, even to close friends, what this book is about. A college friend, who is an artist in many media, wrote to say that she had finally framed and hung examples of her best work on the walls of her home—a type of self-juried retrospective. In congratulating her, it occurred to me that, in writing this book of letters, in which I am assembling a lifetime of thoughts and experiences with literature, I am doing something similar. As I write these letters to the authors who have marked me throughout my intellectual life, I am working at figuring out what they have been saying to me and perhaps to others—a kind of taking stock of where I've been, where I am, and where I might be going next.

*

I have been haunted by the image of a famously talented writer who was said to have "wasted her brilliance writing copy for cereal box-es." An inveterate clutter-bug (my family is missing the throw-away gene), I have come to recognize my unfortunate tendency to hoard everything—including my own words. Time for a change? This letter to you, Dear Reader, is part of that effort.

Franz KAFKA

July 3, 1883-June 3, 1924

Franz Kafka instructed his literary executor, Max Brod, that everything he wrote was "to be burned unread." We are fortunate that Brod did not comply with his friend's request. Although relatively unknown during his short lifetime, Kafka is widely considered one of the most influential modern writers. The eldest and only surviving son of his upper middle-class Prague family, Kafka felt terrorized by his tyrannical, overbearing father—a successful businessman who constantly threatened his sense of self-worth. Kafka felt like a poor "fit" in many areas of his life. As a university student, he switched from chemistry to law, and ended up working long hours in the insurance industry. In addition to the tuberculosis that killed him, among Kafka's other health woes were boils, migraines, depression, anxiety, and insomnia. Even as a Czech-born Jew, Kafka considered German his mother tongue, and identified with German culture.

Dear Franz,

I fell for you in Shoshana Felman's class at Yale, where I sat in on my famous colleague's seminar. You were a new passion of hers, and soon to be mine. What blew me away was your "Letter to His Father." Anyone who has ever felt misunderstood by an authority figure can relate to this extended letter. Even though it was never sent, it has had an extraordinary effect on so many of us over the years.

Although I was just an auditor in Felman's course, I decided that I would write a paper for it. My first thought was to write a letter to you about what I had learned through reading your work. It has actually taken me twenty years to do that. The medium of the letter seemed particularly apt given the importance of letters in the life of a reluctant "man of letters" like you. But I subsequently changed the focus of the 1996 paper and wrote on a less-studied piece of yours, "A Report to an Academy." I called it "On Dropping One's Trousers at The Academy: A Public Forum Goes Private, As Ape Bares All." Felman had left Yale by the time I sent the paper to her—and it didn't surprise me that she did not immediately reply. But when more than a year later she wrote back to apologize for the delay, and to say that she felt that my paper was "absolutely brilliant," I was thrilled. I will be telling you more about that paper soon.

In class, Felman used to talk about the importance of the signature in both literal and metaphorical terms. Although composed of individual letters of the alphabet, a signature on a letter marks its author. The signature on a letter is, nevertheless, much more than a sign-off. The letter itself can be viewed as a unique type of signature in ways that an email or a blog cannot. This contention—that physical, hand-written letters have a certain indelible magic and author's presence to them that has, sadly, been lost in the digital age—is at the heart of my book of letters. You, who had wanted Max Brod to burn all of your work may be surprised to learn that my discovery of you, which came late in my life, is largely behind my drive to write this book.

You came into my life again when my son, who conducted interviews with fellow writers for *The Daily Beast* magazine, asked for my help as translator for an interview with Jacqueline Raoul-Duval, the French-speaking author of *Kafka in Love*.

Jacqueline Raoul-Duval's *Kafka in Love*, (originally *Kafka, L'éternel fiancé*) which draws on your letters to the women you could never bring yourself to marry, showed me that, in our shared devotion to Kafka, we both understood you perhaps better than the women you left behind. I wonder if you will agree. I wrote to her about this, and we recognized that we are kindred spirits.

Here is part of our correspondence:

Chère Jacqueline,

In my recent message I alluded to a little piece that you inspired me to write. Le voici!

—Best, Diane

In Love with Franz

Jacqueline Raoul-Duval and I are in love with the same man. But we have decided not to fight about it. His name is Franz. If he were still alive, he probably would have found room in his heart for both of us, but without being able to commit definitively to either. That's just the way he was.

Maybe things would have been better for all of us if he had had better luck with respect to timing and genes. Jacqueline and I understand how impossible it must have been to be such a sensitive young man born into a Jewish family headed by a terrifying father who thought his son must have come from another planet. And all this against a backdrop of increasingly virulent anti-Semitism.

Maybe modern medicine could have given him more than the fatal dose of morphine for which he begged to end his suffering.

The skin of an artist of Franz's ilk is paper thin. His own

harshest critic, he is convinced that his work is not measuring up, while at the same time remaining at all costs totally committed to it. It was hard for the women in his life to come to terms with this.

And yet, he somehow managed to find the women he needed in his life to make his mark. That mark was long in coming, but once it did, there was no turning back.

I often wonder how he would have responded to his own success. Would it have spoiled him? Confused him?

I like to think it would have made him happy. When one writes so close to the bone, even a little understanding from others can go a long way.

Jacqueline and I would have offered him this. And we still do.

—Diane Joy Charney February 3, 2013

As you can see, that was several years ago, and it is thanks to you, Franz, that Jacqueline and I have become friends and writing partners. You may have had a hard time finding your own soulmate, but in our case, you turned out to be quite the matchmaker. I have done a number of translations of her work, and we love to compare ideas about you and other authors. In her memoir, *Nuit de Noces,* Jacqueline reminded me that you and Marcel Proust, another recipient of my letters, had been in Paris at the same time, and might have crossed paths. You are certainly doing so in my book. I am often amazed at how much in tune Jacqueline and I are on so many literary questions, and today offered a striking example.

I had never mentioned anything to Jacqueline about that one and only quirky paper I wrote about you. But today I forwarded to her an article by Rafia Zakaria from *The Guardian* newspaper, "Franz Kafka's virtual romance: A love affair by letters as unreal as online dating." The subtitle was: "His love letters were sent by post rather than email, but Kafka's affair with Felice Bauer recoiled from reality in a way that has become familiar in the internet age." Of course, email and the Internet will be foreign concepts to you, and my guess is that you would find them as nightmarish as so many other aspects of modern technology. And what would you think of having your face on the statue of a giant, 45-ton rotating head by Czech artist, David Cerny? A photo of this stainless-steel, mirrored bust that is located in a busy Prague shopping center accompanies the *Guardian* article, and I have also seen a video of the head in motion on the Insider Art web site. Be that as it may, as soon as I saw the title of the article, I felt sure that there would be a reference to Jacqueline's wonderful book about you, but this was not the case.

The *Guardian* journalist tells the story of your five-year largely epistolary relationship with Felice that included hundreds of letters, two engagements, but only a handful of deeply disappointing meetings. As a veteran of many years of a long-distance relationship, I can relate to the disparity between the controllable persona as constructed in writing, and what happens during more direct contact. It's easy for painstakingly constructed letters to become rehearsals or even substitutes for so-called "real life."

By the way, this project has brought home to me some of the reasons why I am the one who is writing letters to you, and not vice versa. Writers like you and Flaubert cast your lot with your writing. You resemble the Olympic superstars I've just been watching at the 2016 Olympic Games who are always going for broke. The long distance running legend Mo Farrah falls, gets up, neutralizes a Kenyan and Ethiopian strategy to squeeze him out, and still manages to win the gold. Something similar can be said about the great writers like you who hung on to go the distance: In the tug between life and work, there was no question that work had to be the priority. Despite the fact that both you and Flaubert eluded marriage, I had already noticed how far apart you and he are from the point of view of character, confidence, and general savoir-faire. Yet when it comes to your writing, you are in agreement about the need for a room of your own. This is clearly demonstrated in Jacqueline's brilliant comparative study of you and Flaubert on literature and love that was published in my translation by *Versopolis*. In your final letter to your two-time fiancée

Felice shortly before dying you wrote: "I am forever fettered to myself, that's what I am, and that's what I must try to live with."

In his final letter to Louise Colet, Flaubert writes: "I was told that you took the trouble to come here to see me three times last evening. I was not in. And, fearing that your persistence might provoke me to humiliate you, wisdom leads me to warn you that I shall never be in." Soon after, Flaubert published *Madame Bovary*.

The question of talent aside, I see that I have never had what it takes to prioritize work over life. I have been happy to be a small fish in a big ivy-covered pond. And to be a fervent fan of a number of those who choose to do otherwise. Most of the authors, you included, to whom I have written were not so concerned with pleasing an audience, or even having one. But I am grateful to be able to have read you all, and to call myself your admirer.

On the theme of being a little fish in a big pond, unlike you, I have been lucky to have jobs I love. I once wrote about myself in the context of my work of helping others to write. The piece was called:

On Being an Inner Voice

So, what's it like to be a Writing Tutor? I've been thinking about why I'm sure this is the best job at Yale. As a start, consider all the temptations of the Blue Book, and how many lifetimes it would take to work your way through our seductive course catalogue. Well, to be a Writing Tutor feels like a risk-free way of being able to take every course at Yale.

But that's only the beginning. As the Writing Tutor, if I'm lucky enough to "connect" with our freshmen, I have the chance to work with them over the four years of their Yale career. What a privilege it is to watch the way students, during their time with us, grow as writers and thinkers!

Then there's the issue of personal style and character. I sing alto. Although I've been a serious musician all my life, when I decided to take up a string instrument, I chose the viola, which in French (my academic passion) is translated as "l'alto." There was a strategy behind my choice of this instrument. My sense is that skilled violinists are easier to come by than violists. Further, although my husband, son, dog, and cats would probably disagree, I've always had the feeling that, even in the wrong hands, the viola never sounds half as wretched as a poorly played violin. And now for the clincher: Every quartet needs one, so even a mediocre player like me can have opportunities to play alongside talented Yalies who make the sound that I can only dream of producing. Because I know how to blend, I try my best NOT to play any unintended solos, which leaves me free to imagine that I have the luscious tone of my stand partner, who might be an amazing player from the music school, as was often the case during our concerts.

In fact, it's rare for the viola to have even an intended solo. Violists generally play a supporting role, and to be an inner voice can give an entirely new meaning and sense of access to a piece of music I think I already know well. Similarly, to help students find their own voice that will allow access to their ideas, showing them to best advantage, gives me great satisfaction. And to be able to build on what is sometimes our initially hesitant relationship is often a delight.

My office, from which no one gets out alive without hearing my "Be like Perry Mason, the lawyer who always wins" spiel, is full of touchstones—reminders of these Yale relationships that go back to 1984. Even though it's been more than 50 years since I was a freshman, I remember as if it were yesterday, the terror I felt at having to write my first college paper. Coming from Middletown High School which, just as it sounds, was neither here nor there, did not help my confidence. I try to make my office feel like a cozy refuge for those convinced that Yale Admissions made a big mistake letting them in here, and that they'll soon be found out—which is just about everyone. For parents to leave their brilliant kids with us for four years has always felt to me like a sacred trust.

In an article from the Escapes section of the *New York Times*, I was moved by the words of a Williams College alumnus who had bought a vacation house close to the campus to be near his son, a Williams undergrad. As an empty-nester, I could definitely relate to what he said: "College towns have such energy. You have all these kids breaking away for the first time, and there's a thirst for knowledge that seems to permeate everyday life. Something about the combination of education, excitement, and fresh, new beginnings makes these towns really vital. They have a culture and community that transcends their small size, and you really do feel younger and more alive when you're here." This dad, who might have been talking about our college, figured out a way to remain close to the town and the son he loved. Although my married son has, for a number of years, lived abroad, I take heart from the students who come my way as they make their own way in the world.

Franz, I find it heartbreaking to contrast the nurturing and loving attention my colleagues and I so naturally give to our student writers with what you had to endure.

But back to the present. You and I have a rendez-vous. It's August 15, when all Italy shuts down for the Feast of the Assumption, and "Happy Ferragosto" is the greeting of the day. This is fine if all is going well, but it's certainly no time to have an accident or illness that requires medical attention. (We found that out the hard way three years ago when on Ferragosto my husband slipped and busted his leg.) Or to find out that you've run out of a key ingredient for that dish with which you were planning to impress your Ferragosto visitors.

This year's Ferragosto turned out to be a day full of surprising serendipity of the sort you might appreciate. Let me explain.

One: In the midst of my writing about you, I googled "Kafka and Swimming" and discovered "The Great Swimmer," a piece of yours that I had never seen before.

Two: And because it was 90 degrees and my Czech friend, Pavla, was hosting two longtime girlfriends from the Czech Republic, she wrote to ask if they could all come here to swim. In an email titled, "It's Czech Visitor Day at the Charneys," I answered without hesitation: "Franz Kafka and I will be here all day, and to have some Czech chicks for company would please him no end. Their male consort is also welcome."

Three: Your "Great Swimmer" piece features an Olympic swimming champion at the very time when, once every four years, as is the case at this writing, many of the world's eyes are on the Olympic swim competitions.

There's quite a difference, however, between your unlikely champion swimmer and American swimming legend, Michael Phelps, who ends his Olympic career with the largest number of medals in Olympic history. As they do in this excerpt from your "Fragments," everyone may be shouting to him, "Hail the great swimmer! Hail the great swimmer!" But unlike your protagonist who wins the swim competition, Michael Phelps does know how to swim, he knows why his country sent him to represent it at the Olympics, and he appears to speak and understand the language of his home country.

Because "The Great Swimmer" piece only appears as one of your hard-to-find "Fragments," I'm going to quote it. As is often the case in my encounters with you, I don't pretend to understand what is going on here. But I can't resist thinking about it. You do this to people. We become charmed and bewitched by what appears to be your natural charisma, you have us in your grip, and then you run the other way as fast as your legs can carry you. The equivalent of this happened with all but one of the women who loved you. But even after all the false starts and broken engagements, Felice Bauer said, "Franz is a saint." (Zadie Smith in the *New York Review of Books*, "F. Kafka, Everyman"). Like it or not, we are all in your thrall.

"Hail the great swimmer! Hail the great swimmer!" the people shouted. I was coming from the Olympic Games in Antwerp, where I had just set a world record in swimming.

I stood at the top of the steps outside the train station in my Hometown—where was it—and looked down at the indiscernible throng in the dusk. A girl, whose cheek I stroked cursorily, hung a sash around me, on which was written in a foreign language: The Olympic Champion. An automobile drove up and several men pushed me into it. Two other men drove along—the mayor and someone else. At once we were in a banquet room. A choir sang down from the gallery as I entered and all the guests—there were hundreds—rose and shouted, in perfect unison, a phrase that I didn't exactly understand. To my left sat a minister; I don't know why the word "minister" horrified me so much when we were introduced. At first I measured him wildly with my glances, but soon composed myself. To my right sat the mayor's wife, a voluptuous woman; everything about her, particularly her bosom, seemed to emanate roses and the finest down. Across from me sat a fat man with a strikingly white face, whose name I had missed during the introductions. He had placed his elbows on the table—a particularly large place had been made for him—and looked straight ahead in silence. To his right and left sat two beautiful blond girls. They were cheerful and constantly had something to say, and I looked from one to the other. In spite of the more than ample lighting, though, I couldn't clearly recognize many of the other guests, perhaps because everything was in motion. The waiters scurried around, dishes arrived at the tables, and glasses were raised—indeed, perhaps everything was too well illuminated. There was also a certain disorder—the only disorderly element, actually—in the fact that several guests, particularly women, were sitting with their backs turned to the table and, further, in such a way that not even the backs of their chairs were between them and the table, but rather that their backs were almost touching the table. I drew the attention of the girls across from me to this, but while they had otherwise been so garrulous, now they said nothing, and instead only smiled at me with long looks. When a bell rang, the waiters froze in their positions and the fat man across from me rose and delivered a speech. But why was he so sad? During the speech he dabbed at his face with a handkerchief, which was quite understandable in light of his obesity, the heat in the room, and the strains of the speech itself. But I distinctly noticed that the whole effect was merely a clever disguise, meant to conceal the fact that he was wiping tears from his eyes. Also, although he looked directly at me as he spoke, it was as if he weren't seeing me, but rather my open grave. After he had finished, I, of course, also stood up and delivered a speech. I felt compelled to speak, for there was much that needed to be said, both here and probably also elsewhere, for the public's enlightenment. And so I began:

"Honored guests! I have, admittedly, broken a world record. If, however, you were to ask me how I have achieved this, I could not answer adequately. Actually, I cannot even swim. I have always wanted to learn but have never had the opportunity. How then did it come to be that I was sent by my country to the Olympic Games? This is, of course, also the question I ask of myself. I must first explain that I am not now in my fatherland and, in spite of considerable effort, cannot understand a word of what has been spoken. Your first thought might be that there has been some mistake, but there has been no mistake—I have broken the record, have returned to my country, and do indeed bear the name by which you know me. All this is true, but thereafter nothing is true. I am not in my fatherland, and I do not know or understand you. And now something that is somehow, even if not exactly, incompatible with this notion of a mistake: It does not much disturb me that I do not understand you and, likewise, the fact that you do not understand me does not seem to disturb you. I could only gather from the speech of the venerable gentleman who preceded me that it was inconsolably sad, and this knowledge is not only sufficient, in fact for me it is too much. And indeed, the same is true of all the conversations I have had here since my return. But let us return to my world record."

I could attempt to tease out some bits for comment—how the fat man hiding his tears might represent your mostly terrifying father, but with whom you imagined in your last letter to him, sharing a beer near the swimming pavilion. And how those two beautiful blond girls at the fat man's side might resemble your dear sisters. And how the intense focus on the voluptuous bosom of the mayor's wife that "seemed to emanate roses and the finest down" might evoke your mother. And how all of this unexpected swimming success might represent your own disbelief at some of your own success, despite your feelings of total alienation. And how the sinister-sounding (not honorific) comment about the acclaimed swimmer's ride to the celebratory banquet, "An automobile drove up and several men pushed me into it," recalls K's execution at the end of *The Trial*.

With respect to the language question, in your Swimmer story, except for the "inconsolably sad" fat speaker, no one seems disturbed by the mutual lack of comprehension. Gilles Deleuze and Félix Guattari, cite "The Great Swimmer" in their highly regarded work about you, *Kafka: Toward a Minor Literature*. There they delve more deeply into the role played by your dual-language heritage.

In your Swimmer piece, I find echoes of several of my other letter recipients, notably Albert Camus (this swimmer and Camus' Meursault might speak the same language) and André Aciman.

But back to my own Ferragosto swim guests from Czechoslovakia. When I asked them what they recalled about you from their school days (Were you presented to them as a local hero?), I got some blank stares. These women who are around fifty and who grew up under communism said they were more likely to have heard about Russian heroes and to have been forced to study the Russian language than to have learned anything about you. One says she vaguely remembered visiting a temporary exhibit focused on you in the context of the mistreatment of Jews in Prague. She recalls the notice outside the exhibit that warned about its potentially disturbing content, but she went in anyway. For her, the content of the exhibit is hazy; similar to the effect on the great swimmer of the ceremony that purported to honor him, all she remembers is that she emerged "inconsolably sad."

What I heard from my Czech friends fits with what I learned in a 1989 *Chicago Tribune* article by Paula Butturini. There's more than one reason why you were not a big feature in the Czech school curriculum:

> Sixty-five years after his death, Franz Kafka's nightmarish tales of anxiety, arbitrary oppression and faceless authority are about to be reissued in the city of his birth. But scores of living Czechoslovak writers remain off limits, their books unavailable, their names unmentionable. By Czechoslovak standards, the decision to lift the ban on Kafka, one of this century's outstanding authors, is a triumph of the changes sweeping the East bloc as a result of Soviet leader Mikhail Gorbachev's reforms.

Do you recall that at the beginning of my letter I referred to a quirky-sounding paper I wrote about you for Shoshana Felman's Yale class, "Literature and Testimony?" I later submitted it for consideration at the Modern Language Association annual convention. I'm going to take a risk by showing it to you and asking you what you think of it. To tell the truth, I'm not so sure what I think of it now, twenty years after the fact. But here goes.

On Dropping One's Trousers at the Academy: A Public Forum Goes Private, as Ape Bares All

What better place to talk about "A Report to an Academy" than at the Modern Language Association convention? And on the topic of public versus private language, no less! Here's the story of an ape who goes from being wounded, captured, and enslaved, to being invited to speak to an Academy. Isn't that the ultimate revenge? And at the end of his report, he modestly points out how well he's learned his lessons from the many self-appointed teachers he's "used up." Henceforth, he does his own hiring, and now when he rings, his manager "comes and listens" to *him*. At the end of it all, he's able to say, "I achieved my goal." Wouldn't we all like to do as much? Yet despite what appears an enviable position, a price has been paid. There's no "free lunch"— not even for such a uniquely talented creature.

"...I am made unlike anyone I have ever met; I will even venture to say that I am like no one in the whole world. I may not be better, but at least I am different." Although said by Rousseau, this apparent reveling in one's originality can be applied to this former ape who has successfully learned to "play the game." It could apply as well to the ape's creator, Franz Kafka. There is perhaps an irony in that Kafka's "noble savage" has not only found a "way out" of captivity, but has come out "on top" due to his ability to mimic his human captors. This imitation, however, was only a means to an end. The ape is careful to point out, in any case, that a "way out" is not the same as freedom. This resourceful personage recognizes that since there can be no freedom for him (what poses as freedom is, frankly, a mixed blessing, anyway), he has found the ultimate coping mechanism: The ability to adapt. Maybe there are lessons here for all of us?

"A Report to an Academy" is full of traps and tricks. First, the duplicitous nature of the title: This short piece does much more than report. Moving slyly from the public sphere of reporting and giving testimony, it can be viewed as a private confession—an indirect auto-biography—one that sheds light on many of the perplexing aspects of other Kafka texts. And like all confessions, it has a hidden agenda. It is a story that begins with a wound (actually, two). But these wounds scar over as the victim proceeds through the various stages of adjustment to his initially inarticulate captivity. Although skeptical of his ability to remember his former life, the ape recovers enough of his past story to help him recover from his trauma. At the end of the process, he finds he has brought about a total reversal in the power structure.

But let us begin at the beginning where the ape addresses the "honored members of the Academy" who want to know about his past—what went into his evolution (regression?) from captive ape to guest of honor:

"*You* have done me the honor of inviting me to give *your* Academy an account of the life I *formerly* led as an ape" (emphasis, mine). The lines of demarcation between the human and ape camps are clearly drawn, with "apedom" having been definitively abandoned. The protagonist accepts the closing of this door of memory as a necessary privation: "I could never have achieved what I had done had I been stubbornly set on clinging to my origins, to the remembrance of my youth" (*The Basic Kafka*, Washington Square Press Pocket Books, 1979, p. 245). As the protagonist submits himself to the yoke of his new "forced career," he feels "more comfortable in the world of men and fitted it better." The opening through which he had once come is now so "distant" and minuscule that even if he could get back to it, he "should have to scrape the very skin from his body" to crawl through: There will be no "going home" again. While noting their common ancestry, in a backhanded compliment/insult, the erstwhile ape states that he feels just as far removed from his ape ancestors as do the gentleman of the Academy (p. 246).

The mocking tone continues as one of the primary rituals of civilization, the handshake, comes under ironic fire. In saying that he hopes to "add frankness in words to the frankness of that first handshake," the ape recalls the shameful history of the betrayals of trusting natives by those in power. By alluding to "the *line* an erstwhile ape has had to follow in establishing himself in the world of man" (my emphasis), the speaker calls attention to the phony role-playing lines he has had to master en route to his current "unassailable" position.

By portraying the "leader" of his ambush as hiding ignominiously in the bushes, the ape shows his own capture to be the result of cheap shots. The particular sensitivity and vulnerability of this creature is underscored by his being "the only one" of an entire "troop of apes" that was hit. His status as chosen victim is further highlighted by the sites of his wounds: the cheek, which he must not have had time to turn, and "below the hip." It is unclear whether the second wound is in the rear (the other cheek), or, as the nickname "Red Peter" may imply, in the genital area.

In any case, with tongue firmly in (albeit wounded) cheek, the victim of what he describes as a "wanton" shot denounces the hypocrites who dare criticize his predilection for taking down his trousers to "show where the shot went in." Unlike them, and unlike the author, he professes to be "open and above board," with "nothing to conceal" (p. 247).

What follows is a type of gestation period inside a "three-sided cage nailed to a locker; the locker made the fourth side of it." It will be from this site, which recalls Kafka's drawing of the three-sided enclosure from *The Trial,* that the ape notes: "I came to myself." Among the several allusions to the slave trade are the ape's desire to see the "windbag" author who criticized his so-called "exhibitionism" have his "fingers shot away one by one," and the posture-contorting conditions of the cage. This gestation period gives way to a rebirth of sorts: "there was a gap running through the boards which I greeted with the blissful howl of ignorance... But the hole was not even wide enough to stick one's tail through... (p.248) Yet after what sounds like an infant's first cry, like a good baby, "he reportedly made uncommonly little noise." Following a rebellious, *angoisse*-filled period of feeling forsaken and beating his skull against the locker, further Christ-like images abound: He was "pinned down...motionless with raised arms...Had I been nailed down, my right to free movement would not have been lessened" (p. 248). Out of the depths of his despair, a logical conclusion emerges: Since according to those in power, the only place for apes is in front of a locker, "I had to stop being an ape."

Following a Camus-like philosophical musing about the distinction between a "way out" and freedom (which he recognizes as vastly overrated), the role reversals continue, as the individual in the cage begins to observe closely those on the outside. In retrospect, his memories show a charitable view of the next "calm" stage, as he realizes that his survival depends on finding a way out, but that flight is not the answer. One thinks here of the dilemma of Kafka himself over how to live, as expressed in his letters and fiction: Flight into marriage would not prove to be the solution; a total commitment to the writing life would be his best hope. For the ape, outright attempts to escape to so-called freedom are full of risks, all of which come down to the "freedom" to be devoured—a fate one reserves for those deemed "other." No, he concludes: To adapt is the only way.

Perhaps in the way that those in the powered majority tend to resemble each other, all those on the other side of the cage look alike to the captive: "The same faces, the same movements, often it seemed... there was only the same man" who "walked about unimpeded" (p. 251). One is reminded of how largely the tyrannical presence of his father loomed for Kafka. But whereas in real life, Kafka was always stymied and silenced in the face of this ultimate authority figure, here, his fictional creation figures out that to imitate these fools—an easy task—will be his ticket out.

Despite some initial repulsion and misadventures, through a combination of motivation and attentiveness to his models ("such a student of humankind no human teacher ever found on earth"—a paraphrase from Rousseau about his own uniqueness), it becomes second nature to indulge in the vices (spitting, smoking, drinking) that the student-ape observes as the hallmarks of civilized man. For successful, crowd-pleasing mimicry of man, all it takes is to swig whiskey, throw away the bottle, rub the belly while grinning, and to befoul oneself in one's own cage.

Like Kafka's effort in the "Letter to his Father" to be his own devil's advocate and offer excuses to temper his father's cruelty, the student-ape takes a charitable view of what looks like sadistic reprisals from his teacher for his occasional failure to make the grade: "He would hold his burning pipe against my fur...but then he would himself extinguish it with his own kind, enormous hand" (p. 252). Unlike Kafka himself, this recipient of the wrath of his mentor has a skin thick enough to minimize pain. Once the ape's "artistic" performance of emulating a human bursts forth to the narcissistic delight of all, there is no turning back: "The line I was to follow had been decided, once for all." The lesson is clear: To model oneself on one's master leads to approval and a type of freedom. "One learns when one has to... when one needs a way out; one learns at all costs... One flays oneself at the slightest opposition" (p. 253).

In an exchange of identities, his first teacher's reaction was to be nearly "turned into an ape" himself, and temporarily "taken away to a mental hospital." Whereas in "The Judgment," the terrifying father accuses the son of wanting to kill him and imposes a definitive counter-sentence of death by drowning, here the newly empowered "top dog" considers it "fortunate" that his mentor was soon "let out again." Yet despite the exhilaration the ape gets from his new "enlightenment," the modest-sounding claim to having nearly "reached the cultural level of an average European" is very reminiscent of Kafka's downplaying, in the "Letter to his Father," of his own educational accomplishments. This was in response to his father's acknowledgment of them: "... You have always regarded me as particularly diligent. It would be more correct to say that I studied little and learned nothing... The sum total of knowledge is extremely pitiable. Particularly in comparison with almost all of the people I know" (p. 220).

Kafka's own modest expectations as expressed in the aforementioned letter are in stark contrast to the ape's empowered position at the end of his report. In this "lawyer's letter" that becomes "the trial" of the father, Kafka charges his father with making his failure a self-fulfilling prophecy ("You are unfit for life") and with placing him in a no-win position with double-binds at every turn. Kafka's movingly expressed aspirations are a far cry from being the guest of honor invited to speak to an Academy: "It is, after all, not necessary to fly right into the middle of the sun, but it is necessary to crawl to a clean little spot on earth where the sun sometimes shines and one can warm oneself a little" (p. 225).

In spite of "a success that could not be increased," the ever-sensitive ape-performer's attempts to share his life with the "half-trained little chimpanzee" from whom he takes "comfort as apes do" only saddens him: "By day I cannot bear to see her for she has the insane look of the bewildered half-broken animal in her eye; no one else sees it, but I do, and I cannot bear it" (p. 254). One thinks here of Kafka's combination of overwhelming love, empathy, and guilt with respect to his mother (whose first allegiance is always to her husband), and of his own verdict in the "Letter to his Father" that he is "mentally incapable of marrying" (P. 230). The ape's portrait of conjugal life is probably what the author feared life would be for the wife of Franz Kafka, whose first allegiance would always be to his writing, if he could continue to write at all. As Camus, in his penetrating thoughts on Kafka notes, "Sisyphus was a bachelor."

Why is "A Report to an Academy" so interesting? In an undergraduate course where this text was read, we all laughed when someone proposed that every Yale graduate student thinks he's an ape, but is trying to hide it: Each worries that he's not as good as the others and will be "found out." Yet he still has the pain/consolation? of thinking he's better than the others, and that no one will recognize this. No one offers greater insight than Kafka into the whole concept of how being chosen (whether like this ape, like the Old Testament Sarah to bear a long-desired son, or like Abraham to sacrifice that son) can become a punishment. We students of literature know what Kafka means when he exposes the double-edged sword of being the "top student."

Readers of Kafka also know that the usual course of events in his work is like the scenario of his "A Little Fable" in which the mouse laments the way the world is getting smaller every day. At first the world seems so big that it inspires fear. Then as the walls begin to narrow, the reassurance gives way to renewed panic: "I am in the last chamber already, and there in the corner stands that trap that I must run into." The cat, of course has the answer that gives the illusion of freedom: "*You only need to change your direction*, said the cat, and ate it up" (p. 157).

Choice in Kafka is usually presented as an illusion. To anyone seeking the right path, the typical answer would be a version of the previously cited cat's exhortation: "Give it up! Give it up!" (the title of one of Kafka's shorter stories). Regardless of how one chooses to live his life, what direction one takes, how one uses his allotment of time and energy, in Kafka's world, the outcome is the same: to be devoured by the stronger. But, aha! What if there were a way to give the impression of having become the stronger, but without completely "selling out"? He who figures this out is sure to be the academy's honored guest. They'll all want to find out how he did it. There always appears to be a market for the morbid fascination with our idols' private stories. We want to know how to become them, or at least to console ourselves (after delving and finding the "dirt") that the price is too great—that we are better off where we are.

In Kafka's writings, we repeatedly see a tortured, difficult protagonist who continues to torture himself and be an accomplice to his pathetic fate. Here, in "A Report to an Academy" it's the opposite— the underdog appears to get the upper hand. Why? Is this really the case? How can it be that a crafty victim-turned-apostle who is merely seeking a way out of his own misery upends the power structure and emerges as top ex-ape?

It is particularly ironic that the role of spreading the word is left to a formerly inarticulate ape, who, like the author, moves from a position of feeling voiceless to mastering the public language, and then to inventing a private one that is capable of arousing shocks of recognition and admiration in a diverse audience.

As is the case of the prize-winning Olympic swimmer who has no idea why he won, no one would probably be more surprised than Kafka to see how, in speaking about his own particular case, he succeeds in profoundly touching a global audience. But isn't this what every writer of transcendent appeal does?

*

Back to you Franz. I find it hard to believe that it's been twenty years since our first encounter. I think of you as a recent passion of mine, but I also have a sense that you have always been speaking to me. I'm grateful to have had this chance, thanks to you, to revisit this old paper that has been longing for a wider audience. By the way, how necessary is an audience? What if Felicia and Max Brod had followed your directive to burn most of your work? Thanks to your mother's intervention, your unsent "Letter to His Father" did not reach its stated audience. But that did nothing to diminish its power perhaps for you, and certainly for the rest of us.

*

I thought I had ended my letter above, but then, as often happens when I am trying to close a letter to someone like you, something comes my way that begs to be included. I think you will see what I mean. What follows is my answer to a precious message I wrote in response to my Writing Partner's comments on what I wrote about you.

Dearest Jacqueline

I can see why you made the association between what I wrote to Franz and your own experience. From what I read (present tense) and I have read, I see that it is not easy even to be a widely acknowledged genius. It must be even worse to be a genius who is not, in his lifetime, acknowledged for his gifts. A similar sadness comes through poignantly in the following words from a letter exchange between another great man who was a genius in his field and the woman he loved, but could not bring himself to marry:

> Unhappily, my nature prevents me from enjoying life, except superficially at brief moments, and it prevents me from allowing happiness to anyone who stays near me. I have lived with guilt in the place where love should have been—and still don't know why I live most of the time in dissatisfaction and with a depressing sense of having squandered and left unused, such gifts as I had. Had you lived near me...you would have lived to share a wreckage of hopes.

This feels as if it could have been written by Franz to most of the important women in his life. To see it is a hopeful reminder that in writing my own letter to Franz, I am perhaps striking a chord with which others can identify. Despite the sadness of the situation, to know that I may have struck such a chord would temper that feeling of sadness.

Albert CAMUS

November 7, 1913-January 4, 1960

Albert Camus, born in Algiers into an impoverished family, won the 1957 Nobel Prize for Literature. His L'Étranger *is ranked number one on* Le Monde's *"100 Books of the Century." But Camus also excelled in ethics, politics, philosophy, journalism, theatre, soccer, tuberculosis survival, and more. Camus was an infant when his father died in World War I, and to support the family, his partially deaf mother cleaned houses. He masterfully conveyed the estrangement of man from himself and from an alien universe. Although often associated with existentialism, communism, absurdism, Camus' lifelong commitment was to the humanitarian ideals of justice, moderation, dignity, fraternity and truth.*

Dear Meursault,

I've been in constant conversation with your creator, Albert Camus, since our first encounter when I was a 16-year-old student.

It wasn't exactly love at first sight, a *coup de foudre*, sort of thing. At first I didn't know what to make of him—found him very strange, indeed. But sometimes a lifelong affair starts out that way.

You may have been guillotined long ago, but you are often on my mind. And when that happens, I feel the need to drop you a line. I am feeling closer to you than ever. But unlike you, I've been put on notice about my mother's situation: At 92, my mother is on borrowed time. How long will she be with us? Well, she looks good, but her heart could give out at any moment.

Maybe I'll still end up like you, confused and traumatized enough to say, "Aujourd'hui maman est morte. Ou peut-être hier. Je ne sais pas." ("Mother died today. Or maybe yesterday. I can't be sure.") But I can't say I wasn't warned.

Unlike you, I'll be trying not to kill anybody else and lose my head over the inevitable. Even so, it's hard not to be greedy and to wish for better news. On the other hand, when the long-suffering mothers of friends were dying, I recall saying, in empathy, "it's hard to know what to wish for."

That's what I'm thinking as I go about my daily business of trying to salvage what's left of my aging peaches, before disposing of the rest.

Once a week, Sunday comes around. Like today, which makes me want to send you a note. I think I understand why you never liked Sundays, but I must respectfully disagree. Here in Umbria, where you might not have lost your head, Sunday is my favorite day. Except maybe on September 1, the start of bird hunting season when anything with wings (but that doesn't sing) is fair game.

Some might think me crazy for suggesting that you, a man condemned for not having remembered whether your mother died today or yesterday, could have gotten a fair shake in mother-worshipping Italy. But here they might have understood how an only son could have been so disoriented by his mother's death that he lost all sense of time.

Though Sunday is no longer the day to find everyone in Italy's churches, it certainly remains a family day on which no one else would intrude. In fact, that's probably what I like best about it. I could do without the gunshots, though. As you know too well, guns combined with a merciless sun can bring nothing but heartache. Although the bird hunt here has a long tradition, as a lifelong bird lover, I hope the hunters miss their target. I wish you had not become a target, either.

I see that I'm not the only one with you on my mind. I've been hearing great things about Kamel Daoud's first novel, *The Meursault Investigation*, that my son says he's giving me for my birthday. According to the review "Algerian Writer Kamel Daoud Stands Camus' *The Stranger* On Its Head" (John Powers for NPR Books), "this tour de force forever changes the way you see Camus' novel." I also see that because I have been on leave this semester, I missed hearing the author speak at Yale this fall. Maybe after I read his book, I will want to write Daoud a letter, too.

Who would have guessed that I would be writing to you all my life? And why is that? As close as I feel to you, I think I need to go directly to the source. Albert, have you been listening?

*

Dear Albert,

I first encountered you as a 16-year-old student at l'Université de Montréal, when we were reading your *L'Étranger (The Stranger)* under the guidance of Professeur Pierre Pagé, who was way too handsome to be a priest. I had no clue what was going on in there, but to be alone in a foreign country for the first time, I, too, felt like a stranger. It was a first contact, but I sensed at the time that it was the start of a life-long infatuation. To try to come to grips with your text is a long-term project, and little did I realize that I would teach that very book at Yale University for many years.

When you were killed in a suspicious car accident (some suspect the KGB, and if your publisher, Gallimard had not been at the wheel, others might have thought suicide), an unpublished manuscript was found with you. An agreement was made that the text would not be published while your wife was alive. Your children chose to publish it after their mother's death. Your wife had said that you would never have allowed it to be published as is, because it was too personal. She knew that you would always write large and then cut away, but this text had not been trimmed. That manuscript that subsequently became *Le Premier Homme* was more autobiographical than anything you had written, and it re-opened international dialogues about you, albeit well after you had won the Nobel Prize. It granted access—a chance to crawl inside your head, in a way that had never been possible before. I love that book, and intend to read it again and again.

It's too bad that you died too soon to know author André Aciman, who might have been thinking of you when he wrote, "The better the writer, the better he erases his footprints—yet the better the writer, the more he wants us to intuit and put back those parts he chose to hide."

In 2002, I left a *pensée* flower and a stone on your grave at Lourmarin, but I never got to tell you how much your work has kept me company for so many decades. This is my chance.

*

Let's go back in time. At 16, I'm the youngest student at the French university. It's 1962, the year of bombs in mailboxes. The radical movement of French separatism is centered at *l'Université*—a fact nobody had mentioned in the promotional materials for L'École Française d'Été—and one that I hoped my parents would not discover until after I had persuaded them to let me study in Montreal. Montreal is just beginning to metamorphose into the cosmopolitan city it will become: The *Métro* is sprouting; islands are being connected to the mainland in preparation for Habitat, the International Exposition that will put Montreal on the map.

It's all very exotic to an innocent born in St. Paul, Minnesota, and raised in Middletown, New York—a place which is, just as it sounds, neither here nor there. Middletown is best known as the BIG city in the Borscht Belt of the Catskills.

As I meander through the side streets of Montreal, Paul Verlaine is my favored companion, especially on rainy days: *"Il pleure dans mon coeur /Comme il pleut sur la ville/ Quelle est cette langueur/ Qui pénètre mon coeur?"* It is here that I learn to be alone—a rehearsal for my 1966-67 Junior Year in France.

Highlights of that 1962 summer experience included my somewhat lost innocence of being in the front seat of a masturbating taxi driver who was driving a bunch of us girls to a Montreal restaurant; and my Montreal boyfriend's burly, shy friend posing as a famous—but not to me—Canadian hockey player of the same name. I now recognize that French summer boyfriend Gérard's calling me a potential Madame Bovary was a bit self-serving: He could tell that I was excited to be with him, but that I didn't intend to sleep with him. Kissing an older French dental student was one thing, but I fully intended to return to my Middletown boyfriend as the same relatively virginal "innocente" I had been at the beginning of that summer. Gérard may have been, as a jealous friend proclaimed, "the best-looking thing around here in pants!" But he wasn't getting into mine.

But back to you, Albert. Your prescience never ceases to amaze me. In today's cyber-dominated world, it's become a cliché to say we have to unplug ourselves and learn to "be in the moment." But you figured that out long ago, and where I live in Umbria, the Chianina cows soon to be beef have mastered this art. I am trying to watch and learn.

To bury our noses in our smart phones gives the illusion of connectedness. My students love to brag about pulling all-nighters, and so-called grown-ups pride themselves on being perpetually busy. To look at the number of domains in which you excelled—ethics, politics, philosophy, writing, theater, soccer, tuberculosis survival, and more—one can see that you knew how to keep busy. But you also understood the trap of busyness for its own sake. As you put it so simply: "Life is short, and it is sinful to waste one's time. They say I'm active. But to be active is still wasting one's time, if in so doing one loses oneself."

*

Flash forward many decades to 2015. I'm wondering what you would think about "Serial," a recent American radio podcast that attracted over five million obsessed followers as it unfolded in so-called "real time." "Serial" is a true journalistic whodunit about a teenager jailed for life after being convicted, on slim evidence, of murdering his girl-friend. As revolutionary and new as "Serial" is touted as being, it may ring a lot of bells for your readers—at least for this one.

Who hasn't, at some point, felt like an outsider, on the margins, estranged? As in *The Stranger*, the murder trial of young Adnan Sayed demonstrated how evidence can be twisted to suit the prosecution's desired story line—forcing puzzle pieces to fit, even when there are too many of them—and how the accused's intelligence, as was the case for Meursault, can become a weapon against him.

Like Meursault, Adnan, having spent 15 years in prison before becoming the focus of "Serial," still comes across as a naïf. What Ad-nan says he wants most is to be seen as a person again, not a monster.

At one point in Meursault's trial, the prosecutor who feels per-sonally threatened by the absurdity of the crime shouts, "Do you want my life to no longer make any sense?" If Meursault would just play the game and say he's sorry, he wouldn't be a threat to others who demand that life make sense—that absurd murders don't just happen because "the trigger gave way." (translations are mine) But Meursault can't play the game because he doesn't even know there is one. In the courtroom, what makes him most sad is to see how everyone hates him and views him as a monster.

This reminds me of Adnan not appearing to understand that his consistent claim of innocence is what's condemning him to a life be-hind bars. At first, in what appears as his naïveté, he could not imagine pleading guilty just to minimize his punishment. Someone more savvy might realize that the hypocritical "just say you're sorry" demanded by well-intentioned moms also makes an impression on juries.

The prosecutor in *The Stranger* loves to make fun of the role of chance as Meursault's explanation for how the Arab ended up dead.

In fact, Meursault is only on that fatal beach by chance, and only has the gun by accident. Ironically, he had pocketed it to PREVENT violence by his trigger-happy friend with the short fuse.

I recently read that you, Albert, said, "If there were a party of those who aren't sure they're right, I'd belong to it." And, "Men are never convinced of your reasons, of your sincerity, of the seriousness of your sufferings, except by your death. So long as you are alive, your case is doubtful; you have a right only to their skepticism." The obituary in *The Guardian* of historian, Tony Judt, mentions that in two of his books, he used quotes from you as epigraphs. One was the first that I mentioned above; the other was "Every wrong idea ends in bloodshed, but it's always the blood of others." To quote Geoffrey Wheatcroft who wrote the Judt obituary, "Camus' words could stand as the mottoes of his (Judt's) own sadly abbreviated but splendid life."

Adnan has adapted well to prison life. Meursault, who ended up literally losing his head, had to learn to do this. He did not understand that deprivation of his hedonistic pleasures was part of the punishment. It seems illogical to him: Why would his smoking or sexual desire for his girlfriend harm anyone else?

While in jail, Meursault concludes that the memory of the details of just one day could be enough to sustain a man for the rest of his life. I wonder if the same could be said for Adnan. As conflicted as I am about what would be the right decision to his upcoming last appeal, I confess to hoping that he will not be condemned only to remember, for the remainder of his life, what life was like on the outside.

I think he would be lucky to have someone like you on his jury.

*

It's probably time to bring this letter to a close. In writing to you, I know I'm writing to someone who understood the value of a letter. And as a teacher, I was deeply moved by the one you wrote after winning the Nobel Prize to thank the teacher who had believed in you.

I speak for myself now when I say that you've been teaching me for years. And to quote you from your own letter to your former teacher, I am grateful for this "opportunity to tell you what you have been and still are for me."

*

(As it turned out, that previous "good-bye" was what is known in music as a "false coda.")

Dear Albert,

Well, it's a new year, and I'm back already. By now you are probably used to my saying goodbye and then circling back with another letter. Here's what happened.

I mentioned earlier that I was told to expect Kamel Daoud's *The Meursault Investigation* for my 69th Xmas birthday. Well, I actually ended up with two copies, one in French, the other in English. As a translator, I think I am going to enjoy the opportunity to compare them. But I'm concerned about what's going to happen to my relationship with your Meursault when the formerly silent Arab who dies on the beach is given a voice. Being so involved with Meursault, I admit that I hadn't paid much notice to the voiceless Arab. In any case, it's not as if Meursault himself actually had much of a voice. Whenever I think of the trial scene, I get sick. After I do some reading, I will get back to you about all this.

*

Mon Cher Albert,

I know I said I was leaving, but here I am again. I even started to write my primary writing partner (who had told me to go to sleep early instead of obsessing about you) that I thought I was mostly done writing to you. But I will never be (which I guess is a big part of my point with this *Letters to Men of Letters* book—you are forever companions). At that moment I had 60 pages left in Kamel Daoud's origi-

40

nal French version of *The Meursault Investigation*, to which I merely alluded in my earlier letter to you, where I said I heard I was getting it for my Xmas birthday, had missed the author's speech at Yale, etc. I was going to do double duty by also reading it in English. I even thought that maybe our flagging book group would go for it.

As I mentioned earlier, I was worried about reading Daoud's book. How was I going to deal with Daoud's decision to conflate you and your protagonist? Come to think of it, in writing to both you and Meursault, would I be accused of doing some version of that, myself?

At least I don't have to worry about being marked for death by those who might read me the wrong way and take offense. I admit that I know only superficially (and largely from the view of the colonizer) about Algeria's political history. Because of this, I found it hard to relate to that important aspect of what Daoud, an Algerian journalist, has on his agenda. Even so, like Daoud's angry protagonist, brother of the nameless Arab of *L'Étranger*, I have, as you know, been carrying Meursault around with me since 1962.

Therefore, just for the record, Meursault and I have a bond that remains intact in the face of Daoud's new view of him. Yes, Daoud's is a brilliant idea and a tour de force, but while acknowledging that, I can be just as stubborn as his and your contrapuntal protagonists.

So, what would you think of Daoud's book? Jizo43 on Amazon thinks you would be pleased. I'm not so sure.

*

Dear Albert,

Yes, I'm back again. You keep popping into my consciousness, and often in the oddest ways, from the sublime to the ridiculous, and sometimes the other way around. For example, who would expect that a comment from a local goat farm owner (via a message from City Seed, the voice of our New Haven community farmers' markets) would make me think of you and your Meursault?

The goat farmer, who was asked about his favorite products,

said "right now my favorite product is our goat milk yogurt which is strained like a Greek-style yogurt. It is nothing but yogurt, and when a bit of maple syrup is added to it, it becomes a lot like Sunday. I love it for dessert." Although I've never tried his goat yogurt (with or sans maple syrup), I think I know what he means. As easy as it is for me who frequently feels like an outsider to channel my "inner Meursault," unlike him, I love Sundays. That is especially true in Italy where, since I have no immediate family, Sunday is likely to be a quiet day. Of course I live deep in the countryside, so I am in no position to observe (and feel excluded from) other families. Furthermore, I realize that families can be a mixed blessing.

But goat yogurt aside, Kamel Daoud's Yale lecture, the very one I had lamented missing, actually presented itself right in my email. A message from our course chair, Alice Kaplan, proudly announced that it had been recorded, and was available via a single click.

On watching it, I could not help but be impressed by Daoud's sincerity and humility, which took me by surprise. When I wrote about this to my French writing partner, herself a North-African native, she had some comments of her own about Daoud's book:

> The two books, Camus' and Daoud's, are as different as the two men themselves, and the history of their country, which includes the colonizer and the colonized.
>
> Camus managed to transcend the world of his impoverished childhood, was saved by his love of literature and his immense talent and brilliant intelligence, became in Paris the perfect, sumptuous Don Juan (six mistresses at the same time, and all as well loved and brilliant, two of whom were renowned actresses!). A journalist, writer, intimate friend of the biggest names. A lighthouse and a tragic death.
>
> And the other, writing in a language not really his own, and who seeks, like the protagonist he invented, to emerge from the shadows, to have a name!
>
> L'Étranger, when it first appeared, was a revolution! The style, its very subject were revolutionary.

My friend goes on to admit that before commenting any further she thinks it would behoove her to reread Daoud's book. But she added: "I only know from a first reading that I didn't feel the intense reading pleasure that binds me to a book and that makes me unable to stop reading it. I recall that I stayed calm from the beginning to the end. It's true that I am one of the colonized, like Daoud, but my maternal language is French, not Arabic. Therefore, our point of departure is not entirely the same."

*

Cher ami, (I hope you don't mind that I'm going to call you that, since "Dear Albert" and "Mon cher Albert" as salutations may have worn out their welcome.)

I haven't read much about your sense of humor, but I confess to having appropriated your very serious "Myth of Sisyphus" to use in a frivolous way. My "Will the Real Sisyphus Please Stand Up" deals with the infinite struggles of an Albert Camus fan to prevent her Italian home from disappearing under a thick cloud of dust and insects. At the risk of offending you here it comes.

WILL THE REAL SISYPHUS PLEASE STAND UP?

How many times have I had occasion to demonstrate my lack of artistic skill in the classroom? Fortunately, he's easy to draw: A stooped stick figure of a man rolling a huge boulder up something that looks vaguely like a mountain. Then an arrow pointing up, and one from the top pointing down. During my many decades of teaching French, this guy keeps popping up. A man for all literary seasons, he never fails to shed light on the conversation.

And not just when it comes to discussing literature. He is equally at home in Bella Italia. Living as I do in the Italian countryside, I share my home with lots of dust, spider webs, and local fauna. Even though I make my dusting rounds several times a day, there is always more to be done.

I'm no great housekeeper, but in America, to have many spider webs and dead insects in evidence is not going to win you the Good Housekeeping Seal of Approval.

But Camus says we must imagine existential hero Sisyphus happy. Why? Because there's that brief moment before the boulder rolls back down the mountain when he gets a respite from his absurd task.

Now one can think of this timespan as a metaphor for our own brief span of life, or as the perpetually existential state of every housewife with a feather duster in hand.

When I commiserated about the omnipresence of webs and dust and the dim view of them taken by Americans, the former surgical nurse from Moldova who occasionally helps me clean just shrugged and said in very good Italian, "What do you expect? You live in the countryside!"

Getting back to me in the French classroom: Perhaps I've been going about this all wrong. The next time I draw Sisyphus, maybe she should be wearing a skirt and have a Dust Buster in hand?

*

And while we are on the topic of frivolous things, I am going to defy my risk-averse self and show you the original opener I was considering for this book. It was nixed as too zany by my most trusted critics, and probably rightly so, but we'll see what you think. And while I'm in this confessional mode, I'll admit straightaway that I am a hoarder. But you probably guessed that already. I hoard objects, which is making it especially painful for me to downsize and divest my beautiful 1907 home of 35.5 years' worth of "treasures" (actually 69.5 years' worth, to tell the truth). But I also hoard my words. How many times have I written on the drafts of my writing students, "Less is more!"? Yet here I am, trying to find a place for words that do not serve their original purpose.

My friendly critics who have my best interests at heart say that to organize this book of letters, I should arrange them in an order chronological to my life and my discovery of the recipients. I tried to listen, but as a life-long rescuer of abandoned stuff (I have tried to justify my hoarding by saying that I see the poetry in everything), I'm feeling sorry for this discarded bit. See what you think. You can be frank. I'm working at developing the thick skin that writers and teachers need in order to keep going.

POSSIBLE OPENER FOR *LETTERS TO MEN OF LETTERS*

(The list that follows was an answer to the self-imposed question, "Can you name the important addresses in your life?")

336 Pleasant Avenue, St.Paul, Minnesota
131 Highland Avenue, Middletown, New York
River Campus Station, Rochester, New York
Résidence des Étudiants Maplewood Avenue, Montréal
1 Rue le Goff Paris 5e, France
Swift Avenue Apartments, Durham, North Carolina
Carolina Avenue, Durham, North Carolina
10762 Riviera Place, Seattle, Washington
Kihei Apartments, Maui, Hawaii
181 East Rock Road, New Haven, Connecticut
5 Rue Saint-Jacques, Pau, France
38 Rue Émile Zola, Paris 15e
Boulevard St. Germain, Paris 5e
22 Rue St. Pétersbourg, Paris 8e
1 Rue St.-James, Neuilly, France

Do you ever imagine that you could knock on the door of a former home and find everyone and everything as you left it?

Or dial Diamond 2-2048 and your father's secretary would answer? (Never mind that he would be 95 and unlikely to still be diagnosing the skin woes of a tri-state area.)

What about your encounters with the authors who formed you? What if you could write to them? (Never mind that most of them are long dead and unlikely to reply quickly.)

Last night I saw the film *In Search of Memory* about Nobel Prize winner, Eric Kandel's research on how memory works. My stubborn memory has a mind of its own. Maybe yours does, too? If so, you might not consider a leap the following: I just signed up for Professor Kafka's seminar. I think it will go nicely with the one Professor Nabokov is teaching.

But as a French literature major, I absolutely have to take Professor Proust's class, even if it means having to commute to his cork-lined room.

And I'm wondering what I can say to worm my way into Camus' class, which is sure to be oversubscribed. I might have a better chance of getting into Flaubert and Balzac's classes, since they are being held in a bigger venue.

Course selection time at Yale—always a moment of great expectation!

What could she be talking about? Isn't she supposed to be the teacher?

Well, yes, you could say she is, but she knows how to strategize like a Yale student. Further, even after decades of teaching, she's still studying these writers. And even if she tries to be an auditor and gets closed out of their course, she will never give them up. In fact, she's been in constant conversation with them via letter. You'll see what I mean.

Here's another little piece of which it's hard to let go. Earlier I asked why I find myself so obsessed with your Meursault. Although the circumstances are very different, I had a long relationship with someone who, against all odds, went from being our town's most promising scholar to being the only US physician since the doctor who treated John Wilkes Booth to be arrested for accessory to murder after the fact. Other parts of his trajectory included being pursued by the FBI, jail, and lastly, a distinguished career as an honored humanitarian. One day while at the post office, I was stunned to see his face on a "WANTED" poster. (Inspired by that event, I wrote a poem called "Wanted," but I will have to show it to you some other time, since at the moment, it's packed out of reach.) In our small town where it was not easy or a social asset to be more intelligent than nearly every-one else, he knew what it was like to feel "Other." Unlike Meursault, however, his life journey had a rise, fall, and rise. But although given the right circumstances and an expert lawyer, it's possible to redeem oneself in the eyes of the law, implacable leukemia will not be denied. This feels like the right moment to finally say "adieu" to him, and "au revoir" to you.

Eugène IONESCO

November 26, 1912-March 29, 1994

Eugène Ionesco, although born in Romania, spent most of his life in France where, in 1970, he was elected to the Académie Française. His first play, La Cantatrice Chauve *(The Bald Soprano, which has no soprano, bald or otherwise) has been playing continuously in the same theatre since its 1950 opening. Self-alienation, estrangement, and the impossibility of communication find a unique form of expression in the black humor of Ionesco's tragicomedies.*

Dear Eugène,

Alice Kaplan, author of the intellectual memoir, *French Lessons*, and chair of Yale's French Department describes in her recent *Dreaming in French*, how transformative the semester abroad experience is to women of letters. It certainly was for me.

During the 1966-67 academic year, I lived in Paris and saw several plays a week, including five by you. Our charming, dynamic theatre teacher, Madame Chauvet, arranged a private meeting with you and our class at your favorite bookstore, La Pochade. On your arrival, when the owner who was your friend asked what he could offer you, you replied without hesitation, "Un Scotch!" Madame Chauvet's charisma was such that she was an inch away from getting us a meeting with the reclusive Samuel Beckett, but more about that later. I'm not sure whether her being the daughter of a distinguished Sorbonne Professor helped or hindered her success in persuading important people to meet with us. But your new play *La Soif et la Faim* which we had just studied and seen was being performed at La Comédie Française. She made sure we saw all of your plays of that season, including *The Bald Soprano*, *The Lesson*, *Le Roi Se Meurt* (*Exit the King*), and *Rhinocéros*.

Forty years later, it was a special thrill to bring my own students from the Yale Program to the little Left Bank theatre where your *La Cantatrice Chauve* and *La Leçon* have continued to play for six decades. Each time I start to teach the timeless *Rhinocéros*, whose important message continues to resonate with today's Yalies, I like to make a point of going around the room to shake everyone's hand. Then I can announce that they are all in "direct" contact with Eugène Ionesco, because I had shaken hands with you at La Pochade in 1966. To be an old dinosaur has its advantages! (I try to gloss over my having asked you about the possible symbolism of the color blue, a predominating element in Robert Hirsch's Comédie Française production, which was NOT the type of question you liked to answer.) Please forgive me.

There were many moments during that year when to live around the corner from the Pantheon with the Peguillan family felt like living in one of your plays. I realized this especially after seeing *The Bald Soprano* in which the figure of the "pompier" (fireman) has a funny cameo. Since little boys of my generation used to want to grow up to be a fireman, it came as a surprise to learn that to the French, the fireman, with his elaborate uniform and helmet, has the reputation of being a comic figure who is not very bright.

The Peguillans were proud of their apartment's description in Sartre's autobiography, *Les Mots*. There were a lot of things that my roommate Karen and I did not understand about our family's vast apartment, which had probably changed little from young Sartre's days. Among them was that while we were eating dinner together, we would often hear the front door open and close, followed by footsteps traipsing through to the kitchen area. This was in 1966, back in the days when two-hour dinners were the norm, and conversation was sacred. But nobody ever wanted to talk about the mysterious visitors.

One evening, instead of the mere turning of a key followed by footsteps, dinner was interrupted by very loud banging at the front door. Who should it be but a gaggle of fireman who looked straight out of a Ionesco play requesting permission to drag a length of fire hose through our hallway! Apparently there was a fire upstairs on the top floor that had historically housed the servants of these elegant buildings. Except for our tiny, posh elevator, the only access to that floor would have meant a six-story climb up a nasty, wooden back stairway, so the enterprising firemen had chosen another route.

A small, smoky fire had started in the room of Mme. Jannot, the old woman who had been Monsieur's nanny. Although she no longer worked for the family, out of respect for her, they allowed her to keep her room, and to take the fancy elevator to our fifth floor. Madame had her own key to our apartment so that she could pass through the kitchen and only have to walk up one flight. Aha! So that's where that perpetually locked door in the kitchen led! One day when we saw it open, Karen and I could not believe our eyes: What lay beyond that door was a world entirely removed from our upper-middle class luxury.

The fire was fortunately brought quickly under control, but the former servant's life savings, which she had been keeping in a box under her bed, were lost; however, our ever-loyal French "father" replaced it all.

We later found out that the heavier foot falls we used to hear belonged to the elegant, young Monsieur Favarel, the art student who, although coming from an aristocratic family, had rented one of the top-floor servant rooms, perhaps the better to experience the life of a starving artist. I think that he, too, would have made a good addition to the cast of one of your plays.

On a different topic, from the standpoint of my decades of teaching French, I want to thank you for your thoroughly unique effort to make a textbook, *Mise en Train* (1969), that we French profs could enjoy. Although it was not in use for long, I loved teaching from it. Its surrealistic skits and dialogues put the humor from the nonsensical Assimil method (at which you poke fun in *The Bald Soprano*) to good use. As I recall, my Rumanian grandmother had no sense of humor, but it's reassuring to know that some of her countrymen like you did.

Another surrealistic Paris experience in which I cannot accuse you of having played any part involves my memorable dinner with a surprisingly lecherous actor (known for being the French film voice of Beatle George Harrison) and the actor's more famous TV-star mother. I say "surprising" because it was my very dear and proper Eastman School of Music piano professor whom I presumed was a closet homosexual who had told me to look up this family. And since the actor lived with his mother, I figured it was safe to go there. Further, I might have made some unwise assumptions about the actor's sexual orientation.

I discovered my error when against my better judgment, I accepted the actor's offer to drive me home. Fortunately, I was able to make a quick enough getaway. When on my return from my year in France my piano teacher asked me whether I had contacted the "actor family," I did not tell him the whole story. I think he would have been shocked to learn that he had unwittingly set me up with a French-speaking Beatle who would try to take advantage of his student!

Yale's spring semester is coming right up, and I will once again be teaching *Rhinocéros* in its lesser known but original short story form. My adventurous course chair, Françoise Schneider, who likes to change things up far more than I do keeps threatening to remove it from the syllabus, but I always fight back. Even the most casual glance at today's headlines shows how timely your play still is. The tyranny of the destructive masses to which individuals like your anti-hero, Bérenger, stood up is a metaphor that will never go out of style. You understood the solitude of someone who risks all to say "no" in the midst of the collective hysteria produced by a Hitler. Or the courage of principled, non-egoistic whistleblowers who know something is wrong and act to correct the problem. Or even those willing to brave the fashion or the political correctness police.

As you demonstrate, we humans are weak and all too vulnerable to the seductions of brute force. To side with bullies can give the illusion of safety. In a 1970 *Le Monde* interview you yourself said, "I have been very much struck by what one might call the current of opinion, by its rapid evolution, its power of contagion, which is that of a real epidemic. People allow themselves suddenly to be invaded by a new religion, a doctrine, a fanaticism... At such moments we witness a veritable mental mutation. I don't know if you have noticed it, but when people no longer share your opinions, when you can no longer make yourself understood by them, one has the impression of being confronted by monsters—rhinos, for example. They have that mixture of candor and ferocity. They would kill you with the best of consciences." I wish it were not so, but it is hard to imagine how anyone could help but see how timeless your observations are.

Although during that year in France I saw the incomparable Jean-Louis Barrault in Paul Claudel's *Partage de Midi*, I am sorry that I never got to see him in the role of your Bérenger in the 1960 production of *Rhinocéros* that he directed. But just by looking at the stills, I can imagine how perfect the part must have been for him. No one could play an Everyman (or any other role, for that matter) as well as Barrault.

I'm guessing that you would have been surprised to see what

American comedian Gene Wilder, who died just yesterday as I write this, made of the role of Bérenger, aka Stanley (opposite Zero Mostel's tour de force as "John") in the American Film Theatre's 1973 production of your play. Why they changed Bérenger's name to Stanley is anybody's guess, but having seen *Rhinocéros* several times, I'm wondering if you would have agreed with the harsh criticism of this film version. The way Mostel transforms himself into a rhino before our very eyes, and without special effects is astounding. He won a Tony award for the Broadway production. What would you have thought of Laurence Olivier as Bérenger in Orson Welles' London production? And of Maggie Smith as Daisy?

As part of our study at Yale, we compare the very different ending of your story version of "Rhinocéros" with that of your play. We know which you preferred, and I agree with you, even though the Yalies usually go for the less complex, more climactic drama of the play. I and my students also usually have a different opinion about the possible heroism of your protagonist. They tend to view him as weak for having admitted that he was tempted to become part of the crowd, but something about his essence made him incapable of joining the proliferating herd that surrounded him. According to some, true heroes are not supposed to have doubts. To others, a Bérenger honest enough to reveal his internal struggles over the right thing to do is more deserving of our empathy and admiration.

And speaking of honesty, I am not embarrassed to admit that in your honor, I have a collection of rhinos in varying forms. I can't wait to show my new students the latest addition, which I confess that I swiped from my granddaughter's set of plastic wild beasts. As part of my legacy, some day I will be returning it to her along with the rest of my collection. That includes the anatomically accurate plastic rhino I bought at the Peabody Museum gift shop when I worked there as a volunteer in 1976. Even though from casual inspection, it is hard for a non-expert like me to determine the sex of this rhino, I have named him "Eugène."

Due to his age, he seems to have suffered a detached paw, which I have dutifully saved. In any case, a resilient fellow, he is able to stay upright on just three legs.

But back to my two-and-a-half-year-old granddaughter. I hope that some day she will read your play and love it as much as I do.

PS: I know that I will be tempted to add more to this letter, but I find it more than serendipitous that it currently contains 1966 words. Nineteen sixty-six was the year we met, so I'm taking that as a sign to stop right here.

FLASH!: As usual, I was only kidding about leaving you. Among the very generous gifts given to me by the Yale French Department at my retirement event was a treasure that might have made you smile. It came "wrapped" inside an elegant, rolling Tumi suitcase-travel ensemble in my favorite colors—the ones that set off to perfection my magic flying shirt that I wear on every trip to keep the plane aloft.

When I opened the enormous package that contained the suitcase and matching carry-all, it felt VERY heavy. How could this be? Our clever department administrator, Agnès Bolton and my teaching colleague, Soumia Koundi knew the answer, since they were the smart shoppers who had selected the gifts.

As I was fumbling around trying to open all the hidden compartments in my sexy new travel gear, Agnès came to my rescue. Inside the luggage, thanks to the inspiration of Course Chair Françoise Schneider, was a stunning sculpture of a rhinoceros made of Kenyan soapstone!

This was the perfect gift for many reasons: It will be a wonderful reminder of you and of how much I have enjoyed your company during my 33 years of teaching at Yale. In your honor, I have named him Eugène.

What? If you read closely my letter to you, you probably saw the reference to his predecessor, the plastic Eugène that I had stolen from my granddaughter. But now, with a semi-clear conscience, I will return that one to her.

Now I, who find it difficult to leave home, can travel in style, and while I'm away, your namesake Eugène will stay behind to guard the fort. He, too, is a homebody, so this arrangement makes everyone happy.

Vladimir NABOKOV

April 23, 1899-July 2, 1977

Born into an aristocratic family, Vladimir Nabokov spent his childhood in Russia prior to the Revolution. Although best known for his 1955 novel, Lolita, *Nabokov was a man of many talents—poetry, translation, literary criticism, tennis, and scientific illustration. The best-known writer to be an acknowledged expert in butterfly genitalia, Nabokov fulfilled his dream of identifying a new species.*

Dear Mr. Nabokov,

Warning: I am about to use some words that not even an inventive wordsmith like you will recognize, but perhaps you will be intrigued. I can't quite believe it, but through the miracle of a modern phenomenon which (Luddite that I am) I don't understand or really appreciate, I've been able to spend some time with you this morning. I'm talking about Facebook, where, thanks to clicking on something I saw under my son's listing, I stumbled on your drawing of a map of James Joyce's *Ulysses*. As often happens on Facebook, one thing led to another and I found myself face-to-face with a convincing YouTube version of you in lecture at Cornell, as channeled through actor Christopher Plummer.

I can't help but feel the serendipity of it all. Although I didn't actually study at Cornell, I did visit classes with my boyfriend during his four years there. I had known about your Cornell lectures on literature which I enjoyed reading. But to have a chance to "be there" and hear you speak about one of my favorite authors, Franz Kafka, was an unexpected gift.

In truth, I haven't read much criticism about *The Metamorphosis*. But as I listened, I sensed how much of Gregor Samsa's transformation (from sole family wage-earner in a soul-crushing job) into a beetle mirrors what I know about Franz. First, his body—the mixture of vulnerability and semi-protection of Gregor's armored shell. Then there's Gregor's naïveté and surprising toughness of spirit in thinking he can continue, even as a three-foot beetle, to work to support his ungrateful family who, even including his beloved sister, does not hesitate to renounce him. Having always been made to feel as if he were from another species, Gregor seems accepting of his new carapace. Once locked in his room that will become his death chamber, he experiences a certain relief akin to that of the writer for whom a room of one's own is essential. In Kafka's too brief life, one imagines, or hopes, that the act of writing in solitude offered at least some respite.

At the beginning of this letter, I mentioned serendipity, and I'm not sure whom to credit for what I am about to say—you? Professor Nabokov? Franz? Gregor? Some other power?—but as I was thinking about the beetle, I heard a loud buzzing at the bedroom window. The source sounded pretty big, so I grabbed my trusty transparent "Michelin Man" cup and postcard from a former student that constitute my bug relocation system, and zoomed in for a closer look. After "cupping" the flailing creature, I found myself face-to-face with the biggest beetle I had ever seen. Thrashing about on his back, he was easy to imprison. Even though I had promised my mother not to take any more insect photos, how could I resist? If he were a butterfly, he might have ended up in one of your collection boxes, but now that I've taken a few shots, I'm going to release him. This is just one way you and I are different.

The next button I press takes me to video footage of you reading your own *Lolita* and naming what you consider the greatest books of the twentieth century. My first reaction is to note how well Christopher Plummer had "nailed" you in his performance. My second is what an actor you, yourself, are! As the first lines of *Lolita* trip off your tongue, first in English, and then in Russian, I am spellbound. No stranger to strong opinions, you don't mince words when denouncing Thomas Mann's *Death in Venice* as "asinine," Pasternak's *Dr. Zhivago* as "vilely written," or Faulkner's masterpieces as "corncobby chronicles." In fact, you come up with quite a metaphor to burst the bubble of what many consider "great books": "The same sort of absurd delusion as when a hypnotized person makes love to a chair." Although you refer to the first half of Proust's *In Search of Lost Time* as "a fairy tale," you list it as Number Four on your own Hit Parade of literary greatness. Numbers One, Two, and Three are Joyce's *Ulysses*, Kafka's *The Metamorphosis*, and Andrew Bely's *St. Petersburg*. That last work does not ring a bell, but now I'm curious....

My next click on "Nabokov Tweaks Kafka's *The Metamorphosis*" "speaks" to me, I think, because of my work as a translator, editor, and teacher of writing. To see your spot-on cross-outs and steady improvement of the pictured English translation is impressive. And to think that English is not even your native language! Although Franz would have been outraged by the mere fact of them, I found your sketches of Gregor Samsa as a beetle (used to excellent effect in your

Kafka lecture as dramatized by Plummer) very winning.

Next stop on my Nabokovian cyber-journey: I watch you marveling over the different book covers of your *Lolita*. I've had fun comparing the covers of the various translations of my son's books, but it must be different when those books are your own "babies."

Although it would be hard to say which is the favorite of my recent visits with you, the two-part, "Vladimir Nabokov on *Lolita*: Just Another Love Story" is right up there. What fun to see you rub shoulders with the elegant, cigarette-wielding critic, Lionel Trilling, under whom my husband was lucky to study at Columbia.

*

The morning after...

Since the time we spent together yesterday, life intervened. But I was happy to get up early today because we have another rendez-vous. However, unlike the thrill of a new relationship, ours feels more like what sometimes happens at fortieth high school reunions when former couples who haven't seen each other in decades suddenly find themselves feeling young again. It's hard not to be seduced by someone who knew you way back when, and with whom a get-together feels like a way of recapturing lost time. Actually, I have to admit that this has been happening a lot to me lately, as I reconnect with my literary passions.

It's too easy, however, to be tricked into remembering just the good parts. That's why I decided to go back to my old notebooks and well-marked texts, using them to re-experience some of the magic evoked by the nymphet while she was still an ideal.

Speaking of nymphets, I watched with interest the sly, Cheshire grin on your face during the discussion with Lionel Trilling. And when the interviewer asked about what it felt like to have coined a word like "nymphet," you looked like the cat that swallowed the canary. I, too, make up words all the time—a hobby that's hard for we who love word play to resist. When something is all bollixed up, it's "gabbosh-

somewhere in the shade."

The more I observe you, the more odd coincidences pop up. The beetle on the window sill was one thing, but in the middle of the video, "*Lolita* My Most Difficult Book," as I watch you in pursuit with your butterfly net in hand, two things strike me. First, I see a bearded gentleman who looks very familiar to me refer admiringly to your excitement at entomological exploration, and then to his shock at realizing that after your daily shared expeditions, you spent your evenings writing *Lolita*. When I saw the genial, smiling professor identified as Charles Remington of Yale University, I was reminded that when I first moved to New Haven, I had worked under Professor Remington as a volunteer in the entomology department. This was before the days of computers, and I helped by using an especially fine pen to label, in nearly microscopic lettering, the mounted insect specimens.

The second light bulb that went off for me was realizing that the author on whom I wrote my dissertation, André Pieyre de Mandiargues, was also quite obsessed with insects, as was I when I first moved into the abandoned stone farmhouse we renovated here in Italy. "Abandoned" is not quite the right term, since many generations of insects convinced that this was THEIR house had never left. I'm thinking about the connection between writing and the eye that likes to focus on small elements of the natural world.

Another thing I am recognizing in the course of these letters—one that probably shouldn't have surprised me—is the number of overlapping links among the recipients of my correspondence. When writing to you, I find constant flashes of Flaubert, Balzac (I hadn't thought about how you and he both love to write about obsessive individuals until critic Edmund White mentioned it), Proust, and Kafka. In the same video where White spoke about you, A.S. Byatt, in her brilliant critical remarks about *Lolita,* confesses to having become drunk on the precision of your "sensuously colored" language—how in your word games you managed to master "from the outside" American culture and language. She especially admires your naming everything, like Adam, and the lists that reveal your understanding that "language creates the world."

Byatt compares Humbert's way of celebrating in words Lolita's inner organs and body parts to the portraits of the beloved in sonnets. These, as well as a brilliant series of fragmented close-ups of Lolita that focus on markers of her childlike identity (taken from the Hollywood film), recall for me the Renaissance "blazon" tradition of highlighting various parts, as opposed to the whole, of the love object.

Back for a moment to those note cards of yours—dinosaur that I am, I have always written papers on note cards. (Perhaps this is a vestige of what we were taught in junior high via a "bible" called *How to Write Your Term Paper*, a perennial best-seller in the state of New York. With the advent of computers, most of my fellow Baby Boomers and their kids moved on and ditched the notecard method. But during our recent divestment process, even when making many painful decisions about what to discard from our house, I couldn't bring myself to forsake the notecards from my dissertation. They will be coming with me to my next home.) In any case, when starting this project, the first thing I did was go in search of note cards. You can't imagine how hard I had to look to find the ones I am using as I write to you now.

I think you will forgive me if I take advantage of our mutual affection for these notecards to allow me to backtrack a bit. I know that you liked to shuffle yours around for maximum flexibility. More about that when we get to your last work, *The Origin of Laura,* which had only existed on note cards until cobbled together after you were gone. You probably got tired of talking about your method, but the rest of us remain interested. You used to say that you could start a work anywhere because "the pattern of the thing precedes the thing," allowing you to "fill in the gaps...at any spot" you happen to choose.

I love your comparison of the way you write to creating a painting that does not require one "to work gradually from left to right for its proper perception." Your method allows you to direct your "flashlight at any part or particle of the picture when setting it down in writing." You don't begin a novel at the beginning or necessarily reach chapter three before chapter four. Chronology is overvalued, and what can look like chaos to someone else, isn't, because your text already exists "in invisible lead." The true artist can make time cease to exist.

As I write this letter to you and to other men of letters, I wish I could say as confidently as you that an order will emerge. In the meantime, I'm taking the risk of heading back to my notes about you from various periods.

I do feel that I have been lucky to have had two Vladimirs in my life. My auditing of Vladimir Alexandrov's Yale seminar on you made me fall for you, whom, despite having gone crazy for *Lolita*, I had never really studied. This was at the very start of the email era, and I found this medium of letter writing to be liberating. I would not normally have had the chutzpah to write to a professor like Alexandrov, but email made him more approachable. He and I corresponded about some of my ideas about you, and we became friends. I joined the Nabokov Society and loved exchanging ideas with fellow Nabokovians on the Zembla web site where we "met."

Here come a bunch of favorite bits from my course notes that I'd like to share with you, and my riffs on them. Please imagine them as being on note cards that will miraculously arrange themselves into a coherent order. The first concerns your ideas from *Speak Memory* about the need for a legacy, for tangible proof that "our existence is not but a brief crack of light between two extremes of darkness."

Since I have always thought of common sense as a good thing, your antipathy to it is giving me pause. You say that it is "common" and that it "cheapens all." Maybe you didn't need it because that was the province of Vera, who thought of everything?

My notes tell me that for you, there are two types of truths—a human one, and a transcendent. Only the artist can have access to the latter. A privileged being, he has his own sense of time. This means that one can't focus on one's gift if distracted by the mundane. The artist needs to have the magic preserved. This is where to have the right selfless partner can help.

What would our friend Kafka say about that? Neither he nor Flaubert could pull the trigger on marriage, but Kafka managed to write despite the demands of a day job he detested. Although I love my work of helping others write, and I get some of my best ideas in the course of my job, I do find it very hard to master time well enough to write about life while living it.

For example, right now I am surrounded by my two pre-nymphet granddaughters, age 1 and 3, which leaves barely enough time to fill a notecard. I heard you say, while explaining for the umpteenth time, that you and Humbert are definitely not one and the same, that you had hardly any experience of being around little girls. Like you, I'm the parent of an only son, so this is a new phase for me. I'll let you know how that works out.

I want to get back to your sense of the advantages and disadvantages of the artist who has a hyper-consciousness that is at odds with so-called common sense. An artist has the vision to see what's not apparent and can convey it to others. The poet-mage Victor Hugo knew a thing or two about that, but your version is different. For you, space and time as separate categories disappear, and time stops during the timeless moment that the germ of the future work of art appears. An example you give is how, in choosing to rescue a child from a burning building, you would have also brought out her favorite toy. Why waste precious seconds to save a doll? That's too common-sensical a question for the artist who has the ability to enter imaginatively into another being's world.

More about noblesse oblige: The true writer must convey in words the shock of his rapturous inspiration—to "unpack" what was compressed into a rapturous moment. The artist, like the madman or the monster is therefore "Other"—always the odd man out. All three can take things apart, but only the artist can supply the missing piece of the puzzle to reconstruct the idea. Your widow used the term "otherworld" to convey how much this key term applied to you who had a foretaste of the immortality to come. What we think of as death is not inevitable, and art and nature are not opposites. You are always in search of the "aha" experience, and the fatidic patterning you see in nature and elsewhere is more thrilling than threatening. I wish I could do that, too.

Hence the capital importance for you of the prefix "re," something I have written about in the context of Proust. The struggle is to recapture, reconstruct, resurrect, and remember a previous experience. This is why as you write, you see yourself as the scribe of a divinely-inspired "script" that has already been previously thought out and organized.

This brings to mind something I saw from favorite writer Roger Rosenblatt in a *Time* magazine article from December 28, 1998 titled "The Story of the Year:"

> People know a good story when they hear one. We are a narrative species. We're stories as individuals; our DNA writes the plot, sometimes the theme. It is thought that children acquire language to tell the story that is already within them. Only a few weeks ago, the pure-science linguist, Noam Chomsky, in another change of mind, said he now thinks a divine power gave us language in a single, inspired stroke.
> (well, maybe that "us" does not include everyone—I know you will bristle at any attempt to compare you to the herd.)

While I am poking fun at you a little bit, let's talk about Freud, that "quack from Vienna" who tries to inflict his dreams on you—those dreams you "don't have... that he discusses in his books"—and about whom you never have a good word to say. "Crude" and "medieval," might be the least inflammatory of the adjectives you have applied to him. The previous batch of invective is from a *NY Times* interview of January 30, 1966, where you also refer to a number of writers of great books as "formidable mediocrities." And how about this: "Freudianism and all it has tainted with its grotesque implications and methods appears to me to be one of the vilest deceits practiced by people on themselves and on others."

I understand that you don't want to see the "strings" behind a magician's tricks. But here's my gripe. I think you fail to recognize how what you consider the bugaboo of psychoanalysis actually privileges and values the patient's view, no matter how skewed or at odds it may be with the "objective," common sense "facts." I would have thought that that might have put you a bit more in Freud's corner.

(Full disclosure: I am married to a child psychiatrist, but unlike most of his colleagues, he's no fan of psychoanalysis, either).

And what about your delight in the repetition of patterns and in creating puzzles designed to be solved by the reader who is especially attuned? Is that so different from Freud, the close reader who liked to identify patterns of behavior? Do you resent him for reducing men to predictable patterns that destroy the magic of nature with which you identify?

In *Speak, Memory* you go so far as to say that to follow thematic designs through one's life should be the true purpose of autobiography. How does your own unique destiny jibe with these patterns? I know you're no fan of Darwin, either, for his putting blind faith in scientific forces. The patterning you seem to favor is transcendent and perhaps from some divine force. Your beloved butterflies demonstrate it, as does your own life. As an artist, you are somehow able to penetrate the gaps, chinks, and fissures in the prison of time to see the confluence of seemingly far-flung events. All of this is a bit mystical and hard to put together, but maybe it's OK for us to remain in the dark while accepting the wonder of it all.

While I'm free associating, maybe it's time for a weird association: I just noticed that my notes about you were written in a type of notebook I think you would have loved, called Circa Notes. These elegant notebooks, of all sizes, come readymade with a special type of hole-punch and individual rings that allow you to reposition the pages while they still remain "bound." Freedom, flexibility, yet still some security. What could be better?

On the theme of free association, who but you could have managed to elide past, present, and future in the image of a baby carriage? I'm talking about the moment in *Speak, Memory* where you mention a home movie of a time that predates your birth.

You describe yourself as "a young chronophobiac who experienced something like panic" when seeing "a world that was practically unchanged—the same house, the same people—and then realized that he did not exist there at all and that nobody mourned his absence. He caught a glimpse of his mother waving from an upstairs window, and that unfamiliar gesture disturbed him, as if it were some mysterious farewell. But what particularly frightened him was the sight of a brand-new baby carriage standing there on the porch, with the smug, encroaching air of a coffin." A baby carriage as encapsulator of the life cycle? BINGO! Now that you've said it, who can ever look at one of those hearse-like perambulators in the same way?

I was about to say that you need a break from me when a *Guardian* article (September 26, 2015) on Alfred Brendel's "Music, Sense, and Nonsense" perambulated in my direction. The impressed reviewer suggested that in this collection of essays and lectures, Brendel's delving into the minutiae of performance and editions would not be a hit with the herd—a word you like to use to refer to the kind of reader you disdain for moving his lips when he reads, all the while understanding nothing. I think you would have been in sympathy what Brendel had to say about his recordings, which he considers "simply the fixing of a moment." And this from a man who devoted six years to recording the piano works of Beethoven!

Brendel thinks that the emphasis on making the perfect recording means less risk-taking, and can hinder an artist's development. "People expect an artist to develop, and yet they are only too ready to impale him, like an insect, on one of his renderings." (I'm sure that this metaphor was not intended to disparage devoted lepidoterists.) "The artist should have the right to identify his work with a certain phase of his development. It is only the continuous renewal of his vision—either in the form of evolution or of rediscovery—that can keep his music-making young."

You have already compared your method of writing to the medium of painting, but these musical comments also remind me of your way of writing and rewriting—of never wanting to stop tinkering with even your most hard-won words. To write, like making a musical recording, fixes a moment in time. However, it is the search for *le mot juste* that matters (and perhaps it's even wrong to use the *le mot juste* expression in the singular).

Brendel's book represents "40 years of thinking and talking about music," with occasional glances "back at his former views." In my current Letters to Men of Letters project, in a small way, I find myself identifying with that description. And I, a lifelong serious pianist, have had, like Brendel, some hearing loss. His, however, cruelly "makes it difficult for him to listen to the piano." Yet he manages to say something I find very profound: "Hearing has its own memory."

Like Brendl, you who lost so much never complained. Instead, you figured out how to make memory speak.

Marcel PROUST

July 10, 1871-November 18,1922

Marcel Proust was born into an upper-class Parisian family headed by an authoritarian physician father and a wealthy Jewish mother. Plagued by asthma from the age of 9, the sickly Marcel, who became a recluse after the death of his parents, found refuge in his cork-lined room. Despite the initial difficulty of getting his work published and the challenge of its nearly 3000 pages in 7 volumes, À La Recherche du Temps Perdu (Remembrance of Things Past) *has been heralded as one of the most significant literary achievements of modern times. Part II,* À l'ombre des jeunes filles en fleurs (Within a Budding Grove/ In the Shadow of Young Girls in Flower), *won the 1919 Prix Goncourt.*

Dear Marcel,

We have a lot to discuss, and I owe you an apology or two. You and I have had a thorny relationship ever since, as a graduate student, I was forced to swallow every word of your novel. Now I see that my negative reaction was a youthful and rash rush to judgment. It's no accident that the concept of the madeleine figures so prominently in the writing of authors like André Aciman, whom I so admire. And I see that it also underlies my own writing and, specifically, the enterprise of this book.

I often refer to my memory as "Proustian" because of the way, for better or worse, my past is so present to me. When I recall an experience, even one very far back in my 69 years, the sensory details are there—what I was wearing, the sounds, scents, tastes, textures.

What I'm about to tell you is in keeping with the "now-and-then-and-now" theme of my letters, and I think you will understand. I'm currently appreciating you more thanks to a new biography by Benjamin Taylor, *Proust: The Search*. But even before that, I came across some evidence that our relationship was changing for the better. I'm also reminded that to teach a challenging author like you can lead to a much greater appreciation by the teacher, herself.

In the course of trying to write a short article for those who don't know much about you, I started putting things together in a way that ended up helping me.

Until now, I hadn't looked at this piece that I called, "On Taking Tea with Marcel: Lost then Found," for a few years, and I am wondering what you will think of it.

*

On Taking Tea with Marcel: Lost, then Found

What if everything that ever mattered to each of us could be restored? Regained? Resurrected? Although everything we have the illusion of possessing is actually "on loan" during our lifetimes, what if it could be recovered? For what, and by whom, do we wish to be remembered? How can we be reassured, in the face of our own mortality? If we have artistic aspirations, to what extent does living one's life in the moment conflict with recording it?

In reflecting on Proust, I can't help noticing how often the prefix "re" reappears; to satisfy me, any inevitably clumsy attempt at an English title for Proust's *A la Recherche du Temps Perdu* has to incorporate it. *In Search of Lost Time* is the awkward attempt at translation that really gets my goat. I imagine Proust turning over in his grave: "Does anyone really think that I would have taken the trouble to write these 3,031 pages if I'd had the idea that time was 'lost?'" Even the wily wunderkinds of American advertising who came up with "Some things in life are priceless; for everything else, there's Mastercard," understand how to exploit the tension between our hunger for increasing amounts of "stuff" and for something which will endure.

One thing that has endured is my attempt to come to grips with this text. It was force-fed to me in graduate school, where I read every word, but found it indigestible—not my "cup of tea." And yet, even barbaric force-feeding can yield something as divine as foie gras; lobsters gobble garbage, yet their flesh tastes sweet. Maybe that is why, in my teaching, I've been on a mission to introduce Proust in jewel-like bites that will feel like little marvels, instead of what the French colorfully call *un étouffe-chrétien*—enough to choke a Christian. What could be more fitting than to use the verb *"digérer"* to talk about the miraculous way morsels of a humble madeleine tea cake could produce an explosion in the mouth that would spark what many consider the most remarkable text of the century?

A case in point: I recently dined at one of England's few four-star restaurants, The Fat Duck, where Chef Heston Blumenthal stands ready to startle the palate of those who might cast a skeptical eye toward such menu items as the Douglas Fir Sorbet or the Bacon and Eggs Ice Cream. In the middle of each table was an elegant brochure requesting information on unforgettable taste memories from childhood, which the chef proposed to use as inspiration for new dishes. I found myself wondering what he would do with the cherry popsicle my sweet grandfather used to buy me at the corner candy store. It was always a dilemma: Keep the twin sides of the popsicle intact and risk it melting all over Pleasant Avenue? Or break it in half, tackling each side separately, which would make the pleasure seem to last longer. There was also the choice of whether to lick it delicately, or to aggressively suck the colorful juice out, admire the change of hue, then bite what remained: Big decisions for a 3.5-year-old. There's an embarrassing coda to one of those journeys. So excited about getting the popsicle, I failed to remember to go to the bathroom first and ended up peeing in my pants on the way back. But my Russian grandfather, a pants-presser by trade, ever the Good Humor man for whom a 5-cent popsicle was an extravagant expense, never held it against me. The passage to America had devoured all his rubles, but he was rich in stories of his soldier days taking stray bullets for the Czar, and colorful old-country customs like cutting a hole in a raw egg to suck out its contents. Ah, those pre-salmonella days!

In Proust's novel, the young Marcel recalls his bedtime anguish at being separated from his mother, a trauma that drives his search to regain what felt like a pure, perfect love. Blocked by a threatening, authoritarian father, this maternal love finds expression in Marcel's relationship with his grandmother. A key element of Proust, with which it is easy to identify, is that we have two types of memory: voluntary and involuntary. Through voluntary memory, we can choose to remember a particular time, place, or person. Involuntary memory, however, is more capricious. After Marcel tastes the madeleine offered by his mother, what explodes in his mouth feels like the taste of salvation itself, returning him to what had seemed lost: his childhood in Combray, in the south of France.

Here are the basic elements of this key scene. One bleak, wintry day, the beloved mother of a tired, adult Marcel offers him some lime-blossom tea accompanied by an ordinary, shell-shaped tea cake, called a madeleine. At the first taste, he feels literally transported back to his childhood visits to Combray, when he used to eat tea-soaked pieces of madeleine with his aunt, Tante Léonie. Far more than a mere memory, Proust here experiences an ineffable pleasure—an epiphany that makes him feel as if he has transcended the limits of time—as if the past had been reborn, annihilating along with it, any fears of mortality (the translations that follow are mine):

> At the very instant the mouthful of...cake crumbs touched my palate, I shivered, attentive to what was happening within myself. A delicious, singular pleasure had invaded my being, without offering any hint of its origins. It immediately made me feel immune to all the vicissitudes of life... I had ceased to feel mediocre, contingent, mortal... From where did it, this powerful joy, come? What did it mean? It is clear that the truth that I am seeking is not in it, but within me... I put down my cup, and look inward. It's my own spirit that will find what I seek... And suddenly, the recollection appeared to me. This was the taste of the little piece of madeleine that...Tante Léonie used to offer me, after having dunked it into her own...tea... But (even) when nothing of an ancient past remains, after the death of beings, the destruction of objects...their scent and taste persist, like souls, remembering, waiting...hoping to support, on their nearly imperceptible droplet, the immense edifice of memory.

Proust draws a comparison between this experience and multi-colored Japanese paper flowers that slowly "bloom," when placed in a bowl of water. Like them, his seven volumes will emerge from this extraordinary cup of tea.

To reflect on Proust puts one in intimate touch with the loss of our previous selves and identities. But there's a flip side to this, a potential consolation: What poses as our mutability is an illusion; what seems profoundly changed, really isn't. Proust reminds us that the clutter with which we surround ourselves is a misguided attempt at insulation from death. But paradoxically, this clutter, in distracting, stifling, and "burying" us, as opposed to paring ourselves down to our essence, produces a kind of death. Two particularly beautiful passages underscore the need to create a space that will allow us to cut through our busyness to attend sensitively to what matters. Here is the first:

> ...I begin to once again perceive, if I listen closely, the sobs that I had summoned the power to hold back in front of my father, and which only burst forth when I found myself alone with my mother. In fact, however, these sobs have never ceased; and it is only because life around me is quieter now, that I hear them once again, in the way that everyday noise can cover the sounds of church bells so thoroughly that one might think they fail to ring during the day, but that they only resume ringing in the evening silence.

Here is the second passage I want to cite:

> I find very reasonable the Celtic belief that the souls of those we have lost remain captive inside some simpler being, an animal, a vegetable, an inanimate object, in effect lost to us until the day, which for many will never come, when we find ourselves passing close enough...to enter into possession of the object in which they are imprisoned. They then tremble, call out to us, and as soon as we recognize them, the spell is broken. Delivered by us, they have conquered death and return to life with us. So it is with our past. In vain we try to regrasp it; all conscious efforts on our part are fruitless. It is hidden beyond reach, in some material object (in the sensation that that material object would offer us) that we would never suspect of having this capacity. As for this object—it is entirely dependent on chance whether we would encounter it before we die, or whether we would never meet it at all.

As I think about these evocative passages, a question comes to mind: Is it easier for an aging Baby Boomer to appreciate Proust, than for a college freshman? At the elite university where I teach, narrow specialization is the name of the game. It is unfashionable to be interested in literature as lessons for life, but I am stubborn and don't mind being considered what the French might call *un zèbre*. Well, here I sit, decked out in my stripes, to offer the possibility that, like all classics, this is a work that can be accessed, albeit differently, at various stages of life.

Indeed, most of my students do seem to "get it." Inspired by our brief encounter with Proust, one student zeroed in on some essential questions: "Where does time go? Who's in charge of it? If time is lost, is the search for it worthwhile? What really matters?"

According to Proust, the answer to this last question is *memory*. The images of those who matter to us return because, in reality, they have never abandoned us.

One has the potential to relive the past, thanks to privileged moments, and one never knows where the next catalyst will be: Two things can appear to have no relationship to each other, but perhaps a link will later be revealed.

Another student, inspired by our dip into Proust, chose to meditate on two photos of herself with her father. In the first photo, the summer prior to her departure for a trip to Ireland and then to college, she and her dad are cozily seated together at a cafe. She feels like a queen, but recognizes that, because she is at the point of making an important transition, this will be the last time the two will be able to sit together in such a carefree way. In the photo, the dad's finger looms large as it points something out to her, marking "the last moment when I would not question the direction in which my father would guide me." The second photo shows a twisting Irish roadway, emblematic of her wilder encounters with the unexpected: abandoned castles, glasses of Guinness, intriguing accents. She finds herself looking petite in both photos, especially in comparison to the orienting hand of her father but notes that the two snapshots reflect the difference between a girl who follows the directions of others, and an independent navigator.

In our highly digitalized, hyper-documented age, the role of photos in life and literature raises interesting questions that can blur the lines between voluntary and involuntary memory. Coming from a family of fanatical photographers, I often think that I have my own version of a Proustian photographic memory. As I look at most photographs of myself, I have what feels like total sensory recall of the scene. Maybe it's just an illusion prompted by the photo itself, but I don't think so. In the face of an evocative photo, I literally feel transported back to a different time and place. Any distance between me and the scene at hand seems to disappear. Another thing that amazes me about certain photos is the way I always seem to look natural and unperturbed in them, even though I can often remember feeling quite stressed at the time. Since I am not very good about keeping in "traditional" contact with people who are important to me, I rely on photos to feel "in touch," and to complement the mental conversations I have with my soul mates. Photos, both literal and those in my mind's eye, help me maintain the illusion that those about whom I have been thinking can sense the connection.

In a wonderful seminar that my colleague, Evelyne Ender, allowed me to audit, called "Writing and Memory," we talked about the role of the photo as a memory prop that has the potential to offer a recognition/witnessing of the self—the ability to see things that we couldn't acknowledge otherwise—that allows us to get past "blind spots." As I say this, I think back to all of the 8mm movies my father used to take of us kids under those hot, blinding, hand-held lights that were the height of technology in the 1950s. After a while, they'd start to emit a burnt smell, and when they were turned off, there'd even be some smoke. It's a wonder none of us ever got hurt from them.

In the Writing and Memory seminar we also talked about the photo as a metaphor for remembering; the fact that a photo is always a record of a past moment; the need to remember that there is an eye/I behind the lens. Does a photo steal the memory away? Replace it? Enhance it? Stifle it? Fuzzy memories can gain clarity from a sharp photo (and vice versa). A photograph appears to offer evidence of real events—to record the way things really were, to offer an objective historical truth. But is this an illusion?

Can there be memory outside of language? Does one need to be able to say "I remember," in order to remember? Freud would say that we're overly interested in the visual because it's the least threatening of the senses.

In my own classes, two questions I posed stimulated intense discussions: In looking at a photo do you stand OUTSIDE the memory as an observer? Or do you remember yourself from WITHIN the scene?

Among the things my students have cited as their own petite madeleine: "The rock song, *American Pie*, and the legendary Red Chevy of my father's youth;" "the clink of my mom's ever-present gold bracelets;" "the perfume of the California pine trees inside and outside the home of my grandfather during our Xmas visits;" "the books I constantly reread—impossible not to think of the circumstances when I first read them." I hadn't thought about it before, but this *Letters to Men of Letters* book that I am currently writing is very much in tune with that last "petite madeleine." As one for whom all of France feels like a personal madeleine, I consider myself lucky to have found a vocation that allows me to relive, on a daily basis, my passion for French literature and the accumulation of the formative experiences that I have had with the French.

The astonishing variety of uses to which the madeleine incident has been put no doubt far exceeds the number of Proust's actual readers. I wonder what Proust would think about popularized manifestations of his ideas, such as the recent comic book versions of his work; a classic perfume from the House of Worth called "Je Reviens;" the self-help bestseller, *How Reading Proust can Change Your Life*; or even a pop psychology book, *What Flavor is your Personality*, that promises to help you discover who you are by looking at what you eat: "Which snack food do you like best?...Your answer tells you more than just what you like to crunch."

After initially being appalled by an article touting the Proustian implications of Martha Stewart's monthly musings for her magazine (from Combray to the homey pleasures of Nutley, New Jersey seemed like quite a leap), I found myself backing down, and thinking that perhaps I shouldn't be so dismissive. Another example: British perfumer, Jo Malone, is in Proust's debt for this ad, entitled "ALL SHE DOES:"

She makes ordinary things like fried eggs or toast with jam special, and when you beg her for her secrets she just smiles and says it's a pinch of herbs, a hint of spice and something she can't remember. When she goes out at night she smells like the delicious scent of gardenia lingering in the balmy air of summer, and you wait gladly on the promise of her kiss goodnight when she returns home. THANK HER.

Perfumer Jo Malone's Oedipal conflation of what could have been Marcel's mother with her besotted son who anxiously awaits her goodnight kiss is right on the money.

One might argue that, with today's sophisticated anti-anxiety medications and anti-aging surgical techniques, a work like Proust's might never have emerged at all. In a recent lecture, *Where Have all the Hysterics Gone?*, distinguished analyst Elizabeth Young-Brehl noted that, because in our increasingly permissive society there are fewer and fewer taboos, there is less repression than in Proust's day. Like the artist who needs to stand back from the canvas, Proust needed to isolate himself. Only through art, and alone, could he penetrate his own multiplicity. Perhaps today, the reclusive, asthmatic, homosexual Proust, who spent much of his life in his cork-lined bedroom, would have felt less need to establish the type of private cocoon propitious to the creation of a work like À *la Recherche du Temps Perdu*. Without the benefit of psychotropic drugs, Proust discovered that as exciting or emotionally draining as events can be in "real time," retrospection offers the opportunity to process what has transpired, and to put to rest what might have been overwhelming.

Of course I'm feeling remiss about all that I have not included in this meditation on some aspects of Proust. But I am encouraged by this comment from Susan Sontag's *Against Interpretation*:

> Our task is not to find the maximum amount of content in a work of art, much less to squeeze more content out of the work than is already there. Our task is to cut back content so that we can see the thing at all. The aim of all commentary on art now should be to make works of art—and by analogy, our own experience—more, rather than less real to us.

In summary, Proust pulls the rug out from under us, but in a good way, persuading us that:

~ What we think we've lost—we haven't.
~ What we think we know—we don't.
~ The truth is always right there, but we can only access it when we are ready to hear it.
~ What appears a shared epiphanic moment can be a mere illusion.
~ We carry in our bones what matters: Traces, scars, body memories.
~ Despite the multiplicity of selves with which, as we age, we seem to have lost touch, there is a coherence to our life.
~ All small towns and families have a lot in common.
~ Ghosts can be friendly.
~ Places and objects can have an aura.
~ Time is not money.
~ "The more things change, the more they stay the same" is not a mere cliché.

The above is my own list of some of the things I am beginning to grasp thanks to Marcel Proust. And here's another infiltration from popular culture, compliments of Stephen Sondheim's *A Little Night Music*:

"Every day a little death."

Every day a little death? Who would expect a line like that in a song from a musical comedy? Nothing puts one in touch with loss, like immersion in the work of Marcel Proust. And yet, nothing can prove quite as consoling. When is a good time to be separated from everything you hold dear? If your answer is "never," then Proust has a lot to offer you.

*

Back to you, Marcel. In terms of the "then" and "now" of our relationship, we are about to get closer to the latter. I want to tell you about what my home institution, Yale University, did to celebrate the 100th-year anniversary of the publication of your *Swann's Way*. The French Department sponsored a marathon reading of this first volume of your 7-volume novel. From November 16 to 17, 2013, students, scholars, and guests took turns reading a 10-minute passage in the language of their choice. Readings began Saturday at 7:30 AM and ran until 3:30 AM on Sunday. You probably would have felt right at home, since a special highlight was the setting: a full-scale recreation of your cork-lined bedroom.

A favorite student and future Rhodes Scholar, Benjamin Mappin-Kasirer, whom I helped with his prize-winning senior essay on you and the weather ("Concordance des temps: Marcel Proust et la météorologie"), was the main student organizer of the event. He had offered me a chance to sign up early to read, but I was too disorganized to take advantage of that privilege and was closed out. Of course, I stopped by anyway, and was able to hear a few of the readers, who got to choose not only their passage and the language thereof, but also the position from which they would read. Some elected to recline on the bed, others paced. There was also quite a range of clothing and acting skills. When I arrived at the purpose-built setting, a lovely blond was doing her reading in Polish!

I was pleased to see that the next reader was doing his reading in native French. Had you been there, I'm guessing that you would have been more excited to find this young man sitting on your bed than the pretty blond. In addition to his great accent, this spiffy reader had a pair of shocking pink sunglasses coolly tucked into his shirt.

As I was leaving, a very nervous young Yalie who confessed to not knowing much about this guy named "PROWST" was just arriving to read his selection. At least he deserves extra credit for having had the foresight to sign up in advance.

I'm thinking that you yourself would have been very pleased to see this evidence of how your legacy has endured. And I'm pretty sure that of the two teas on offer, you would have chosen the *tilleul* to accompany your madeleine.

And speaking of madeleines, do you think a pot could be one? I've written a piece called, "May Your Future Be As Bright And Shiny As These Pots" that I think of as an homage to you. I certainly couldn't have written it without you. Henri Bergson has said that for you, the present does not exist. It is made of the past. A key word for you is "circularity." My notes from Wallace Fowlie's course at Duke University elaborate on this: "Proust lives in the past in search of his childhood. His nostalgia for the purity of that time is a main theme of his novel." I wonder if you will agree that my piece below reflects these elements. Although I wrote it a few years ago, and it refers to a long-ago period of childhood, adulthood, and loss, it remains totally present to me. I will be coming back to the links between you and Fowlie, my revered professor and erstwhile dissertation director, that have just been crystallizing for me. One never knows where involuntary memory is going to lead!

Here is another place you have taken me. What do French cocoa and Cordon Bleu pots have to do with linden tea, madeleines, and involuntary memory? Please read what I've written below.

I'm betting that you will understand.

May Your Future Be As Bright And Shiny As These Pots

I am thinking about endings as I stand here in 2012 making myself some very fancy French cocoa that had an expiration date of "best by May 16, 2005." I have been known to do stuff like that, especially when the expiration date police are not watching.

This particular brand of cocoa, a requested birthday present of some eight years ago called La Parisiennne, is described as "silky swirls of cream gliding, intoxicating and arousing." According to the blurb on the fading package, the maker of this sensual product trained at the Cordon Bleu where her responsibilities while working at the Hotel Crillon in Paris included making this ambrosial drink. And here she is having created in the spirit of this memory, "a Parisian style of chocolat chaud for those who want to bring a taste of Paris home."

Well here I am in my New Haven kitchen channeling my inner Proust, and something has made me reach for this box that has about two more servings of this transformative product.

One thing about which I had no doubt was the pot in which I was going to prepare this delicacy. I received two Cordon Bleu pots of incomparable quality as an inspired wedding present way back in 1970 from my beloved piano teacher, Mr. Borenstein, with whom I had spent most of my childhood and beyond. Like my memory of Morris and Emily Borenstein, these pots have stood the test of time. Morris' wife, Emily, the multitalented pianist, poet, teacher, and all-around genius mother of a good friend wrote the unforgettable note that accompanied them: "May your future be as bright and shiny as these pots."

Well, the 1970 pots are no longer so shiny, but they still work brilliantly and one of them just proved that it can still make a mean chocolat chaud worthy of all the hype on the box. It is so rich and delicious that I even I, chocolat-o-mâne that I am, cannot finish it in one sitting.

Mr. Borenstein died a few years ago at 91, his mind still sharp enough to be a master bridge player, and it is hard to believe that he is gone. He imprinted generations of pianists, four in my own family, with a lifelong love of music, and his spirit is always with me.

My 87-year-old mom and I talked to Emily a few times over email and on the phone from the nursing home where she moved once her own health problems became too severe to manage. We received word that she died last week, and my sister drove some distance to represent our family at the service in her honor.

Every time I spoke with her I reminded her about these pots which I will continue to cherish to the end of my own days. Maybe some day they will become a legacy for my musical son and daughter-in-law.

As for the "Couture Cocoa," I am looking forward to drinking the second half of it soon. To tell the truth, I can't remember what it tasted like when I first got it back in 1984, but even eight years after the fact, it remains intensely memorable.

Sometimes the expiration police are wrong.

*

Yes, cher Marcel, I am back again.

À propos of our mutual attraction to certain hot beverages, I am quite a tea fanatic. My kitchen shelves are full of all types, but because of my sensitivity to caffeine, herbal infusions work best for me. I see that one of my favorite companies, Mariage Frères was founded in 1854, so you could well have enjoyed one of their elegant brews, perhaps at the Ritz or the Crillon. But whenever I drink tea, I have two involuntary associations: One to my beloved Russian grandfather drinking his strong tea in a clear glass with perhaps a spoon-full of jam as sweetener; the other association is of course to you.

You may recall that I said earlier that I would be coming back to the chain of associations that this letter is evoking between you and my Duke professor, Wallace Fowlie. As I mentioned earlier, I've been reading Benjamin Taylor's *Proust: The Search*, which is part of Yale Press's series on Jewish Lives. Some people might be surprised to find you under this rubric, but even though your father was Catholic, having had a Jewish mother, you are considered by Yale Press to have had a Jewish life.

I'm thinking about Fowlie's attraction to you, and your mutual connections to Cocteau. I see that you were 18 years older than Cocteau, while Cocteau was 19 years older than Fowlie. I read in Benjamin Tayor's book how hurt you were when you heard that your former love, young Lucien Daudet, son of writer Alphonse Daudet, had become involved with Cocteau. Even worse, Edmund White, in his biography of you (*Marcel Proust: A Life*) mentions that Lucien Daudet told Cocteau that you were "an atrocious insect." You used to be welcome at the Daudets' until they became aware of the infatuation between you and their son. White quotes Daudet Senior as saying, "Marcel Proust is the devil!" And that was even after you could have gotten yourself killed in a duel trying to defend the honor of Lucien, after a flamboyantly gay literary critic, Jean Lorrain, intimated that you and Lucien were having an affair. You surprised everyone by remaining calm and scheduling the duel for the afternoon when it would not interfere with your sleep.

In Fowlie's first memoir, *Journal of Rehearsals,* he talks a bit about being like a star-struck fan when he met the older man-of-the-world, Cocteau. You and Fowlie both demonstrated discretion about your private life, and even the implications of the title of Fowlie's memoir owes a debt to you. Fowlie always needed a period of retrospection to process what was happening in the moment. Impeccable preparation eased his anxiety. He told me he became a credentialed lay analyst "to be of greater help to his Bennington students," but perhaps also to help himself come to terms with his own double identity and sexual preferences, of which it took me a long time to become aware. He was a godlike figure to us at Duke, where I had gone especially to study with him.

During the summer of 1969, after my first year at Duke, I was taking the course at NYU with Thomas Bishop that ended up providing me with my dissertation topic. One day after class, Bishop asked me about what it was like to work with Fowlie, adding with shocked bemusement that in Fowlie's book about Cocteau, he failed to make any mention of Cocteau's homosexuality, something Bishop considered a ridiculous lacuna. Even then, I did not understand the insinuations behind that remark. All my naïve self could say was, "Well, Professor Fowlie may have some problems relating to women."

Of course I considered myself an exception since I and my soon-to-be husband felt like privileged members of his inner circle. He used to come to our house for dinner at a time when Coq au Vin made with a secret ingredient or two—Lipton Onion Soup and Thunderbird wine—seemed like the height of culinary sophistication. This was also when gazpacho made what may have been its first appearance in Durham, North Carolina thanks to a "gourmet" recipe from the *TV Guide.* It was surprisingly good, and I still have my well-worn copy. When Fowlie had us to his Valley Terrace apartment, no madeleines were served, but his own self-prepared "company" dish featured shrimp and frozen peas over rice.

When I learned to make men's ties, I of course made one for him. It was burgundy-colored with what I thought were subtle white flowers, and I was thrilled to see him wear it. He brought me a beautiful heavy silk scarf from his trip to Italy. I once played Debussy's "La Fille aux Cheveux de Lin" for him on the piano, and during vacations, he used to send me letters signed "Michel," a name he reserved for intimates. He sent a number of them while on car trips in his very basic, radio-free, black, "unsafe at any speed" Corvair. Not missing the entertainment or company a radio could provide, he prided himself on his unique method of passing the time on long trips. He had a special, long list of French poems that he would recite from memory. He could actually keep track of the time and miles by where he was in his recitations. Who needs a radio?

Closer to home, I'll never forget the large Cocteau murals he had as one of the few adornments in his all-white, Spartan apartment. These were a gift from Cocteau into which he had incorporated Fowlie's name and a personal message into the design of the artwork itself. That odd conversation with Thomas Bishop about what he considered Fowlie's flawed book on Cocteau got me wondering more about what he was implying about the relationship between the two men. Now when I think back to Fowlie's "Inferno" course, I remember Canto XV where Dante the Pilgrim recognizes as having been condemned to hell as a Sodomite the teacher he revered, Ser Brunetto Latini. I recall the deep poignancy with which Fowlie read the line, "Siete voi qui, Ser Brunetto?" "Are YOU here, Ser Brunettto?"

When I recently wrote a Junior Year Abroad friend, Martha Crockett Lancaster, who also ended up in Duke Graduate School, about our experience in Fowlie's classes, she, who subsequently married a minister, had similar impressions about our teacher:

> I, too, always thought he was just a wonderful professor and, as you said, godlike. I never realized he was gay, but I was so naive back then that I'm sure a lot went over my head. It was a different time and place, and you mentioned that he was a very private person. We could use a bit more of that today, I think. I never went to his apartment, but sure wish I'd seen the Cocteau art. He always seemed to me a Catholic priest

manqué—he just seemed to have that kind of personality and bearing. I know he came to Catholicism as an adult, so maybe if he had encountered it earlier, he would have been a priest. He was, however, like a high priest of literature to me. I still think of things I learned in his classes, and he opened new doors of understanding for me.

Martha's mention of doors takes me back to 1968, the year I, against my better judgment, ended up at a concert in the Eastman Theatre of some guy named Jim Morrison and The Doors. As a classically trained musician of narrow vision, I'd never heard of him, but my friend who had an extra ticket insisted that I should not pass up a chance to hear Morrison. I'd never heard of the opening act, either: A little-known group called Linda Ronstadt and The Stone Ponies. I see now that 1968 was also the year that Fowlie received a letter from Jim Morrison, thanking him for having translated Rimbaud's poems, which Morrison said were important to him. But it was not until 1980 that Fowlie, thanks to a student who gave him Morrison's biography, realized who Morrison was. Once he noticed the parallels between Morrison and Rimbaud, he wrote the book *Rimbaud and Jim Morrison: The Rebel as Poet.* We lifelong teachers are constantly learning things from our students, and I am sure that as an octogenarian, Fowlie got great satisfaction from this opportunity to branch out into such a "with-it" area of popular culture. As for my dip into popular culture and The Doors, my own ears are still ringing from the decibel level of that concert.

One day, toward the end of our Proust class, Fowlie described an interaction he had had with a gentleman who seemed to know a lot about your own reclusive habits, Marcel. They talked for a while, and during the course of the conversation, Fowlie brought up the name of your Swedish manservant, Ernest Forssgren. The dramatic, perfectly timed punch line of that memorable Fowlie lecture came when Fowlie quoted that man's revelation: "But monsieur, I am Ernest."

When I think about you and Fowlie, despite his devotion to you, I see a study in contrasting personal habits. I saw a painting by an unknown artist of you writing in bed in your night cap, tucked under vo-luminous covers, a bedside table and mantelpiece groaning under the weight of what look like tons of perilously balanced sheets of paper. That made some sense of biographer Benjamin Taylor's recounting of how you "managed to lose, somewhere" in your "anarchic bed-room," the page proofs of Ruskin's *La Bible d'Amiens* that you and your mother had been translating. In despair you "forsook the Ruskin project" on which you had spent four years. "The proofs had to be somewhere in that mess. Instead of looking harder," you left on vaca-tion. That was probably for the best, since your enslavement to Ruskin delayed your doing your own work. In contrast, it is hard to imagine anything getting lost in Fowlie's stark, white, orderly apartment.

Here comes a newsflash I just stumbled on. Since this is a book about and composed of letters, you may want to know that your 14-year-old great-grand-niece (who has yet to read your novel) sold, through Sotheby's, 120 items from your personal archive. That includ-ed intimate correspondence between you and Reynaldo Hahn, and Lucien Daudet in which *The Telegraph* tells us that you "lay your heart bare." According to *The London Times* the sale raised 1.2 mil-lion pounds at auction, double the estimate. You may be relieved to know that the diary of composer Reynaldo Hahn, your most loyal friend and lover, a document that writer Benjamin Taylor refers to as "the holy grail" of your biographers, will be sealed until 2036.

So you see, you have lost none of your allure, and you keep ap-pearing on my traffic pattern in unexpected ways. My next-door neigh-bor in New Haven, the formidable Catherine Coffin (1892-1982), was a passionate Francophile who ran a literary salon and had a house full of books personally inscribed to her by practically every major au-thor of her time. Thornton Wilder had been her friend and neighbor, and according to another of my neighbors, the eminent critic Harold Bloom, Thornton Wilder owes a lot to you: "...In fact, without being aware of it and though Wilder is a writer of real originality, he has, in a sense, been a popularizer of Proust." In his *The Bridge of San Luis Rey*, Wilder is said to have drawn on the letters between Mme. De Sevigné and her daughter, whose passionate devotion to each other recalls that of you and your beloved mother, Jeanne. During a visit to Mrs. Coffin's house, I happened to notice a book of Wallace Fowlie's that contained a loving inscription to her. What are the chances of my living next door to someone who had a lifelong friendship with someone who had figured so largely in my intellectual life? Mrs. Coffin lived to be 90, and one of the most eloquent speakers at her funeral on the Yale campus was Wallace Fowlie. For him, this was a return to the campus where he had taught between 1940 and 1945.

On the subject of your ongoing cachet, the latest *New Yorker* magazine has an article that might please you: "How the Proust Questionnaire Became a Prestigious Personality Quiz." I first found out about your questionnaire when I saw it being answered by the author on whom I ended up writing my dissertation, André Pieyre de Mandiargues. You'll be hearing more about that soon. In the meantime, although there is no end to all the things I want to say to you, this letter is at risk of swelling to the proportions of your own *Recherche*. It is probably time to say "au revoir" but certainly not "adieu."

Gustave FLAUBERT

December 12, 1821-May 8, 1880

Perfectionist and relentless seeker of le mot juste *("the unique right word"), Gustave Flaubert was the son of the Chief Surgeon of the Rouen hospital, and of a doctor's daughter. Despite the torment that Flaubert's epilepsy and nervous ailments caused him, they allowed him to abandon law studies in favor of literature. The serialization of Flaubert's* Madame Bovary *earned him few francs, a trial for immorality, and definitive literary fame.*

At age 15, he fell in an idealized form of love with the married Elisa Schlessinger, whom he never forgot. His subsequent eight-year tempestuous affair with poet Louise Colet worked much better on paper than in the flesh. His remarkable letters to her and others, however, arguably reveal more of Flaubert's inner life than any of his fiction. The sacrifices he made for his orphaned niece, the death of his closest friends, and his sufferings from syphilis contributed to the pain of his later years.

Dear Gustave,

The first time I read *Madame Bovary*, as with Camus' *The Stranger*, I definitely didn't get it. But when I was 16, my older French boyfriend accused me of being a potential Madame Bovary. I didn't understand what that meant at the time, but I was pretty sure it wasn't a compliment. Years later, I began to read your letters, and realized that you and Kafka have much in common. Both of you needed women in your lives, but at a distance, so as not to interfere with your art. In your own letters, you both reveal yourselves in ways that differ from and that complement your fiction.

Under duress, you said, "Madame Bovary, c'est moi," a declaration that has many more meanings than are obvious. Many academics like to go on about Emma Bovary's mediocrity, but I prefer scholar Victor Brombert's idea that she thought she was better than everyone around her, and indeed she was! At 16, and now approaching 70, I am still wondering to what extent erstwhile boyfriend Gérard Archambault may have had my number. You and I have a lot to discuss.

In preparation for writing this letter, I've been reading lots of writers' thoughts about you, including those of a Yale freshman reading *Madame Bovary* for the first time. In my capacity as Yale College Writing Tutor, we worked together on her paper for the literature component of Directed Studies, a year-long honors program for select Yale students. This was Jessica's last paper of the year, and although she was initially flummoxed about what to write, she ended up doing an excellent job. I told her that she needn't worry about not "getting" all that was to be gotten from your book, because this was a work to be read and reread at different stages of life. "Yeah, that's exactly what Professor Porter told us all in his lecture. He specified the need to read it at three different times in one's life." Gustave, does every professor say the same thing about your novel?

After our discussion of her plan for the paper, Jessica was on her own. It was very late and close to the deadline when she left my office, and frankly I was worried about what the outcome would be. To her credit, however, she ended up picking a challenging but ultimately successful topic for her essay: a close study of Flaubert's language that she titled, "Conscious Constructs." Eager to see where students take our conversations, I always ask them to let me know how they ended up feeling about the finished product, and what the professor had to say about it.

In response to my email, "You and Mme. Bovary: Who won?" Jessica sent me a copy of the paper with her professor's generous comments. In it, she points out that Emma has no way to express her feelings for her lover except in literature-inspired melodramatic showcases. To quote Jessica,

"I am sure that up there, together, they approve of our love," Emma says wistfully to Rodolphe, invoking the gods to add divine weight to a relationship that has almost no substance (158). Her words are so sappy, but oddly appealing because they create the illusion of uncorrupted nature. Her romanticism is so deliberately constructed. All of it consists of things she has derived from books, which makes her language ultimately deceptive. It might not be true love, but it's certainly true naïveté.

And Rodolphe, knowing better, takes full advantage of that. To him, she is just another novelty to be conquered. He, as an experienced seducer, has heard many a time women's treacly, unfulfilled declarations of love to him. Unfortunately for Emma, who doesn't know how to express her amorous sentiments to men besides in the cheesy lingo of love stories, her genuine affections are brushed off by Rodolphe because he believes them to be another string of empty professions. "He did not distinguish, this man of great expertise, the differences of sentiment between the sameness of their expressions." Emma on the other hand has no idea how to play this game. She has only the overblown language of the cliché. Cheaply spoken words by him can appear to have profundity for her because she doesn't know any better. She's a reader of novels, not of people.

In the end, Emma does not get to keep anything. Not only does she lose her lovers, her husband, and her life, but she loses herself under the layers of her own contrived language.

Well, if that was Jessica's first reading of *Madame Bovary*, I would love to hear what she makes of it a second and third time.

I'm trying to think how old I was when I first read your Madame Bovary. I note that I referred to it in my letter to Camus about my own 16-year-old amorous misadventures of the summer of 1962 while studying French at l'Université de Montréal. That was the summer after my sophomore year in high school, so I'm guessing that I first read it at fifteen the previous year. But I did so on my own, so nobody told me anything reassuring about how much I was, or was not getting out of the book. As a Midwest-born Middletown, New York-raised young girl who liked to read historical romances, I probably found it easy to identify with Emma. In any case, I was hooked. I subsequently got to reread it as a college undergraduate, and then at Duke in Richard B. Grant's class. He did some fabulous analysis of the "tourbillon" ("whirling") as a key image in your book: Emma's dizzying dance with Rodolphe at the ball, the spider web references that occur throughout the novel. Was I getting tired of hearing ever more interpretations of Emma? Not in the least!

I am actually having a great time now rereading my notes about you from many sources: Yale colleagues Peter Brooks, Charles Porter, Shoshana Felman, and my letter recipients Marcel Proust, Jean-Paul Sartre, Vladimir Nabokov, and Franz Kafka, who considered you his favorite author. I'm also recalling having been introduced in 1988 to distinguished psychoanalyst Marcel Eck, father of the head of my host family during one of the periods I was teaching in Paris.

Dr. Eck had written a number of well-received literature-focused papers for the *Nouvelle Presse Médicale*. Knowing how much he and I both loved nineteenth-century French literature, the family thought we would enjoy having a chat, and they were right. The first thing he asked me was who my favorite novelists were. I was quick to pipe up with Balzac and Flaubert, but only one of the two was the "right" answer.

You were his specialty, and he explained that he had written two papers based on Jean-Paul Sartre's controversial 3-volume work on you, *L'idiot de la famille* (*The Family Idiot*). The first was "La psychanalyse de Flaubert selon Sartre" ("The Psychoanalysis of Flaubert by Sartre" from Volume 1, No.10, March 4, 1972); the second was "L'idiot de la famille. La maladie et la personnalité de Flaubert selon Sartre" ("Illness and the Personality of Flaubert According to Sartre" from Volume 1, No.12, March 18, 1972). At the end of our talk, Dr. Eck generously gave me reprints of each of these articles. Although I tend to have nearly total recall of most events like these, my memory of this occasion, beyond being impressed by Eck's erudition, is uncharacteristically fuzzy. My files are currently 3,000 miles away, but those articles will be there on my return. Sometimes it can be useful to be a hoarder!

What I'm hoarding right now are many pages of critical comments about you, but without intending to insult anyone, if I could keep just one, it would be A. S. Byatt's "Scenes from a provincial life." I was astonished to read such a scholarly study in my favorite newspaper, *The Guardian* (July 27, 2002). I see that this article had also served as the introduction to a Norwegian edition of your *Madame Bovary,* which makes more sense. I find it hard to imagine an American newspaper running such an extensive intellectual piece. I especially love her opener:

Reading Madame Bovary for the first time was one of the most terrifying experiences of my life - at least up to that point. I was a very young woman - not even eighteen. I was au pair in the French provinces in the 1950s, and I read Madame Bovary in French, sitting in the furrow of a vineyard. I was like Emma Rouault before she became Madame Bovary, someone whose most intense life was in books, from which I had formed vague images of passion and adventure, love and weddings, marriage and children. I was afraid of being trapped in a house and a kitchen.

Madame Bovary opened a vision of meaninglessness and emptiness, which was all the more appalling because it was so full of things, clothes and furniture, rooms and gardens. The worst thing of all was that it was the books that were the most insidious poison. Recently Madame Bovary appeared in a British newspaper listing of the "fifty best romantic reads." It was, and is, the least romantic book I have ever read. If I have come to love it, it is because now... half a century older, and not trapped in house and kitchen, I can equally sympathize with the central person in the book, who is its author - endlessly inventive, observant, and full of life.

I see that in this letter to you, I've included comments of three young women's first contacts with your book, and I'm thinking that you might like to see an article slyly called, "My First Time: Women Writers Reveal Their Feelings On Being Initiated into the World of Emma Bovary." I say this despite knowing that you profess never to care whether anything related to you sells or not, but I'm not sure I believe you. I think that Byatt got *your* number when she states, while pointing out the similarities and differences between your Emma and Tolstoy's Anna Karenina, "It might even be said that both are physically attractive to the men who invented and trapped them in their stories and that both are punished by their authors, as well as by society."

Byatt mentions "an illuminating paper" by the psychoanalyst, Ignès Sodré, titled "Death by Daydreaming" in which Sodré used Freud's essay on "Creative Writers and Daydreaming" to discuss the particular daydreams of Emma Bovary. That one is also going on my list.

I always like to imagine what Freud would have to say about major figures in literature. Byatt notes that Freud "makes the point that the hero or heroine of the daydream is in a narcissistic solitary world. Emma Bovary's romantic desires are little scenes in which she plays the heroine. She prefers to dream about her first lover, Léon, rather than to see him. Her moment of ecstasy after she has been seduced by Rodolphe is when she is able to tell herself in a mirror, 'J'ai un amant. J'ai un amant'" ("I have a lover. I have a lover."). I had forgotten about that mirror scene, but once reminded of it, I couldn't help flashing to scenes from modern films like *Taxi Driver* and *La Haine* where, even though the motivations may be different, the protagonist talks to himself to boost his image and rehearse a role he wants to inhabit. Many people forget that the next line after "You talkin' to *me*? You talkin' to *me*?" is "There's nobody else here." Similarly, the sense of Emma's alienation from herself and from others is implicit in her excitement at having a lover whose actual presence is superfluous. What would you, Gustave, make of Travis Bickell from *Taxi Driver*? I'm guessing you'd say, "he's no Emma Bovary."

As in the situation mentioned above, your oft-quoted (but perhaps apocryphal) line "Madame Bovary c'est moi!" purportedly has a sequel that often gets lost. "Madame Bovary c'est moi!" is immediately followed by "d'après moi." ("Madame Bovary is myself—according to me"). This is in contrast to what you wrote to your lover, Louise Colet: "'Rien dans ce livre n'est tiré de moi . . . Tout est de tête" ("Nothing in this book is drawn from me. Everything comes from my head."). Byatt notes that you figured out a way to mingle, but not fuse, your characters' relations to the physical world with your own.

I found plenty of quotes from you about the "down" side of writing, such as "Writing is a dog's life but the only life worth living," and the odorously colorful "Sometimes I think I'm liquefying like an old Camembert." I also like the sense of humor in your, "It is splendid to be a great writer, to put men into the frying pan of your words and make them pop like chestnuts." But amidst the pain of your writing process of obsessively seeking *le mot juste*, the one and only "right word," you said, "for better or worse it is a delicious thing to write, to be no longer yourself, but to move in an entire universe of your own creating."

Thanks to his association with you, Nobel Prize-winning Turkish author Orhan Pamuk received an honorary doctorate from the University of Rouen. In his gracious acceptance speech, Pamuk notes similarities between your and his own writing trajectory. Before his first book was published, as a late bloomer, he had been living with his mother who wondered when he would settle down to a more traditional life. Pamuk quotes an exchange between you and your mother about your choice to remain unmarried: "If you participate actively in life, you don't see it clearly: You suffer from it too much or enjoy it too much... The artist must be a freak of nature, an oddity outside ordinary life, a monster of sorts...So, I am resigned to living as I have lived: Alone, with my throng of great men as my only cronies..., with my bear rug as company." Pamuk says you addressed to your mother other sentences very much like those he whispered to himself before he had turned thirty, sentences in which he tried to believe: "I care nothing for the world, for the future, for what people will say, for any kind of establishment, or even for literary renown, which in the past I used to lie awake so many nights dreaming about... That is what I am like; such is my character."

Pamuk recognizes two sides of your character—the one that is "derisive and belittling" and the other that he loves and admires as

a great writer who, within the large canvas and panorama of the novel, discovered a new way to enter—suddenly, with the stroke of a few words—his characters' inner lives. A writer who could approach his characters with the deep compassion and empathy demanded by the art of the novel, and as a result, who could later simply declare, "I am Madame Bovary!" It is not difficult for the reader who admires him to imagine these two Flauberts as lobes of the same heart. I have always wanted to identify with this author, who on one hand felt boundless anger and resentment toward humanity, and on the other hand, nurtured a profound compassion for the same, and understood men and women better than others. Whenever I read his work, I am urged to say, "Monsieur Flaubert, c'est moi!" (Rouen, March 17, 2009)

Before I say goodbye, cher Gustave, the last of your critics whom

I want to cite is another recipient of my letters, Vladimir Nabokov. I just read a reprint of his lecture on your *Madame Bovary*. But if only somebody would invent Time Travel, I'd whisk myself back to 1954 and right into the Cornell lecture hall alongside all the other students in Lit 311, "European Literature of the Nineteenth Century," popularly known as "Dirty Lit" (according to Edward Jay Epstein's article, "An A from Nabokov" in the *New York Review of Books*, April 4, 2013). After seeing photos of the class, I think I would have blended right in, wearing my original saddle shoes from the fifth grade (still my most comfortable shoes, regardless of all the holes). Technically speaking, I would have been only eight years old, but I'm thinking of myself as a college sophomore—even we letter writers are entitled to a bit of poetic license.

Some readers of Nabokov's lecture on you get annoyed by his inability to resist showing his superiority to those dolts who call themselves translators, but whom he considers true philistines. But from the examples he chooses, I think he has a good point. Further he criticizes not just the translator's words, but their decisions to change your punctuation. He's quite the specialist at pointing out the chinks in everyone's armor, but he does so in an amusing, witty way that I think you would appreciate.

Nabokov points out some convincing themes in your book, such as the "layers" or "layer-cake" theme, using as examples young Charles Bovary's ridiculous hat and the over-the-top Bovary wedding cake. I found myself adding to these, Emma's toppling mountains of debt, and her three-layered tomb, among others. Another theme for which he gives numerous examples is the horse theme. Further, Nabokov's remarks made me more aware of your likely symbolic use of color in the novel. First, the greens (the silk cigarette case, the green velvet of Rodolphe's waistcoat, Charles' choice of green velvet for the coffin, the contention that no "greens" would ever grow in Rodolphe's black heart); and then the blues (Emma's long blue veil, the blue arsenic jar, her blue-black eyes, the "azure infinity" of her dreams, the blue haze of the landscape at her funeral).

Nabokov calls your book the most romantic fairy tale whose

prose does "what poetry is supposed to do." He cautions the students never to ask irrelevant questions like "How true is this?"

Finally, how's this for a compliment? "The girl, Emma Bovary, never existed.... The book *Madame Bovary* shall exist forever and ever. A book lives longer than a girl." Of course, the same could be said for his *Lolita*. Unlike those cronies of yours who told you to throw your fiction into the fire, Nabokov would have dismissed their opinion with his favorite insult, "Philistines!"

Come to think of it, you and Vladimir might have hit it off just fine.

Honoré de BALZAC

May 20, 1799-August 18, 1850

Honoré de Balzac began life as Honoré Balssa, the son of a mother 38 years younger than his ambitious father who was intent on moving up in society. Never one to think small, Balzac, with his Comédie Humaine *composed of forty novels and other writings, set out to produce novels that would offer a panoramic view of society. This was after having failed at a number of professions—politician, publisher, literary critic, speculator—and after having been an unpopular, disobedient student who took refuge in books. Balzac excelled at creating ambitious, energetic characters who don't give up, and even when writing potboilers under pseudonyms, he proved himself a skilled renderer of objects with an eye for the telling detail. His diverse admirers include Marcel Proust, Gustave Flaubert, Henry James, Karl Marx, Walter Benjamin, James Baldwin, Roland Barthes and Camille Paglia.*

Dear Balzac,

I'm picturing the literally pocket-sized powder-blue paperback of your *Père Goriot*—the expurgated version, probably intended for impressionable high schoolers like myself, from which anything deemed too sexy had mysteriously vanished. Even without the juicy parts, I was transfixed by it. That was back in Middletown, New York in 1964—a long way from Paris. By the way, when we read Voltaire's "Candide," there was no cleaned-up version available. In order to comply with the school board's idea of decency and not get fired, our enterprising teacher, Madame Van Eseltine, had to tell us which passages to skip: "Students, whatever you do, do NOT, I repeat, do NOT read the following pages..." You can imagine how well that worked!

My literary love affairs have followed a pattern: There's that first, blown-away naïve contact with a book and then, years later, I revisit it and begin to feel that I understand what I'm loving.

When I finally got to Paris in 1966, I saw Rodin's looming statue of you every day, and walked by the places you wrote about and inhabited. That was during my Junior Year Abroad (a rite of passage that probably would have perplexed you, since young ladies of your class and generation tended to have to fulfill their ambitions closer to home).

Indeed, the closest equivalent to which I think you may be able to relate was The Grand Tour, which was more often the province of young gentlemen. Just ask Flaubert about how that turned out for him and his traveling companions. Although they wrote some wonderful letters that we readers have as a souvenir, they themselves came back with some "souvenirs" of their own in the form of syphilis or other diseases that would haunt them, and not in a good way.

But back to you, who didn't have to go far to indulge in some non-health promoting habits—not that you had a choice. Writers driven by deadlines and passion do what they have to do to keep going. Me? One drop of caffeine, and I don't sleep; a few sips of wine, and I'm practically comatose. Some of us are not cut out for 19th-century Paris society, even though we love to imagine it and read your accounts of it.

À propos of that, while teaching a storied Yale creative writing course called Daily Themes—a class that you certainly didn't need—I got the idea of trying to write each of the daily prompts along with my students. That meant coming up with 5 pieces per week times 13 weeks.

The first year, I only managed to eke out a few. I'm wondering what you will think of this one, in which the assignment was to describe a place. On the morning that I wrote it, I looked up and around my bedroom from a cozy supine position—a bit like from where I'm writing you now, albeit in another country. Two years later, I still like this piece that I found myself writing in a "Père Goriot" moment.

In any case, I am indebted to you for helping me with my own writing. I never could have done it without you.

UPSTAIRS, DOWNSTAIRS
NOW WHAT?

From the vantage of bed, I survey my inner sanctum. Formerly on the floor below, we have moved up. I think of the old French boarding houses like Père Goriot's, where each ascension meant the opposite: fortunes depleting, life oozing, spirits dashed.

Is my trajectory so different? This space feels master-suitely luxurious. Self-sufficient. Flooded with light. Honeyed Pear on the walls and ceiling. Playful touches of turquoise punctuate here and there, and the Tudor-ish timbers and shelves gleam dark cherry. Although there's no kitchen, it feels like all I'd ever need.

1907 was a good year to build. Servants used to live up here, and it took some hundred years to realize, "Hey! That's the best part of the house! Keep it for yourself!"

In this space repose some favorite things—better-controlled clutter than elsewhere. Having reached the divestment phase of life, could I be outgrowing my hoarding?

No way around it. Taxes are up, and I may have to move on. This was not part of the plan. I figured I'd be carried out of this house—a soothingly wrenching prospect. When you are a child whose parents were born during the Depression, to downsize feels like death.

I think of my brave Russian ancestors who traded the Old Country for this one. And now, I am poised to do the reverse.

The bottom line? We are just the caretakers. Everything is on loan. It will all end up behind us. If we are lucky, the aura will remain.

*

Four years after writing this piece, I have to admire my own prescience in what I just said above, and I need to heed my own painful wisdom about letting go. According to an article in, of all places, the *Yale Alumni Magazine*, Buddhists understand this. "Sweeping away the mandala teaches the lesson of impermanence: Remove attachment. Everything is going to change." My mantra has always been: Hang on for dear life to everything. You never know when you're going to need it. Insulate yourself! (THAT has got to change!) But maybe it's easier if you're Buddhist, not Jewish? In any case, our beautiful house is for sale, and we will soon be downsizing.

Our son was nine months old when we moved in, and he will celebrate his thirty-eighth birthday this fall. In my fantasies, a nice family (or two) with a French sensibility will fall in love with the house, start a bidding war, offer a cash deal with no contingencies, think (as does my husband) that we have priced the house far too low, and buy it on the spot. This has been a wonderful house in which to raise a child. We have tried to be good caretakers, and our time here is up. I hope we will have left a good aura behind us. At least the new homeowners will be able to see that unlike for Père Goriot, the top floor is indeed the best part of the house!

*

Now, dear Balzac, I want to change gears a bit and tell you about how you and I ended up reconnecting in a different class setting. It was your short story, "The Red Inn" ("L'Auberge Rouge") as taught by my Yale colleague Shoshana Felman, that brought me back to you in 1994. As an undergraduate, I had specialized in French Literature, but the intellectual dynamos around me were all involved in the relatively new field of Comparative Literature. While teaching at Yale, I got a second look at these favorite texts by auditing Comp. Lit courses like Felman's.

"The Red Inn" had all of us in Felman's class mesmerized. (By the way, I think that as an early fan of Franz-Anton Mesmer's ideas about occult magnetic forces, you would approve of my choice of that word.) Although Amazon did not exist at the time, we fans of yours would have been shocked to hear from an Amazon reader who said in her "Red Inn" review: "A short story—probably just as well. This will kill a short space of time, probably good if you are used to sitting outside schools or discos waiting for your kids to emerge. There are better things to read out there" (M. Dowling, Amazon.co.uk). Joe, on the same site, kept his remarks very brief, giving the story just one star, and one word: "Nil." Others piped up to say, "ditto."

Before we talk more about your "Red Inn," a tale within a tale that has what appear to be many digressions, here comes a True Confession that I know you won't mind: I am what Yale Writer-in-Residence, Anne Fadiman colorfully calls "a carnal reader." I'll explain.

My husband gave me Fadiman's book of essays, *Ex Libris: Confessions of a Common Reader*. After hearing her speak at a Master's Tea, I thanked her for writing it and asked her to autography my copy. I told her that her essay, "Never Do That To A Book" really hit home for me because of my and my husband's different approaches to reading. Fadiman divides readers into two categories. She looked me in the eye and asked which type of reader I was, courtly or carnal.

After I told her, she wrote in my copy, "For Diane, Please feel free to spill coffee and muffin crumbs all over this book."

Now, Honoré, if I may call you that, I feel certain that you, like me and Anne Fadiman, would proudly call yourself a carnal reader. Every photo I've seen of you looks way more carnal than courtly. Your white (?) shirt typically appears a bit rumpled, and your mustache does not look as if you just stepped out of the French equivalent of George F. Trumper's, which since 1875 has been offering everything a well-groomed gentleman would need. Moreover, I doubt that you, a keen observer, will take offense at my observations and speculations. I mean them in the nicest way.

Can you tell that I am stalling about getting to why I was so taken with your "Red Inn?" Are you ready for another confession? My well-marked copy (the margins of which are likely filled with brilliant comments and observations) currently resides on a groaning, messy bookshelf in another country. The good news is that I will soon be returning there, but I'm tempted to try something that I would never have imagined myself doing.

I found on the internet a copy of your story that I can read right now. It's true that it's in English, which we French teachers refer to as a *langue barbare*. But maybe it will be good to take a fresh look at it now that we're having this conversation. And if I'm lucky, some of my old insights will materialize along with some new ones. In the spirit of experimentation, let's see what happens.

*

OK, mon cher Honoré. I just finished reading what turned out to be your 15-page story (at Classic-Literature.co.uk, Free Public Domain Books from the Classic Literature Library) ably translated by Katharine Prescott Wormeley (1830-1908), a Civil War nurse and your contemporary who found time to translate your entire *Comédie Humaine*. Unlike the aforementioned Joe, however, who was able to reduce his review to one negative word, I'll bet I have taken about 15 pages of notes. Now I have to decide what, if anything, to do with my current complicated ideas on the subject. When I get back to my dog-eared French copy, I can compare them with the old ones. Regardless,

I've been having fun reflecting about my process.

One thing I noticed for the first time is your dedication of "The Red Inn" to Monsieur Le Marquis de Custine, who, I learned from en.m.wikipedia.org, "became known as France's most distinguished and notorious homosexual." Victim of a savage homophobic attack by soldiers he, during his marriage, established a lifelong romantic rapport with the Englishman, Edward Saint-Barbe. "Even though the literary salons, as opposed to the society salons, remained open to Custine, many...who were friendly with him sneered...behind his back." I see from another source that he and you, "who had a weakness for aristocrats" had a long friendship that lasted until your death. ("Balzac and the Marquis de Custine" by Francis J. Crowley in "PMLA" Vol. 58, No.3 Sep.,1943, pp.790-796.) You and Custine may seem like an odd couple, but I can see how your openness to delving into all forms of sexuality, and your personal and literary preoccupation with insider-outsider status could be part of the attraction.

Here are a few things that have come to mind on this reading of "The Red Inn." I'm reminded that although with you, what you see is not to be confused with what you get, many readers who don't seem to notice the irony of so many of your comments are satisfied with the entertainment value a story like this can offer. This diverting effect mirrors the story itself, which is set in motion by a coquettish request for an after-dinner frightening story, but that ends up giving all concerned way more than they bargained for. In this story that has multiple frames, we hear about a man who was framed for a murder he likely did not commit. To entertain his dinner guests, the unnamed Narrator repeats a story he once heard badly told by a German merchant named Hermann. In your story, each man has a "treasure" about which he feels guilty, and the way you go about focusing on the unconscious nervous habits of each one anticipates what Freud would "discover" about the psyche after you were long gone. There are many gaps alluded to in this story that foreshadow those that will later become the key issue in trauma theory.

According to the unnamed Narrator, Hermann the egocentric raconteur and original source of the story claims to have heard the tale directly from the story's French protagonist, Prosper, who had been condemned for a horrific murder he had been tempted to commit, but did not. Yet this would-be murderer who struggled but stopped himself in time feels as guilty as if he had, in fact, done the deed. Prosper judges himself guilty for merely having dreamt about committing a crime that would have given him enough wealth to help his impoverished mother. He allows himself to be convicted on the most circumstantial of evidence, whereas it is obvious that his "friend" who disappeared at the same time as the money, is the true guilty party. Hermann presents himself as an empathic friend who offered the condemned Prosper consolation and a sense of absolution. He also fancies himself a reliable observer of who is guilty and who is not. But Dr. Balzac, we know who the most reliable observer of the lot is, *n'est-ce pas?*

Hermann, who takes it upon himself to avenge the injustice by ferreting out the true murderer (who happens to be among the listeners), has his own moral concerns. In your multi-layered story there is plenty of guilt, ambition, greed, hubris, and self-punishment to go around. You call into question the motives of Raconteur Hermann the self-appointed Avenger when Hermann reveals his own anxiety about marrying the innocent heiress who happens to have become rich through the ill-gotten gains of her murderous father. The odd behavior of Hermann's future father-in-law and likely murderer seated at the table reveals his own guilt by his nervous reaction to Hermann's story. You, Dr. Balzac, repeatedly call attention to the gaze of the unnamed Narrator who has a passion for interpretation. Indeed, YOU are the true provider of the post-prandial entertainment.

Further, you have your Narrator say things that could have come from the mouth of a Freudian analyst. This Narrator (you?) calls himself "a seeker after *impressions*." Of Hermann's story, the analytic Narrator states, "I now write it down in my own way..." While relating what Hermann said, the Narrator jumps in to notice details like "the slight trembling of the hand and a moisture on the brow" of the truly guilty guest whenever the name of Prosper, the falsely accused murderer, is mentioned. In the quoted words of Hermann, we hear, in the context of his after-dinner entertainment story, pseudo-analytic observations of the tableside murderer like "unable to disguise altogether some secret apprehension, or possibly some anxious care." Hermann declares that the "perfectly natural motions" of the listener-murderer he hopes to trap "were noticed by me, only."

We expect psychoanalysts to be more perceptive than the average listener, and to be capable of making interpretive observations such as this one of a story's falsely accused protagonist: Prosper "believed himself both innocent and guilty...He judged himself; and he felt that his heart was not innocent after committing that crime in his mind." Did this sort of remark of yours inspire Freud's theory of the super-ego?

Prosper feels so guilty that he has even convinced himself he might have committed the crime not just by his intent, but while sleepwalking. The story, anticipating Freud's theories about the Unconscious, alludes to "the terrible agony of the too sudden reunion of our two natures separated by sleep." The gap in Prosper's consciousness about the crime is in harmony with what will be later known in Freudian circles as trauma theory. Poor Prosper who has been framed becomes feverish during his struggle NOT to commit a murder from which he could profit financially and fulfill his dreams of pleasing his mother.

Your Prosper "begins to plan a crime theoretically," but he becomes his own judge when he says, "Deliberation was, undoubtedly, already crime." In doing so, this character anticipates the quite modern concept that one can be legally innocent of a crime but be what Comparative Literature professor Arnold Weinstein calls "psychically guilty." The usual order of events is that one commits a crime, and then is punished. But current psychoanalytic thinking suggests otherwise— that guilt can *precede* the crime. And in this counter-intuitive-seeming scenario, the perpetrator commits the crime *in order to be punished.* Further, your Narrator will, with his self-vaunted "divinatory skill" appropriate Hermann's story: "I have written it in my own way..." This Narrator will take credit for "anything poetic or interesting there may be" in his self-proclaimed superior version of the story. But you make fun of him, too, by implying that his version of the story is just as tainted.

Freud would have had a field day with so many details of the story, and I would love to hear him try to get to the bottom of it. The murdered man's stolen treasure was stored and will be carried off in a heavy case. The room where the murder will be committed had been thoroughly secured against any intruders, making it clear that any trouble had to have come from within—an "inside job." They just happened to pin it on the guy who hung around long enough to look and sound guilty. In "The Red Inn," you, Dr. Balzac, refer to the "moment before sleep, when images arise confusedly in our minds and when often, in the silence of night, thought acquires a magic power." In dreaming about what he could do with all that wealth, the ironically named Prosper who will be condemned fails to distinguish between the idea and the act. A divided character whose conscience is too strong, Prosper double-judges himself for his unconscious wishes. As is the case with the primal scene of a trauma, the crime is committed while Prosper sleeps, so for him, the central traumatic event of the story is missing.

There are many additional ironies in the story, not the least of which is that in trying to restore order by imposing the law and executing Prosper, society commits a further crime. Society has what may look like scrupulous rules to be followed in the event of a murder, but the outcome of their application can be wrong. Another gap is Prosper's absence of testimony on his own behalf. He can't be his own witness because he had a lapse of consciousness. He does a far better job of defending his obviously guilty friend who has gone missing along with the treasure. He in effect "passed judgment on himself and did not find his heart pure, after committing the crime in his thoughts." He even finds himself guilty of killing his own mother, who he is sure will die if she thinks he's a murderer. Dr. Balzac, where were you when this poor man needed your help?

What I find intriguing about these details is how you, Balzac, appear to intuit what will later become psychoanalysis. Or is it the other way around? Which came first, the chicken or the egg? We know that Freud came up with many of his theories based on the literature he read. Numerous sources mention that on his deathbed, the last book

Freud read was one by you.

To come back to Hermann's vows to be the Avenger, after his Avenger status is mentioned, a more meta, analyst-like voice stands outside the action to comment: "Often the avenger is as cowardly as the victim." Hermann the Avenger shows himself to be guilty of the same self-serving reasoning as the evil side of Prosper. If Hermann marries the heiress he loves (even though her rich father is a murderer) and uses the money for good, will he be absolved? And Honoré, what about you, yourself, who profits from so brilliantly portraying so many vices? Do you feel guilty about this?

The punchline of your story implies that Hermann, the conscience-stricken lover is responsible for his own dilemma: In seeking the truth about whether the father of his intended was indeed a murderous profiteer, he ended up being hoisted by his own petard. His hunch was right that his father-in-law-to-be was indeed the murderer in question. Is the moral of this complex story that we are all guilty? That no one is without sin? That ignorance is bliss? That we shouldn't try, as Hermann did, to play God by exposing the murderer? Are we seeing here an anxiety on the part of you, yourself, as the inventor of characters like Hermann (Everyman?) who do that?

Critic Peter Brooks states, in his introduction to *The Human Comedy: Selected Stories*, that you were in fact haunted by the belief that you might be creating too much—"overreaching, usurping a power that should only be wielded by God the Father."

How do you feel about that?

Well, Honoré, our time is up for today, but we can talk more about this whenever you are ready.

*

Dear Honoré. Yes, some time has passed since our last visit, but I'm still here, and I have more to say about your "Red Inn." Here's my two cents.

In addition to the unexpected order in the notion that guilt precedes the crime, you've now got me thinking about some other

111

reversals of order.

When I first read your "Red Inn," it was before my study of Kafka's *The Trial*, but five decades after my first brush with Camus' Meursault in *The Stranger*. Now I'm thinking about what these authors might make of your character, Prosper, and, for that matter, of Hermann the ostensible narrator of your story who reminds me a lot of you. In each of these three works, there is some version of a trial.

In *The Trial*, Kafka's Josef K is caught up in a nightmarish, incomprehensible system that appears to have judged him guilty, but for an unnamed crime. It's not as if he has much of a choice about whether to be executed for this unspecified crime, but even if he did, he would likely have accepted the punishment. Indeed, he does not protest when taken away by two men to have a knife driven into his heart.

Meursault on the other hand has to be persuaded that he is guilty of a crime punishable by guillotine. The so-called logic of traditional rules of crime and punishment completely eludes him. Furthermore, as I think about it, with respect to the theme of crime and punishment, mothers play a key role in Camus', and in your story, as in the life of Kafka himself.

I'm sure I need to think more about the role of the mother in Kafka, in general. His *Letter to His Father* remained unsent as a result of his mother's intervention. Although she frequently tried unsuccessfully to protect Franz from the outsize wrath of his looming father, it's never been entirely clear to me just whom she was protecting by imploring Franz to promise not to deliver that letter.

The role played by Prosper's mother in what transpires in your "Red Inn" is similarly ambiguous and multifaceted. Yes, as we learn in Hitchcock's *Psycho*, "a boy's best friend is his mother." And when your mother is poor, to have within reach a treasure that could make her life easier is a huge temptation, as is the appealing idea of being her savior.

But what if she, like Hermann in your own story, knew that her benefit had come from ill-gotten gains? And that the price might be her son's life and the shame of having produced a son who would violate everything she had taught him? Execution might seem preferable to the humiliation of having to face such a situation.

Let's return to Meursault's mother in *The Stranger*—the mother he loses his head over because he allegedly didn't care enough to know which day she died. We know little about her except her presence/absence in the first line of the novel. Yet she will become a pretext used by those pretending to care about her to justify taking the life of her "monstrous" son.

Oh, dear. We mothers have a lot to answer for, right, Sigmund and Honoré? (But not necessarily in that order?)

Here comes one last word—and this time I mean it—about how prescient you have been in marking both reader and writer. Although you were born too soon for Netflix, I think you would have loved an irresistibly compelling recent film adaptation of Margaret Atwood's *Alias Grace*, which also artfully plays with the tension between technical innocence and psychic guilt. This film does so in a way that makes it impossible to know the extent to which the seductive and aptly-named Grace Marks is a murderess, a victim, or both. According to the publicity for the trailer (https://youtu.be/hMj_wraH3Ms), "Famed murderess Grace Marks told the man who came to study her mind that she'd lost her memories. But it could be that she'd rather not remember." Like the budding psychiatrist who in the film tries to get to the truth, we the audience are putty in Grace's hands. The same can be said for the rapt audience for Hermann's after-dinner tale, your "Red Inn."

Jean-Paul SARTRE

June 21, 1905-April 15, 1980

Considered one of the leading public intellectuals of the period after World War II, Jean-Paul Sartre received, but declined, the 1964 Nobel Prize for Literature. In his theoretical writings, novels, and plays, Sartre expressed his vision of existentialism as a response to an absurd, godless world. For Sartre, freedom, authenticity, and responsibility are key words. Good intentions mean nothing—man defines himself solely by his own actions.

Dear Jean-Paul,

There have been many Jean-Pauls in my life, but you're the only one in whose bedroom I have slept. You're probably wondering what I'm talking about, so I will explain.

During 1966-67, my Junior Year in France, I was living at 1 Rue le Goff, near the Pantheon and had read, in your autobiographical book, *Les Mots,* that this was your former address and the very apartment in which you grew up. You described very clearly the elevator and many features of the building. By that time, you had moved not too far away, and although you were very much on my mind because I was reading your work, our paths did not actually cross. But from what I know about your sloppy personal and libidinous habits, it's probably much better that I shared the bedroom with fellow blond Hamilton Junior Year in France student, Karen Watson of Binghamton, New York. Regardless of who or what wasn't in our room, the text of your play, *Huis Clos (No Exit)* would become part of my curriculum at Yale, and I never tired of teaching it. Apparently, you never tired of it, either, since towards the end of your life, you included it on your short list of works for which you wanted to be remembered.

In fact, *No Exit* was the first work that Yale students in our Intermediate-Advanced French used to encounter. Early in our study, I would pass around the scroll from a fortune cookie that said "The road to hell is paved with good intentions." That's not quite the most famous line of your play, "L'enfer, c'est les autres" ("Hell is other people"), but to many of those students, living as they were in overcrowded dorm rooms, that line immediately made sense. In the midst of our discussions, which happened to coincide with our study of the conditional tense, I came up with an assignment that worked well.

As a lighthearted *devoir* I asked the students to write me a paragraph that would complete the sentence, "*Pour moi, l'enfer serait...*" ("For me, hell would be...") and another for "*Pour moi, le paradis serait....*" Then after they had corrected their efforts, I divided a sheet of paper in half, and recopied a selection of the best parts of their respective heavens and hells. I numbered each set of comments but preserved everyone's anonymity. I made copies for all and we read them aloud in class. It was great way to get to know them (and each other) better. And also a way to showcase their work while allowing them to compare it in a friendly way to that of their peers. It offered a chance to say interesting things while learning new vocabulary ("extra credit for using the new vocabulary and target grammar!"), and to put into practice the grammar we were reviewing. I turned it into a guessing game where I encouraged them to guess who might have written what, but I never spilled the beans.

Throughout the semester I used variations of this technique to share excerpts from their best work, and it was a hit with all of us. Further, to have a page of elegant French with lots of good ideas about what we were studying proved to be an ego boost for them, a good study tool for exams, and a nice souvenir.

My *"Trois Choses"* ("Three Things") assignment was another efficient approach designed to combat the fact that with such a rich curriculum, we always felt rushed. Whatever other assignment happened to be due on a given day, I asked my students to always come prepared with at least three things to say about the day's reading—a key word or phrase that had caught their eye, a question about something they weren't sure they'd understood, anything surprising they had observed. That way if called on, nobody ever needed to feel on the spot about having something to offer. I sometimes used to have them break up into 3 small groups where for five minutes they would compare each other's "three things." This allowed us to cover a lot of ground while giving everyone a voice and a stake in the class discussion. I would call on each group in turn to summarize their findings, which I would record on the board. In truth, I would have been happy to spend the entire semester on your "Huis Clos." But that's why it's a good thing that I was just one member of a teaching team, and not the truly brilliant course chair, Ruth Koizim, who was the decider of the curriculum.

I think it's important and relevant for students to hear a bit about existentialism, and I'm ashamed to say that for many, our course was the first place they did. They tended to feel unsettled about what was going on in "Huis Clos," so I liked to stress what I see as the positive aspects of your ideas. Of course, they didn't always agree about the positive part:

In Sartre's view, there is no God. (Oh, no!—the upset begins!).

But this allows you to be free. (Hmm...but there must be some strings attached).

All that counts is what you do. You alone define yourself by your actions. (Oh, dear! You mean I can't blame my parents?)

Sartre thinks that the bastard is the freest of all. (Are you kidding? How could that be? My parents give me a lot of freedom. They even let me make my own decision about whether to come to Yale or Harvard!)

In this absurd world where there is no afterlife, you and only you are responsible for the actions that will define you. (But this is making us nervous. That's not what they taught us in Sunday School.)

To their virgin ears, it was a lot to swallow. But this is what happens when you come to college. You had some useful things to say about relationships, too: When you're attracted to another person not for his or her self, but because of how that person makes you feel about your own self, this is not a good thing. You illustrate this clearly in *Huis Clos* when you have Inès, the lesbian who wants Estelle, the coquettish murderer of her own baby, to join forces with her against the third person in their perfectly tailored hell. Knowing that Estelle feels lost without a mirror, Inès says that Estelle can look into her eyes and see the reflection she craves. Of course, the third member of this infernal *ménage* à *trois*, Garcin, will intervene to make sure that this potential coupling will not occur. But if Estelle hadn't already been in hell for good reasons, to look to another person to define herself would have landed her there, anyway.

In that Intermediate-Advanced level of French at Yale, we tended to use literature as a pretext for studying the language. But while stressing enough of the grammar to prepare the students in my section of this multi-section class for the group exams, I much preferred to focus on the ideas. And there were plenty of them, since after you, we did Camus' *L'Étranger* and "L'Hôte" from *L'exil et le royaume*

(*Exile and the Kingdom*), André Gide's *La Symphone pastorale*, Giraudoux's "La Guerre de Troie n'aura pas lieu" ("Tiger at the Gates") and *L'Apollon de Bellac*, Raymond Radiguet's *Le Diable au corps (The Devil in the Flesh)*, Joseph Joffo's *Un sac de billes (A Bag of Marbles)*, the film *Jules et Jim* via Pierre Capretz's incomparable approach, and even Goscinny and Sempé's *Le Petit Nicolas*. In recent years, the curriculum has veered into cultural studies and works by contemporary francophone authors, but I liked the original, which I taught for decades without ever tiring of the material.

Enough about my attempts to teach about you. I'm trying to picture you, Jean-Paul as a high school teacher. Or a meteorologist. Or a prankster. Or a man who had simultaneously many attractive young mistresses to whom you made your "rounds," in addition to some very kinky ménages à trois situations of your own that included a nineteen-year-old Jewish Algerian whom you adopted as your daughter. Or your young self as the victim of bullies. Actually, the last one is easier to imagine than the rest. Maybe that's why you refused to keep quiet about inequalities and injustices. I see, however, that in 1941 you took a teaching position at the Lycée Condorcet in Paris that became available because the Jewish teacher you replaced had been forbidden by Vichy law to continue teaching. It's clear that you were a man of many parts.

I've tried in vain to understand the ins and outs of your relationship and ultimate break with Camus. Although you and Camus worked together at "Combat," he said of you, "Sartre was a writer who resisted; not a resister who wrote." Ouch!

Whatever I do, I find that my heart is with Camus, and I don't think it's because of his physical allure. (I have to admit, however, that the photo of a young Camus that adorned the program for the recent Camus: A Stranger in the City conference dedicated to him on the 70th anniversary of his "one and only trip to the USA" took my breath away. What a face!) But somehow you did manage to get the prettiest and smartest girl in the class to be your life partner, so go figure! But your relationship with her, as explored in the shocking 2005 Louis Menand *New Yorker* article, "Stand By Your Man, The Strange

Liaison of Sartre and Beauvoir," exuded more than a whiff of Laclos' *Dangerous Liaisons*.

Yet even though New York did not organize a glamorous conference about you, you have gotten serious appreciation in recent years. In fact, I've been tiptoeing around you throughout my own letters to men of letters. You have felt like the elephant in the room, having extensive connections to so many of my letter recipients—Flaubert about whom you obsessed enough to try to write three volumes on him (your *The Family Idiot* that remained unfinished at your death); Romain Gary whom you praised; Ionesco, via my story of the fire in your (and my) Paris apartment at 1 Rue le Goff.

I had forgotten but was reminded by my Paris roommate Karen's journals that during our 1966-67 year abroad, our French "brother," Bertrand Peguillan, now a novelist, translator and researcher was, like you, a self-proclaimed anarchist. In fact, he probably got the idea from reading you. According to Karen, he and his anarchist buddies had an idea for something he wouldn't have called a prank, but that sounded like the one you orchestrated to convince the French public that Charles Lindberg would be stopping by the École Normale Supérieure to get an honorary degree. According to several sources, thousands showed up only to find a Lindberg lookalike, and the mess resulted in the resignation of the director of France's most prestigious school. But when you were arrested in 1968 for civil disobedience, you were pardoned by none other than Charles de Gaulle, who said, "You don't arrest Voltaire."

As for the young Bertrand, who is the same age as me and Karen, here's what he and his idealistic posse were discussing in 1967: "After supper, Diane was reading and I was in Bertrand's room hearing about this big secret project that the anarchists have in mind to spring on Paris. It involves getting ahold of loud speakers in a big department store, telling the people that they could take what they wanted, using tear gas and distributing leaflets. (Rather tame in terms of the terrorism of today, n'est-ce pas?)" I have Karen to thank for that quote from her journal.

Flash forward to more current information about Bertrand. I see he was quoted in *The Chicago Tribune* of November 15, 2015 about the Paris bombings:

> Several blocks away, outside La Cosa Nostra, a small Italian restaurant attacked minutes after Le Carillon and Le Petit Cambodge, Bertrand Peguillan, 69, was more blunt [about the reasons for the attack]. "The Bataclan is rock-and-roll," he said. "It's freedom, it's immorality, it's profane."
>
> Peguillan pulled out of his pocket a map he had clipped out of Le Monde newspaper showing the site of each attack. He said he planned to visit every one—just as he did last January after the Charlie Hebdo shootings.

At the end of your own life, you considered yourself an anarchist. For Bertrand, anarchy seems to have been an earlier phase.

But back to the current appreciations of you. *The Guardian* published an article on October 22, 2014 by Stuart Jeffries titled, "Jean-Paul Sartre: More relevant now than ever" ("Fifty years ago, Jean-Paul Sartre refused the Nobel prize for literature. His reputation has waned, but his intellectual struggle is still pertinent"). Jeffries asks,

> How then should we approach Sartre's writings in 2014? So much of his lifelong intellectual struggle and his work still seems pertinent. When we read the "Bad Faith" section of "Being and Nothingness," it is hard not to be struck by the image of the writer who is too ingratiating and mannered in his gestures, and how that image pertains to the dismal drama of inauthentic self-performance that we find in our culture today. When we watch his play "Huis Clos," we might well think of how disastrous our relations with other people are, since we now require them, more than anything else, to confirm our self-images, while they, no less vexingly, chiefly need us to confirm theirs. When we read his claim that humans can, through imagination and action, change our destiny, we feel something of the burden of responsi-

bility of choice that makes us moral beings...The existential plight of humanity, our absurd lot, our moral and political responsibilities that Sartre so brilliantly identified have not gone away; rather, we have chosen the easy path of ignoring them. (https://www.theguardian.com/stage/2012/jan/10/huis-clos-reviews)

Jeffries makes a convincing case for your ongoing influence.

Then there's the Monty Python sketch about you, "Mrs. Premise and Mrs. Conclusion Visit Jean-Paul Sartre at his Paris Home." Whether or not this is funny, to have inspired an elaborate sketch like this implies a certain importance to mass culture.

I'm going to end with one of the best homages to you that I found. In her excellent 2016 book, *At the Existentialist Café*, Sarah Bakewell (author also of *How to Live,* which is about the life of 16th century philosopher Montaigne) reveals much about you and Beauvoir that was new to me. Reviewer Lara Feigel (*The Guardian* March 17, 2016) calls Bakewell's book "the most engaging work of philosophy I have read." I knew from many persuasive sources that you were blamed for your commitment to Marxism despite the terrible events taking place under the communist regime. But Feigel points out that Bakewell gives a more nuanced account of your struggle to balance your ideals with the cruel reality of Stalin's policies:

> Though Sartre certainly fetishized violence, he did not enjoy watching the Soviet Union's casual disregard for human life. But he stubbornly believed in the necessity of overcoming what he viewed as squeamishness about death, placing the greater good above the mere individual life. Increasingly, this put both Sartre and De Beauvoir under a severe strain that their critics may not have seen. Sartre in particular was addicted to drugs....
>
> Sartre comes out of this book well, despite his selfishness, his bloodymindedness and his contradictions. He once said that it was important to ask how every situation looked

to "the eyes of the least favored," and to take their side. This stance led him to change his mind frequently and to make mistakes. But it also resulted in a compelling willingness to assess each situation anew and to think always from first principles.

Jean-Paul, how you yourself appear in the eyes of others—a pre-occupation that would have been anathema to you—has varied over the years. On the other hand, 50,000 people came to your funeral. Is hell always other people?

Whenever I am in Paris, I make a point of stopping in front of our former home, 1 Rue le Goff, Paris Vième. In my mind's eye, I see a plaque above the entrance that reads, "Sartre slept here, and so did I."

CHRISTO

June 13, 1935-May 31, 2020

Both born on the same day, Christo Vladimirov Javacheff and Jeanne-Claude Marie Denat de Guillebon (who died November 18, 2009) were environmental artists who used fabric to wrap buildings, surround bridges, islands, trees, and other elements of nature. The Christos' projects were always time-limited because, as they put it, "Everything in the world is owned by somebody. But "we go in" and "we create gentle disturbances; we are borrowing...space and use it intricately for a short time." Christo liked to refer to his installations as "irrational, irresponsible, useless." Others of us describe them as life changing. The same can be said of his death.

Christo and Jeanne-Claude at the Wrapped Reichstag. Berlin 1995. Photo: Wolfgang Volz

(En route to *The Floating Piers*, Part One)

Dear Christo,

This is not my first love letter to you. I'm sure you're used to getting letters from crackpots, but not necessarily from someone who used to think you were one.

But that's an older story—back to that later. At this point, not only do I think you walk on water, but you are going to let the rest of us join you. So right now I want to live in the present and tell you what's on for today, 1 July 2016.

But before we bid arrivederci to the topic of craziness, I admit to being a total nut case whenever I have to leave my nest. I have to say, however, that today's departure is different—the least crazy in memory. I credit you for that. You have set a good example and made me a woman on a mission.

I probably should have thought ahead of time that to set out on a 6-hour voyage to your *Floating Piers* right after Part One of a root canal, and in a newly repaired (we hope) 14-year-old car, might not be so smart. But you know all about life on the edge. With your short-term projects that can take decades to prepare, you may understand better than anyone the need to carpe those diems. So car issues, root canal, agoraphobia, and all those rumors about overcrowding be damned, my husband and I set off to catch the last two days of your *Floating Piers* project.

This may sound frivolous, but in my packing, I made a point to include a pleated orange top that would not clash with the way you outfitted your *Floating Piers*, and that reminded me of your other projects.

There were signs on the highway warning that parking for the Christo event was closed. The web site said a number of discouraging things: That trains were being delayed or turned away, that there could be a wait of hours or more, with the possibility of never making it onto the *Piers* at all. Then there was the ominous weather report about potential storms causing a shut-down of the *Piers*. All this is not music to a neurotic woman's ears. In a 1989 poem, I described you as "the winner of the Woody Allen look-alike contest." Well, you may look like Woody, but as I read this, I see that I'm the one who thinks like him.

"So what?" I once heard you mention, after saying how many decades you had been attempting to get permission to wrap the Reichstag, "All my projects have several times 'no.' I am [sic] very stubborn man."

I kept that comment in mind as inspiration at each of the literal roadblocks we encountered en route to the *Piers*. We had to circle back around a traffic rotary several times before an impatient police-woman would even inspect our reservation that would allow us to get to the apartment we had rented. It certainly didn't hurt that we had with us our Italian artist friend who knew just how charm her countrymen. Phew! We're getting closer...

(Getting closer! En route to *The Floating Piers*, Part Two)

Then came the stormy, gray weather that threatened to close the *Piers* before we could even sneak a peek. And also a decision to be made: Should we wait on line for the shuttle buses that might never arrive? And just to bring us to another line that might never end? Or take the suggestion of Roberto, whose apartment we'd rented, to wait, perhaps forever, for a boat ride to the *Piers*?

Here's where some of my worst anxieties—the ones that make it hard for me to leave home—rear their ugly head. As I look at the churning water, I, who have been known to get seasick merely by imagining a water scene, am having second thoughts. Maybe a long wait on endless serpentine lines under what could turn into a blazing sun might not be so bad? At least if I arrived by shuttle bus, I wouldn't worry about taking a misstep on or off the boat, losing in the process, this iPhone that contains all my notes for this writing project, not to mention my priceless hearing aids.

A possible sequel to the aforementioned neurotic worries: Let's just say I somehow managed to make it onto the *Piers* without myself or my belongings falling into the lake. Would I feel seasick once on the *Piers*, themselves? What about the sun? Woody and I, we don't tan, we stroke. Would my back and sea legs hold up during the 3-kilometer walk? Well, guess what! Something—actually, it was YOU, the master of temporary displacements! (and not all those years of therapy)—who made me put all those concerns aside. En avant! AVANTI! Full steam ahead!

So how did we actually make it onto the *Piers*? The story was that our landlord Roberto's young friend, Riccardo, co-owner with Francesco of a little motorboat, was out on the water somewhere with his girlfriend, but everyone seemed convinced he would show up soon. After all, it was lunchtime, and they'd probably get hungry. Many unsuccessful attempts were made to text Riccardo, but since it seemed that he was the only way we might get onto the *Piers*, we dug in with a bottle of water, prepared to wait. After four hours, just as we were about to give up, who should appear but Riccardo with a bevy of bosomy beauties that included his mom. So much for all the hanky-panky between him and the girlfriend that we had been imagining!

By now the threat of the storm had passed, the waters had calmed, and it took just the promised few minutes for Riccardo to whisk us to our destination, where helping hands got me off the boat without incident. He even offered to come back to get us later, and would not take any money.

(Time-out for some background! En Route to *The Floating Piers*, Part Three)

Before getting to *The Piers*, I hope you won't mind that we are going to do some time travel. I'm thinking that you who know all about timelessness, delayed gratification, and being in the moment might agree with me that chronology is not always what it's cracked up to be. At the beginning of this letter, I alluded to our older story, but said I would get back to that later. It was important to me to maintain focus on the project at hand. I am always amazed at how you manage to do that, given how many proposals you devote yourself to, often over decades. Once again, you are being an effective teacher to me.

So never mind that it was just July 2016. We are going to zip back to 1989. One of the great perks of being at an institution like Yale is that eventually, most everyone who is anyone shows up, and you can actually talk to them. I had only heard a bit about this artist, YOU, who would be coming to the campus to give a talk at a Master's Tea.

Here's what made me want to go. I had taught French in Paris for the Choate Program the summer after your 1985 wrapping of Le Pont Neuf. I really didn't know anything about you then, but had heard from a reliable and generally hard-to-impress friend about the transformative effect on Paris of your Pont Neuf project. I actually went to the Tea out of curiosity to see you and Jeanne-Claude. As I approached the Master's House at Yale's Calhoun College where you would be, I was still thinking that I would come away agreeing with your detractors. To my surprise, I was completely blown away by the two of you—your integrity, brilliance, tenacity, willingness to take total responsibility (but not a cent from anyone, because you know that financial support always comes with strings attached), complete lack of arrogance, and refusal to do more than create a time-limited "gentle disturbance."

Unlike me, you love transitions and the transitory. You have no interest in leaving a permanent mark or in seeking to own anything. You "borrow" space. Here's how you put it in the interview with Gianfranco Mantegna for the *Journal of Contemporary Art*: "Everything in the world is owned by somebody." But "we go in" and "we create gentle disturbances; we are borrowing...space and use it intricately for a short time."

This is one of the things about you that I find most remarkable. In your modesty and determination only to "borrow" spaces and to create no more than "a gentle disturbance," you are the only man for whom those words are NOT an oxymoron.

And yet, your projects do leave a different type of mark, one with which Marcel Proust would find an affinity. I'm thinking here of the comments by British art critic Marina Vaizey, who is quoted on page 45 of the Taschen book from their Basic Art Series by Jacob

Baal-Teshuva, *Christo and Jeanne-Claude* that I bought at the *Piers*:

> After the work has been put up and then taken down, it remains in the memory of the thousands who will have experienced it firsthand; it remains in the memory of those who will have seen the work on him, on television, in the newspapers. And an integral part is Christo's own portable art, the magnificent sketches, drawings, collages and prints that are both his working drawings and works of art in their own right.
>
> The temporary quality of the projects is an aesthetic decision for the sake of endowing the works of art with a sense of urgency to be seen and a feeling of tenderness that arises from their very transitory nature. It is these emotions of love and tenderness that Christo and Jeanne-Claude want to offer to their works as an added value: A new aesthetic quality.

I noticed at *The Piers* that my fellow walkers were not necessarily the same people I might encounter at a museum. It's true that some skeptics sniped that the reason so many came was because there was no admission charge, and because they wanted to brag to friends that they had done it.

But accessibility is important to you. In comparing what you do to what is the province of museums, you said that "Traditional sculpture creates its own space. We take a space not belonging to sculpture, and make sculpture out of it. It's similar to what Claude Monet did with the cathedral at Rouen." As Albert Elsen put it in the 1990 Sydney exhibition catalogue: "It is in the populist nature of (the Christos') thinking that they believe people should have intense and memorable experiences of art outside museums."

This accessibility extends to a wide array of differently abled people. I read in conjunction with your 1978 *Wrapped Walk Ways* project in Kansas City that a bus full of blind people came, and after walking the walkways barefoot, they said "We saw your project."

This was similar to what happened at *The Umbrellas, Japan—USA (1984-1991)* project, where, to the delightful surprise of the artists, blind visitors said they were able to "see" the umbrellas—to grasp their size by the degree of shade they provided from the sun.

The Japanese sense of vision embraced the concept that, as Jeanne-Claude herself put it, "an umbrella is roof, a house without walls." And that the Japanese would remove their shoes before sitting under them was proof that they understood your intentions for the space.

(And speaking of your intentions, En route to *The Floating Piers*, Part Four)

Of course, you know all about your own intentions for your projects, but in case anyone else is reading this letter, I'm guessing that they might not have had a chance to see the eloquently-stated facts that were part of a brochure for *The Floating Piers*. (By the way, I recall that at *The Gates*, although the friendly "monitors" had similar brochures and even actual pieces of the fabric that they were willing to hand out, one had to know to ask for them. Many didn't.)

"For sixteen days—June 18 through July 3, 2016—on Italy's Lake Iseo, 100,000 square meters of shimmering yellow fabric, carried by a modular floating dock system of 220,000 high-density polyethylene cubes, will undulate with the movement of the waves as *The Floating Piers* rise just above the surface of the water.

Visitors can experience this work of art by walking on it from Sulzano to Monte Isola and to the island of San Paolo, which is framed by *The Floating Piers*. The mountains surrounding the lakes offer a bird's eye view of *The Floating Piers*, exposing unnoticed angles and altering perspectives. Lake Iseo is located 100 kilometers east of Milan and 200 kilometers west of Venice.

A 3-kilometer-long walkway extends along the water of Lake Iseo to form *The Floating Piers*. The piers are 16 meters wide and approximately 35 centimeters high with sloping sides. The fabric continues along 1.5 kilometers of pedestrian streets in Sulzano and Peschiera Maraglio.

The Floating Piers project was first conceived by Christo and Jeanne-Claude together in 1970. It is Christo's first large-scale project since Christo and Jeanne-Claude realized *The Gates* in 2005, and since Jeanne-Clade passed away in 2009. As with all of Christo and Jeanne-Claude's projects, *The Floating Piers* is funded entirely through the sale of Christo's original works of art. After the 16-day exhibition, all components will be removed and industrially recycled."

I want to elaborate on some of the attributes I mentioned about you a few paragraphs back. The necessary tenacity you describe in the course of the lengthy process to gain permissions for your projects reminds me of the long preparation for an elaborate dinner that gets eaten all too quickly. Or of the long gestation period for the birth of a cherished child (who "borrows" space in the womb?)—especially if one starts at the very beginning of the relationship between the parents. But even then, where is the real beginning? Further back?

At that 1989 Yale Master's Tea, you and Jeanne-Claude spoke eloquently about your quest, begun in 1971 and not to come to fruition until 1995, to wrap the Reichstag. You called the Reichstag a "Sleeping Beauty...Very single...Separate from all the other buildings, sitting very lonely at the edge of the Tiergarten... A Mausoleum" that evoked centuries of German history, "that belonged to all the German people."

To wrap a structure of such breathtaking size and complexity seemed like an unrealizable dream, but I see from my notes that I saw you in October of 1989, and the Berlin Wall came down just a month later. There was a chance...

Meanwhile, back at the Tea, I found myself ecstatically scribbling notes throughout your presentation. Then I went home and feverishly turned them into a poem I called "Willing to Take the Wrap: Christo Comes to Tea."

I knew that you would be on campus the next day for a continuation of your talk, so I went back intending to give you my poem as a gift. At the end of your presentation, I shyly said a few words of thanks to you in French and gave you my finished poem in a sealed envelope. I was pleased with myself for having done something so uncharacteristically bold, but it was my enthusiasm that had emboldened me. I never expected anything in return, but here's what happened.

I guess you liked my poem, because a few days later, I found on my front doorstep a giant, very well-wrapped mailing tube with a return address of Howard Street in Soho. (What could it be? I didn't think I knew anyone there.)

Inside were a number of stunning posters, all signed CHRISTO.

I've been collecting data to write more about you since the day I went to see you at that Yale Master's Tea, certain that you and Jeanne-Claude would be a curiosity, rather than hero material. Instead, you definitively knocked my socks off!

This feels like the right moment to revisit my poem, "Willing to Take the Wrap: Christo Comes to Tea." Forgive me if I zig and zag a bit to include some of the notes I took as preparation for writing that poem. The title of my poem refers to your courageous willingness to take total responsibility for all aspects of your projects, and to the facts that I learned about you first-hand at that Calhoun College Master's Tea. There, you completely won me over, and I found a new hero.

To see you that day made me rethink the way you, unlike me, have never had a problem with investing herculean efforts and decades in a project that might never see the light of day, and that would be subject to a strict time limit. Your projects show understanding of a concept that has always eluded me: "Game over." When the preordained time is up, all evidence of an installation must be removed, the site returned to its original state, and all the materials used are to be recycled.

Although detractors like to refer to the two of you as egotists, you are nothing if not self-effacing. I liked your modest smile when you told us you seek to create what you like to call "a gentle disturbance." In fact, paradoxically, it's the ephemerality of the fully realized projects that is at the root of their urgency and power. It is rare to hear of anyone who has experienced a Christo project, even a blasé Parisian, who does not confess to having been forever marked by their participation in it.

Perhaps the key word is "participation." Whether as a paid witness (you insist that every project employ round-the-clock "watchers" to make sure things go right), or as an observer, every participant gets to feel an integral part of something unique.

I say this as someone who sensed all of the above even before ever being on the scene of one of your projects. The only one I had experienced first-hand was *The Gates* at Central Park, which came very late in my fixation on you. Even though I have never been a fan of New York or of most large cities, I could feel the life-changing effect of your project on myself and those around me.

My young niece (then age 4.75) and nephew (age 1) who had not yet visited museums and were too young to know anything intellectual about you, and even my aged mother who is no museum goer, responded to this event. I doubted they would ever forget it. More about that, soon...

(My poem about you, "Willing to Take the Wrap: Christo Comes to Tea," En route to *The Floating Piers* Part Five)

So much for all the preamble about that poem. So far, only you and Jeanne-Claude have gotten to see it. Maybe it's time to show it to someone besides us three. Because I wrote it before the computer era, I have never actually recorded it in any way other than the piece of paper on which I typed it. And since I only had one copy other than the one I gave you, I was afraid to lose it in coming from New Haven to Italy, so I took a photo of it with my phone. I am going to transcribe it from there now. Here goes.

*

Willing to Take the Wrap: Christo Comes to Tea

His works in progress come via Kodak Carousel
only no one is bored
all eyes keyed
to the hunched figure in jeans

winner of the Woody Allen look-alike contest
the wife encased in grey leather, shocking pink socks
fuchsia striped shirt, flaming orange hair

Wrapping Reichstag, islands, or Pont Neuf he doesn't shirk
"I absorb total liability"
Talks about borrowing, not owning space
His lack of pretense, (no buffoonery), wealth of integrity
amaze

In this age of rushing to make a mark
to cheat time by leaving lasting impressions
he aims for the temporary
creates a gentle disturbance
not a frontier of arrogance
In their urgency to be seen, their vulnerability
these peripatetic projects resemble nomads
not McDonalds

Never mind the universal—herculean effort goes
to the chosen spot
the materials new, useful, recyclable, destined for donation:
a welcoming pyramid of 410,000 oil barrels
gleam in the Arab Gulf
like an Islamic mosaic
as war rages

What about the saffron-colored waves of fabric
for the walkways of Central Park
suspended like a golden roof, sensual disorder in all directions
arabesque-ing in two weeks of winter wind?
Takes only minutes to explain,
painstaking preparation to persuade
a 200-page report to reject

Dealing in permissions isn't easy
"It won't cost the taxpayer a thing" can be your best argument
provide around-the-clock monitors
(600 for the 800' Pont Neuf)
as 3 million on the bridge experience the event
sending shivers up the flics

The Yalies listen respectfully, albeit amused
the plump patroness of the arts tries not to look miffed
at his refusal to accept a cent
an artist who understands there can never be "no strings"
that real collaboration doesn't exist—always somebody on top
talks about Prime Time for viewing a piece
and the need not to exceed it
Each project must have a hidden kamikaze dimension
an expedition into the uncharted

This man knows freedom and wants to scream it
beyond all confines
Art need not justify itself
esthetic, though not necessarily beautiful
form, color, a dynamic relation with its site
engagement à la Sartre

This unassuming figure in two-tone brown
pursues since 1972 his compulsion to dress the Berlin Parliament

"All my projects have several times 'no'
I am very stubborn man."

*

Phew! I am very relieved to see that I still like the poem, and hope
that you will, too.

(Are we there yet? Yes! Here at last! En route to *The Floating Piers*, Part Six)

Back to the mission at hand. As pleased as we were to be walking at last on the saffron-colored material of *The Floating Piers*, where we landed was not the transformative part of the experience. Once we had passed through the section of the project that ran through the town, however, everything changed.

As you, yourself, said years ago in an interview with Gianfranco Mantegna (*Journal of Contemporary Art*), at a time when *The Gates* were still an unrealized dream,

> You can see the people change. They start smiling at each other, they start talking to each other. They are in a completely different state of mind. It is very rewarding for us, because they feel that freedom, they feel that they are witnessing something that happens once in a lifetime.

Indeed, it felt like that at *The Piers*, just as it did when we had walked your *Gates* in Central Park. I could not stop smiling. What diversity among our fellow walkers!—people of all ages, shapes, sizes, races, and degrees of physical ability! What joy on the faces of those in wheelchairs and strollers! A family of ducks and a preening swan became show-stoppers. Ditto for the impromptu tango dancers (of varying ability, but no matter) moving to the sound of portable music. Even on the porta-potty-dotted parts of the walkway that ran through the town, we found ourselves watching with fascination the fish going about their banal business, swimming in the clear water. To be there created a hyper-consciousness and appreciation of every encounter.

I had read your thoughts about the enhanced awareness that is an important element of your earlier projects, and those comments can certainly apply to *The Piers*. It's true that it can be exciting to have to focus attention on things we take for granted. To walk on a wrapped surface does require a certain intentionality. I like what you said about your *Wrapped Walk Ways* in Kansas City 1978, a project whose relative simplicity you look on with nostalgia:

> You never watch what you walk on, now everybody was obliged to be aware of how he walked on that fabric, otherwise he would break his neck because there were so many folds in the fabric. In the most ordinary and banal process of walking, suddenly people were obliged to readjust themselves, to rethink how they moved through that space, think every path, think every step.

Jeanne-Claude added a poetic postscript to this idea,

> and maybe from the first time they watched their children take their first steps, they became conscious of their feet.

You like to say that there is nothing useful about your projects, but Paola Crestan, our Italian artist friend who came with us to *The Floating Piers* (who by the way, is not much of a museum-goer) helped us put into words what we were feeling: "Non è utile ma è un simbolo della possibilità di congiungere—di creare un ponte di incontro fra le persone." Although Paola's comments, like most things, sound better in Italian, I translated them as: "*Floating Piers* may not be useful or necessary in the traditional sense of those words, but they are a symbol of the possibility of creating a point of encounter for all people." She added, "Through his vision, Christo did something that didn't seem possible—to unite land, sea, and people."

Paola, an artist who also knows how to paint with words, had another way of putting her impressions: "Oggi la passerella di Christo porterà i colori di tutta l'umanità." ("Today Christo's runway will be displaying the colors of all humanity.")

After our miraculous day at *The Piers*, it was time to "refuel." We weren't expecting to necessarily find great food on this trip, but had some surprises. The first was hearing the disastrous crunch of a fancy Mercedes hitting a pillar in the parking lot of our restaurant, La Pernice, perched high above the lake. Oops! I found my overly-empathetic self thinking that you, who at every stage of your projects have to be ready for all manner of serendipitous events, would have taken that contretemps in stride. I tried to emulate your sang-froid. The lovely restaurant had three fixed (and not overpriced) menus prepared for the occasion: Meat, fish, or vegan. We had them all, and no one was less than thrilled.

The health-conscious Paola, who is accustomed to finding that in Italy "vegan" often equals "tasteless," pronounced "scrumptious!" her carrot-coconut soup, chickpea farinata and basil pesto, and "seriously" chocolate cake. The night view of the lit *Floating Piers* from the restaurant balcony was another highlight.

But then our dessert in the elegant dining room began to be punctuated by raucous cries and moans coming from the adjacent bar. What could it be? You, who love to juxtapose "opposites" like land and sea, ranchers and farmers, Japanese rice paddies and American hillsides, always seem undaunted and able to incorporate everything that happens into the experience of your projects. I'm thinking that you might have liked the serendipity of carrot-coconut soup and a loud soccer game.

When we left, the score was tied at one goal each for Germany and Italy. Even though the final score broke many an Italian heart, we felt like winners. After all, there will be plenty of soccer games. But only one last night of *Floating Piers* on Lake Iseo.

By sad coincidence, the death of Elie Wiesel coincided with the close of *The Floating Piers*. Yet it feels good to hear the words "never again" that we associate so strongly with Wiesel in a less painful context. When you yourself say "never again," I think you mean "there will never be another *Umbrellas* or *Surrounded Islands*" or *Floating Piers* "because they are sublime, unique things."

I am lucky to have a French writing partner, Jacqueline Raoul-Duval, who has just written a moving tribute to Wiesel that I will be translating for the online journal *Versopolis*. When I asked her about you, she said that you have also been a good teacher for her. Although she has only seen your *Pont Neuf*, she has seen many pictures of your other works. Drawing some interesting parallels between you and

Wiesel, she says about you,

> Firstly, Christo teaches us about memory. In front of the
> draped Pont Neuf, I asked myself, "What lies underneath?" I
> could barely remember. From Christo, we learn that we only
> truly see things when we can no longer see them in a literal
> sense. It's a psychological lesson, one that can be applied to
> the Holocaust and the need to remember. That's because no
> one really saw the Pont Neuf until it was draped! A ghost!
> And these ephemeral works, like our lives of which
> barely anything remains—photos, some letters, some clothes
> to donate—this is all part of a formidable lesson! And to
> think that this couple whose origins were so different, the
> Christos, shared so completely their vision for each project!
> Christo taught us to see, to remember, to reconstruct
> through memory; he taught us to pause, to witness and take
> notice, and love while there is still time, before people and
> things disappear.

As someone who recently had to divest and empty her home of
35.5 years, I'm finding that Jacqueline's comments about you are making me think more about the role of memory in coming to terms with
the transience of all things. In writing to Balzac about the task of
learning to travel lighter in life, I wrote, "The bottom line is that we
are all renters. Everything we think we possess is actually on loan."
And you, Christo, are teaching me that there's nothing tragic about
that. Au contraire!

(Echoes of The Gates, En route to *The Floating Piers,* Part Seven)

Having warned you that we would be embarking on some time travel, I am now going to return to the present. My formerly little niece,
Jillian, the one who saw your *Gates* eleven years ago, is now 16, and
on her first trip outside the States. This week, I am getting a vicarious
thrill "cyber-following" her around France. (When I was 16, the clos-

est to France that I could persuade my parents to allow me to get was the French summer program at l'Université de Montréal, but times have changed.) I had told Jillian we were just back from your current installation in Italy. When I asked if she remembered her 4.75-year-old self seeing *The Gates*, she said:

> Yes! I remember that:)
> But who is Christo?

Immersed as I was in writing about you, I found that a delightfully naive question. I sent her some info, a link to https://www.britannica.com/biography/Christo-and-Jeanne-Claude and to a lovely 5-minute video about you and Jeanne-Claude that I found on Facebook (https://m.facebook.com/xtojc/videos/?mt_nav=1)

I also really enjoyed Chris Livesay's 6-minute documentary/interview with you for National Public Radio. (www.christopherlivesay.com) It was fun to see the actual installing of *The Piers*.

With respect to my niece, to try to capture the interest of a teenager excitedly zooming around Paris, and who had just been to the Louvre to say hi to the "Mona Lisa," I came up with this quick answer:

> Wow! What energy you have! You are taking full advantage
> of the city and doing SO much! I am really impressed. The
> Christos are environmental artists who use fabric to wrap,
> surround and enhance buildings, bridges (they did Le Pont
> Neuf in Paris), islands, trees, and other elements of nature.
> Their projects can take decades to get permission, and are
> always temporary. We walked on water for miles last week-
> end on *The Floating Piers* in the middle of Lake Iseo, Chris-
> to's first installation since *The Gates*. It was only up for 16
> days. All parts of it are currently being dismantled and recy-
> cled. The 15 million bucks it cost is paid completely by him
> through the sale of his drawings.

Back to you, Christo. I don't think you would mind a bit that your *Gates* made a lasting impression on a toddler, even if your name did not.

When I wrote about all this to Jillian's parents, her mom responded:

> We all remember *The Gates* so fondly. Avery was only 1-year-old. When we got back in town, I had him in a grocery cart at the local health food store and there was a photo of *The Gates* behind the counter. Avery was having a little talk with me about *The Gates*. I think he started the conversation by spotting the photo and saying "Gates." The lady behind the counter said, "That is the smartest two-year old that I have ever seen!" and I just had to tell her that he wasn't even 2 years old yet!!!

So when is the right age to experience a Christo installation? At your *Floating Piers*, in addition to us Old Farts, we saw many young parents pushing strollers, not to mention pregnant moms who would soon be doing the same. One was even dancing a joyful tango. I can't speak for her baby, but I'm betting that the future mom will never forget that moment.

(Time for a coda, En route to *The Floating Piers*, Part Eight)

This letter has been quite a journey in itself, and I hope that it hasn't ended up feeling as interminable as some of the preparations for your works-in-progress. Like you, I have trouble giving up on a project, and I still have a number of thoughts I would like to add. I wish that I could wrap them up as elegantly as a Christo project, but since I am not optimistic about that happening, I'm going to include them here before saying arrivederci.

Full disclosure: This letter is coming to you soon after an "epic" conversation I had with another of my heroes, Vladimir Nabokov. I am trying to imagine him and Vera promenading down *The Piers*.

Would they have come? And if so, would they have appreciated what you were doing? There are many points at which I think you would be at odds with each other. Unlike your predilection for including them, Nabokov had an aversion to too many statistics and facts that, for him, could destroy the magic of an experience. His violent dislike of what he thought of as Freud's "too much understanding" might not be in tune with what you do. I'm not sure how to understand my passion for you and him.

On the other hand, I have written to Marcel Proust, with whom some of your ideas seem in harmony. In your interview with Gianfranco Mantegna (*Journal of Contemporary Art*), via questions like "Is art immortal? Forever?" you have addressed the need to change people's notions of art. In response to whether the length of time of an installation could be extended, you said, "It is kind of naïveté and arrogance to think that this thing stays forever, for eternity. It probably takes greater courage to walk away than to stay. All these projects have this strong element of missing, of self-effacement, that they will go away like our childhood, our life." Yet, as is case with Proust's madeleine (and the posters with which you gifted me), we can hold onto the memory.

To merely borrow space is a modest endeavor. You compare the vulnerability, temporariness, and fragility of your work to "a nomadic tribe that moves through the desert. They fold their tents and over-night they could build an entire village and the next day they would be gone...Freedom is the enemy of possession, and possession is equal to permanence." This is why the projects cannot stay. Yet, as Jeanne-Claude reminded us, "It is very expensive to be free."

As I free-associate and recognize the links among the men of letters to whom I write, and between my self "now" versus "then," I know that when I next write to Flaubert, I'm going to mention your mutual dedication to precision. Here is an example in the context of your description of a key component of *The Floating Piers*:

> The texture of the fabric, the cloth, is fully dynamic, not
> static. It is not like a bronze, it is very sensual, very teasing

material. You like to push it, to touch it. It is very tactile, that's why all these projects have the quality of inviting you.

Another example of a trait that you and Flaubert share can be seen in the way you speak about the effect of the transient nature of your projects. Even though English is not your native language, you use it very precisely:

> Your comparison between before and after is very fresh, it is not something you are used to. All this links to that transition existing in the project, the project is in a continuous transition, passing and going away.

Your early description of the future effect of the proposed *Gates* turned out to be right on target:

> The project is very ceremonial: When the wind is blowing, the fabric becomes like a roof. The project is very festive, very playful, between the strong, restrictive geometry of the gates and the very sensual disorder of the fabric flapping in all directions.

I think that Flaubert or Proust would have been very pleased to have written a sentence like that last one. I know I would.

Jeanne-Claude also had a way with words. On the topic of the recycling from *The Umbrellas*, she said, I imagine with a twinkle in her eye, that "the aluminum from the umbrellas is probably part of an airplane flying in the sky, or a can of ginger ale.

I'm no artist, but I'm going to close by referencing two close friends who are, and whom you have influenced. One, Paola, who was literally able to accompany me to *The Floating Piers,* just sent me a photo of her latest watercolor, "Walking Barefoot on Christo Dahlias." It is a gently exuberant explosion of the colors we saw together at *The Floating Piers.* The other friend, Judy, an artist in many media who is in the midst of a family health crisis, was unable to come to Italy. But even so, we made the journey together, in spirit. What you have to say about so many things, especially about temporariness, resonates with my favorite piece of her art. In her wispy calligraphy, she created a card that reads,

Teach us to number our days
that we may get us
a heart of wisdom.

The next time I write you, maybe it will be on one of Judy's cards.

Romain GARY

May 8,1914-December 2, 1980

Diplomat, prolific novelist, war hero, film director, and husband of American film actress Jean Seberg, Romain Gary was born in Vilnius, Lithuania. Although the Prix Goncourt is to be awarded only once to an author, Gary won it in 1956 and again in 1975 under a pseudonym. He also may be the only person to have challenged Clint Eastwood to a duel. Admiring Gary fans have said various versions of how unfair it seems that one individual should have had so much talent. Even so, Gary's dazzlingly accomplished life came to a characteristically dramatic end by his own hand.

Dear Romain,

I came to you in a roundabout way, as a fan of your one-time wife, Jean Seberg, an innocent from the Midwest who was oddly plucked from the wheat fields of Iowa to star in a French production of Joan of Arc, and would later feature in Godard's À *Bout de Souffle*. Everyone agreed you were a genius—a polyglot who won the Prix Goncourt twice by taking an assumed name, a war hero, a diplomat. But maybe you always felt like an impostor?

Some time after your divorce, a long-depressed Seberg was found dead in her parked car on a Paris street. There is a complicated back story about Seberg having been hounded to death by J. Edgar Hoover's FBI agents because of her support of leftist groups like the Black Panthers. You later blew your brains out long before I was able to write to you—and tell you not to go and do something like that. And to think that I was living in Paris at a time when we could have discussed our mutual Eastern European heritage, among other things! (I was about to write "Russian," but after hearing so many different legends about your origins, I was afraid to take the risk.) You, however, have always been all about risk, whereas I can't run far enough away from it. Yes, we are an odd couple.

I regularly teach and have written about your rich and probably semi-autobiographical short story, "le Faux." Once I discovered you, I had to read everything. As anyone who has read your *Promise at Dawn* (*La promesse de l'aube*) knows, you were a man who knew how to write a letter! Indeed, your novel that portrays a mother-son attachment of similar complexity to those in Roland Barthes' *Camera Lucida*, Camus' *Le premier homme*, and André Aciman's recent *New Yorker* piece about his deaf mother, is composed of wartime letters between a singularly devoted mother and her war hero son. I have never gotten over my shock at the surprise ending. And to think that you who were so accomplished and so loved—the *raison d'être* of such a mother—could have felt so estranged from yourself! I see that a new film version of this unforgettable book, starring Charlotte Gainsbourg as your mother, opens in France on December 20, 2017. The trailer already has 161,787 views. Yes, you are still irresistible.

Flash! Once again you, in your guises of "enchanter" and "chameleon" have left me enchanted! I who have never understood addiction, feel addicted to you, including the countless myths you created of yourself. It defies all logic, which I guess is what happens with true addiction. Each time I found a new reference that purported to tell your real story, I said to myself. "Yes! That's the one I will read!" But after much research and having listened to the words of your biographer and former lover, Myriam Anissimov in the truly enthralling 2014 interview with Zoé Varier, "Romain Gary, le Chaméleon" on her "L'Heure des Rêveurs" program (https://www.franceinter.fr/emissions/l-heure-des-reveurs/l-heure-des-reveurs-06-juin-2014), I feel sure that Anissimov's books are the ones for me.

On the program, this woman who comes across as smart, psychologically astute, and sensitive seems to "get" you better than anyone, and I'm not surprised that you went for her. She offers plausible theories to explain your initial exoticism to the easily hoodwinked reading public, claiming that your books seemed to have a greater affinity with American masters like Philip Roth, Saul Bellow, and Bernard Malamud than with the French tradition. The 54 minutes of that program flew by, enhanced by well-chosen music, excerpts of you yourself speaking, and the intelligence of the articulate interviewer who asks the right questions but knows when to get out of the way—a masterpiece!

Without any pretentious gobbledygook, in the face of your "complexity," "incredible ambivalence," and flair for the grand gesture (who else would have challenged Clint Eastwood to a duel because he had a fling with their wife?), author Anissimov gives convincing evidence for your being bipolar. She observed your depressed states of near-total immobility, as well as the feverishly productive ones during which you could work in the morning on a book written under your own name, on another that you would be writing under a pseudonym in the afternoon, after which you would go out on the town the same evening. She also reports your saying the equivalent of "I will never get old. I have a contract with the Guy upstairs."

I've had a longstanding critical interest in the reliability of the narrator in confession. In the current mania for memoir, the Lie in all its forms can be a central issue: The personal myth, *le Beau/Pieux Mensonge*, the Little White Lie, the small exaggeration, the nose-extending whopper—the Pinocchio factor. Let's just take a look at the varying versions of the "facts" about you.

In an excellent November 12, 2010 article from *The Telegraph*, "Romain Gary: Au revoir et merci," your biographer, David Bellos calls you "the most glamorous of literary con men," who "wrote novels under many names, won major prizes, and married an iconic actress." In "the strangest metahoax in literary history," one that had multiple twists and turns, Bellos shows how you pulled the wool over the bespectacled eyes of Sartre and Beauvoir, along with everyone else, by winning the Prix Goncourt twice, the second time under the pseudonym of Émile Ajar. The last words of your suicide note, which Bellos terms "an entertainer's farewell," were: "I had a lot of fun. Au revoir et merci."

In Victoria Baena's December 2, 2015 article from *Tablet Magazine*, "The Greatest Literary Imposter of All Time Deserves to be Remembered," here's what she says about you: "He eludes categorization and clear-cut identification... Ultimately Gary succeeded in writing his own history and leaving behind, if not a guarantee of how he was to be remembered, an evident desire to be remembered in a certain way." Baena views your worship of Charles de Gaulle as a stand-in for your reviled, absent father, and your extreme heroic exploits during your years with the Free French as your "first conscious sense of community and an identity other than that of an exiled Jew."

An earlier *Tablet Magazine* article (Oct.31, 2007), "Great Pretenders," by Emma Garman opens with the kind of dramatic flourish you would have loved: "On December 2nd, 1980, Roman Gary lay down in his Paris apartment, a synagogue-sized menorah at the foot of the bed, and put a .38 caliber Smith and Wesson in his mouth. Seconds later, the life of one of France's most celebrated and prolific novelists—a decorated war hero, globe-trotting diplomat, and notorious lothario was over. But this was more than suicide: It was the final act of mythmaking from a man preoccupied, above all, with manipulating the people and events in his life almost as deftly as those in his books."

You certainly had the ultimate stage mother who quite accurately predicted the triumphs you would have on so many fronts—the military, diplomatic, literary, and the romantic: "The most beautiful women will be dying at your feet." That sort of agenda, however, surely comes with a price. Sartre declared your first novel, *A European Education* (1945) "the best written on the Resistance" and even "the first great novel about the Second World War." The game was afoot!

As your novelty with the critics wore off, you felt the need for a new adventure. You said "I am tired of being nothing but myself... there was the nostalgia for one's youth, for one's debut, for one's renewal... I was profoundly affected by the oldest protean temptation of man: That of multiplicity." Thus your alter-ego, the too-successful Émile Ajar of your own invention was born. Your nose got longer and longer as you tried to cover your tracks. To win the Goncourt a second time, you had persuaded your nephew, Paul Pawlovitch, to pose as Émile Ajar, the supposed author of the prize-winning *La vie devant soi*. Then, you felt obliged to have Émile Ajar write a mad, hoax confession in the form of the book *Hocus Bogus*, considered by many to be a masterpiece, in which he pretends to be Paul Pawlovitch confessing to being Ajar. Who would have guessed that the pseudonymous Émile Ajar's winning the 1975 Prix Goncourt for *La vie devant soi* (*The Life Before Us*), a book whose beauty blew me and my students away, would have led to so much more complicated subterfuge that ended up making you feel even more like a has-been?

After hearing that Myriam Anissimov's biography of you was over a thousand pages, I was attracted by the title of Madeleine Schwartz's article in "The Harvard Advocate"—"Romain Gary: A Short Biography." Her opener gets right to the point: "By the time Romain Gary shot himself in the head, the French-Russian writer had published over fifty novels under four different names, directed two movies, fought in the air force, and represented France as a consul. His marriages...had brought him celebrity. He had enmeshed some of France's literary giants in an elaborate hoax that broke fundamental precepts of the country's cultural institutions." (That's not the part of this article that I think you will like, but check out this next image)

"But Gary always saw his own life as a series of incomplete drafts." Schwartz suggests that even as you planned your own death, you remained on the path to self-improvement: *To renew myself, to relive, to be someone else, was always the great temptation of my existence*, read the essay you left with your suicide note. She goes on to say, "It's perhaps no surprise that biographies of the author often seem overwhelmed by the slippery nature of their subject. *Romain Gary: The Chameleon, Romain Gary: The Man Who Sold his Shadow*."

Her punchline might please you: "Gary was one of France's most successful writers, but he lived the life of a spy."

I'm going to end my survey of articles on you by giving a reference to one of the best: "A Chameleon on Show" by Benjamin Ivry (from Jan.12, 2011, but updated Mar. 24, 2015 in *Forward Magazine*). There, Ivry mentions what he calls David Bellos' "insightful new biography" about you, *Romain Gary: A Tall Story*, and summarizes and synthesizes recent events and information about you from 2014 on the 100th centennial of your birth. There was a museum exhibit in Paris of your bafflingly illegible manuscripts, Arte TV showed a stage adaptation of the unforgettable Simone Signoret film of your *La vie devant soi*, and Gallimard came out with a book of essays about you by various writers.

I'm another of those various writers—one who wrote a piece about your intriguing multi-layered story, "Le faux," ("The Fake") that I have taught for many years in my French classes, and I may be the only one to have done so in the context of art crime. My article appeared in the spring 2011 ARCA (Association for Research into Crimes Against Art) *Journal of Art Crime*. In addition to offering great possibilities for conversation in a French class (about it, and you, due to what appear to be its many autobiographical elements), I found that your "Le faux" functioned well as a lens through which to view the 2010 Art Crime Studies Conference. I will omit the specifics of the conference itself, but let's see what you think of the rest.

In your story, a shady, nouveau-riche Neapolitan collector,

Baretta, who earned his fortune selling Italian salami, is in the news for having purchased, for a princely sum, what many believe to be a "fake Van Gogh." Seeking to burnish his image through buying expensive art, Baretta pays a visit to the renowned expert, S, who he hopes will authenticate, or at least not challenge, the authenticity of his Van Gogh. S, also a newcomer to Parisian grand society, has come a long way from his poor Turkish roots. Despite their equally modest backgrounds, however, Baretta and S have very different approaches to the exchange value of art. Among the themes of this richly suspenseful story are an obsession with authenticity in art and in cultural origins, and the valorization of the aesthetic object. (Sound familiar?)

Baretta's request that S refrain from suggesting that his Van Gogh may be a fake go beyond Baretta's hopes to enhance his personal glory by owning such a valuable piece. He also wants to look smart and to protect his investment. He didn't become the Salami King by failing to understand marketing! (Does this ring any bells for you, Romain?)

S, who prides himself on his *total* commitment to authenticity at all costs, likes to think of himself as the defender of the more purely aesthetic issues at hand. As honorable as S appears, his excessive pride raises a red flag and makes him an enigmatic figure. To be complicit in authenticating a fake can be seen as a harm to all. Another way to view this, however, is to see S's refusal as evidence that his reaction was always all about himself—especially his ability to flaunt his own power and influence, and by doing so, to make Baretta look foolish. (In contrast to your own tall, slender self, I'm visualizing the greasy Baretta and suave, dapper S both as short men.)

There's an odd twist to your story in that longtime bachelor S has finally found total (uh-oh—there's that dangerous word again!) marital happiness with the flawlessly (more red flags?) lovely Alfiera. Could there ever be a more perfect wife—the crown jewel of his collection?

In asking that S not say anything to cast doubt on the authenticity of his Van Gogh, Baretta thinks he is making a coercive offer that S can't refuse. But when S declines to budge on the Van Gogh authenticity question, Baretta promises that S will be very sorry. Indeed, his revenge is definitive, as he exposes something about Alfiera: a lack of perfection which results in the ruin of the marriage and the couple's happiness. (This recalls the terrible bedroom revenge scene in *The Godfather* where the bad guy knows just how to skewer his enemy who loves nothing more than his prize race horse.) In his diabolical plot, Baretta, who knows that S will never be able to forgive Alfiera for her deception, succeeds in turning S's obsessive commitment to authenticity against himself.

But what about S's apparent view of Alfiera as his very own perfect "work of art?" Does his "ownership" of her represent his personal desire to elevate himself from the barefoot boy who started out by selling sexy "art" postcards to sailors? Because Alfiera has been surgically enhanced, she can indeed be considered a work of art, if one considers the definition of art as what is arranged, as opposed to what is "natural." Further, as one whose face has been "arranged," Alfiera can be seen as representing the art of the surgeon who crafted her new nose, which restored balance and harmony to the rest of her.

À propos of the above, I've read comments by you and others that there was more than a touch of Pygmalion in your relations with your much younger wife, Jean Seberg, whom you proudly educated by showing her what to read and how to present herself: "You should see what I gave her to read: Pushkin, Dostoevsky, Balzac, Stendhal, Flaubert..." To that, Jean interjected, "Madame Bovary...That could have been me if I had stayed in Marshalltown (Iowa) one day longer."

But back to your "Le faux." So what if Baretta's Van Gogh was a fake? Was the extreme stance taken by S of divorcing his wife worth the unhappiness it caused everyone, including himself? Or was the satisfaction of staying true to his total commitment to what he considered authenticity enough to keep him warm on the long, lonely nights of the rest of his life? What does it mean that S is the only character in the story referred to only by a single letter, instead of a name?

These are some of the questions raised by your provocative story. In thinking more about it in the context of your own personal story, I'm still trying to figure out what you might be saying on both a conscious and unconscious level. That to try to maintain total control of one's image and that of a loved one leads to heartache and solitude? That an extreme commitment to authenticity is overrated? That art or a pretty wife should not be used to enhance personal status? Was it wrong for the flawed woman to acquiesce to her ambitious parents' insistence that she improve her natural appearance so that they could benefit from her attracting a rich husband? Does anyone in this story win?

In the world of art, with respect to a work whose provenance is suspicious, it is in no one's interest to prove that one is dealing with a fake. But what about the world of literature? I have to say that in terms of teaching, you are an author whose stories, both your own personal story and those you wrote, hold extra allure for college students who are in the midst of trying to find their own identity.

As for S and Alfiera, there was a brief window of happiness enjoyed by the couple, but it was based on a lie. In the end, however, there was more than enough misery for all. Fascinating, seductive, mysterious, enigmatic...Does it sound a lot like the Romain Gary story?

In the wake of writing you this letter, I came across the *French Review* article (Vol. LVII, No.2, December 1983, "Emile Ajar Demystified" by Bettina H. Lustig.) She delves into the specifics of how you orchestrated the plan for your second cousin, Paul Pavlowitch, to be the public face of Émile Ajar, the supposed author of the Prix Goncourt-winning *La vie devant soi*. She is interested in your motivations, how the pretense could have remained a secret for six years, what benefits you could ultimately derive from the ruse, and something I hadn't considered before, the reactions and effect on Pavlowitch, survivor and your principal accomplice in the Ajar conspiracy. According to your younger cousin, you had always enjoyed disguises not for the sake of provocation, but for the pleasure of inhabiting another skin. I can relate to that thrill of being liberated from oneself by becoming someone else, but I prefer to do it in a less baroque way: by adopting a name and identity to go with each of the languages I speak. In my letter to Marcel Proust where I talk about Wallace Fowlie, my former thesis director, I noticed that this name change technique also worked well for him.

Let me explain about how foreign language and identity change have worked for me. In Saltillo, Mexico in 1969, I honed my Spanish identity. Since then, whatever I do in Spanish, I am Diana Narro de la Fuente. The name comes from the wife and daughters of my Saltillo family. Although none is Prix Goncourt-worthy, I have plenty of entertaining stories from there, including the Cucaracha/Black Flag/ Anti-Insectos bomb facedowns that suffocated us without causing the dresser-dwelling insectos to miss a beat, the Let's-try-and-kill-Diane's sister-by-tricking-her-into-chomping-down-on-a-red-hot-pepper Caper, the water "purification" system that consisted of a large screen of chicken wire over the rooftop rain barrel to filter out the REALLY BIG insectos, to name just a few highlights.

I needed to be a fluent speaker of Spanish for Ph.D grad school requirements, and worried that two years of high school Spanish from 1963-64 were not going to "cut it." So my sister and I studied at L'Instituto Ibero-Americano for six weeks, mostly because it was cheap. We lived with Señor Alfredo Valdes de la Fuente (about whose Sunday family drives in his big red American Chevy I wrote in my letter to André Pieyre de Mandiargues), his wife Ofelia Narro de la Fuente, and spoiled, racist daughters Señioritas Alma-Rosa and Gloria Narro de la Fuente. Come to think of it, I could have usurped the name of my tutora—a sweet high school girl of darker skin color whom the school paid a pittance to hang out with me in the afternoons—Sara Elia Flores Valdes. With all the machismo down there where, you, Romain, might have felt right at home, it was a nice surprise to see that at least Mexican women get to keep their own names.

My Italian alter-ego emerged in 1972, when, with the help of my Sicilian train-compartment-mates (and some *Let's Learn Italian* flashcards that they found hilarious), I first taught myself many semi-useful Italian phrases on the Trans-Europa Express from Amsterdam en route to Rome. For many years until I moved to Italy, whatever I did in Italian, I was Donatella di Marco, the lyrical name of the daughter of the Italian Consul in Seattle during the 70s, when I lived there. My Italian adventures, which when not making me tear my hair out make me smile, are now recorded in a blog under yet another assumed name, Donatella de Poitiers. To speak Italian and tap dance are the two best antidotes to depression, and there are NO side effects. Niente! But you, Romain, seem to have been a born polyglot, which didn't help you avoid depression. And frankly, I doubt if tap dancing would have saved you, either. Some of us are wired differently.

When my new husband and I finally arrived in Rome in 1972 without any hotel reservations, having memorized my Italian flashcards, I felt ready to swing into action. We daringly allowed ourselves to be "picked up" by a slightly suspicious-looking guy who offered us a room in his home. Despite visions of being clobbered on the head and robbed, Jim and I followed him to our first delightful encounter with an extended Italian family. My own so-called linguistic "genius" notwithstanding, there were a few funny misunderstandings. I was puzzled to hear the name "Louie" bandied about by la Signora in the direction of my own husband, as well as being used to refer the Italian guy, himself. I said in my best hour-old Italian, "No, no. MY husband's name isn't Louie; his name is Jim. YOUR husband's name is Louie." That really took her by surprise. She replied, "No, no MY husband's name is Giorgio!" Then the smart, adorable grandma figured out the problem. She pointed to Jim and to Giorgio, gesticulating wildly, "lui, lui!" The light bulb in my dim head went off: *Lui* means "him" in both French and Italian. Duh...Non capsico niente! I understand nothing! (Too bad there weren't any *Let's Learn Italian* flashcards for that "lui/ Louie" situation!)

On the continuing theme of you-may-have-a-great-accent-but-you-don't-know-as-much-as-you-think-you-do, one of my Italian touchstones is a nifty manual gadget used to foam cappuccino. I've had three foamers in my life. How I lost the first one is one of my best stories, whose punchline is: "When leaving your rented house in Fungaia, never ask your son to 'pitch in and help' by putting your refuse-filled plastic bags in the garbage cans by the road." If you do, be sure you know the Italian word for "cappuccino foamer" (instead of calling it a "gadgetto"—a word you invented on the spot) BEFORE you call your sweet, former landlady to ask in your really nascent

Italian if she happened to find a "gadgetto" left behind in the rental's kitchen, along with "some old cheese and some nice apricots." And in a futile attempt to make yourself sound like less of a pest, you tell her that if she happens to find and want any of those things, she is welcome to keep them. (Huh?)

With respect to the aforementioned story, the poor woman was left speechless. All she could answer was, "Scusi, cara Diana, ma non capisco niente." ("Please forgive me, Diane, but I haven't got a clue about what you're trying to say.") And after hanging up the phone, I was left with no clues about the mysterious disappearance of my "gadgetto"/cappuccino foamer, either. I'm just hoping that the garbage man looked at our refuse deposit before dumping it. It would have been a shame to accidentally junk such beautiful apricots, old but still good cheese, and a really pretty cappuccino foamer. When we rented that same place, Il Mandorlo, a second time, Giovanna was happy to see us again, and was kind enough not to refer to the gadgetto/cappuccino-foamer incident. Italians are like that.

This brings me to my last point. Unlike you, who loved novelty, to be "reborn" here in Italy these past eight years has been enough of recharge for me. I am wondering, Romain, if your life would have been different had your mom made it here, to Italy, instead of to France. As the author of "Emile Ajar Demystified" points out, you could not bear being "pegged" by the French critics who, late in your career, seemed to glory in your fall from favor. You were furious at them for jumping to conclusions about your work without paying you the courtesy of examining it closely and impartially. You figured out what you thought was a good way to give them the finger. To write under an assumed name seemed an ingenious scheme that would prove that you still had more talent in your little finger than anyone else. Well, for what it's worth, I agree with you, and I hope that this letter from a fervent fan proves that.

PS: I have to confess that I lied when I said at the beginning of the preceding paragraph, "This brings me to my last point," but I think you will forgive me. Here comes a loose association. I don't always read closely my *Duke Alumni Notes*, but I need to tell you about an article I found there on imposter syndrome. It arrived just as I was finishing my letter to you, and the headline got my attention: "How a Dean Got Over Imposter Syndrome—and Thinks You Can, Too." I wonder what you would have made of this article—if it would have "spoken" to you, and if it would have made any difference in your trajectory. (https://www.chronicle.com/article/How-a-Dean-Got-Over-Impostor/241863)

The author, Valerie Sheares Ashby, currently Dean of Duke University's College of Arts and Sciences, winner of National Science Foundation awards and several teaching prizes, is a woman of accomplishment by any objective standard. Yet for much of her life, by her own standard, she felt she was not measuring up. She now gives talks aimed at helping those plagued by self-doubt—who feel like frauds who will be found out.

I noticed this phenomenon frequently during my 33 years of teaching at Yale, where even the most gifted students often believed they were lucky imposters who had gotten in by mistake. In helping them with their writing, I took it as my mandate to convince them otherwise, with statements like, "Yale Admissions never makes mistakes. If you gained admission, it means that you can do the work and deserve to be here, so no need to worry." But as Dean Ashby says, "all it takes is one professor in a classroom to embarrass you…one professor to tell you that your question didn't make any sense or wasn't valid. What that tells you is, *there's the evidence that I was right all the time* [about being an imposter]."

So what does this have to do with you, Romain? Well, as it turns out, it's usually the Romain Gary-type high achievers who can be most vulnerable to imposter syndrome—geniuses who need to prove they can win the Prix Goncourt twice, and with two entirely different books.

With respect to imposter syndrome and its possible relation to you, you've also gotten me to think back to pediatrician and psychoanalyst D.W. Winnicott's ideas concerning "the good enough mother." I first learned about this concept in Shoshana Felman's class where, perhaps in connection with Rousseau's *Confessions*, we read Winn-

159

icott's collection of brilliant essays, *Home is Where We Start From*.

Here are some of Winnicott's insights that feel relevant to the connection between the over-achieving hero of your *Promise at Dawn* and his mother, whose ambitions for her son knew no bounds. According to Winnicott, "the good enough mother" starts out by being totally devoted to the baby, sacrificing all for his comfort. But then she needs to pull back so that the child can learn to tolerate small amounts of frustration—a necessary lesson for survival in the outside world. By gradually allowing the child to understand that there is an external reality that will not always conform to his wishes, the good enough mother helps her child gain the ability to live in such a world, but still maintain touch with a world of fantasy, magic, and illusion. Would you agree that your mother was much better at the second part?

It seems logical that the never-good-enough mother is likely to produce a child anxious to perform extravagant, over-the-top feats in an effort to fulfill such a mother's grandiose plans for him. And unless he does so, he will feel like a not-good-enough son. But I'm guessing that this type of talk will not be music to your ears; indeed, you may be as allergic to it as another of my letter recipients, Vladimir Nabokov, who was violently hostile to anything vaguely Freudian. Even so, I hope you won't hold it against me if I, as a mother who has aspired to be good enough, do a bit of further musing on this subject.

I see that to be a good enough mother requires a sense of balance—a willingness to avoid excess, an acknowledgement of the need for separation, and knowledge of when to let go. (By the way, the final two episodes of a series about England's royal family, *The Crown*, that I watched last night showed Prince Philip as the wounded son of an appallingly *not*-good-enough father. Yet Philip repeated, with his own son, Prince Charles, a number of Philip's own father's mistakes and cruelty.)

But let's get back to you. Your own formidable mother, a resilient gambler who bet all her cards on you and was always going for broke, probably did the best she could. She may have been an expert at creating the origin myth of a hero, but you knew the stakes and somehow rose to the occasion. Moreover, after all the exploits and accolades of the hero-son (who in classic hero fashion, completes his circular journey by returning home in triumph), at least the mother in *Promise at Dawn,* in her own way, showed she understood the power of letters as both umbilical cord and legacy.

Although I think I have an intellectual understanding of successful parenting as the ultimate act of generosity—as mothers and teachers we work hard to facilitate independence and *not* to be needed—I'm finding it hard to let go of you.

André ACIMAN

January 2, 1951

Seventeenth-century French Literature and Proust scholar André Aciman, born in Alexandria, Egypt) directs The Writers' Institute of CUNY and the doctoral program in Comparative Literature. The themes of memory, exile, assimilation, and desire find expression in his memoirs, essays, novels, and short stories. The recipient of several prestigious awards, Aciman has lived in Italy and France, and has written, among many other publications, for The New York Times, The New Yorker, The New York Review of Books, *and* The New Republic. *His novel,* Call Me By Your Name, *and its sequel,* Find Me, *have been bestsellers, and the former became a prize-winning film. Guest editor of* Best American Essays 2020, *Aciman is, according to the* Los Angeles Review of Books, *quite simply, "one of the finest essayists of the last hundred years."*

Dear André,

I've been slow to tell you about this book of letters to men of letters that I have been writing, and the key role you have been playing in it. For one thing, you are way younger than Marcel Proust or Gustave Flaubert, and unlike most of the long-dead recipients of my letters, you are alive and, I hope, well. Furthermore, several of my letters to you were actually sent and received replies, so you have a place of honor in my book (pun intended)!

Like those Russian Matryoshka nesting dolls, this letter contains a number of other ones. Let's open the "Big Mother" doll first.

*

By the way, I'm sure that you are a great teacher. I am always learning things thanks to you. Here's just one zany example. In trying to find an image that could convey what was happening with these letters within letters to you, I settled on the nesting dolls, which are part of my Russian heritage, but I had to verify the spelling. One thing led to another, and before I knew it, I found out from Wikipedia that Matryoshkas "are used metaphorically, as a design paradigm, known as the 'matryoshka principle' or 'nested doll principle,' which denotes a recognizable relationship of 'object-within-similar-object' that appears in the design of many other natural and crafted objects." There's even a French connection: The first Russian nested doll set was carved in 1890, but the dolls were presented at the 1900 Exposition Universelle in Paris, where the toy earned a bronze medal. I was wondering what won the gold and silver, but all I could find was the astonishing fact that "Russian sparkling wine defeated all the French entries to claim the internationally coveted Grand Prix de Champagne." Who knew? Russianlegacy.com (which would be happy to sell us some of these dolls) has an interesting marketing statement: "We can see dignity and humility, power and hope for the future, deep sorrow and boundless hilarity in the Russian painted nesting doll...." Somebody there deserves the gold medal for mixed metaphors. (And some letter writer probably deserves one for not getting to the point.)

*

Back to the subject at hand. I opened the 2011 *New York Times Book Review*, and then went in search of your essay on lavender, which swept me away. However, I didn't want to buy your book, *Alibis: Essays on Elsewhere,* because I'm a cheapskate. So I asked the Yale Library to buy it and promptly checked it out. But as I've already confessed, I have a particular style of reading: I'm what writer Anne Fadiman calls "a cannibalistic reader" (not a "courtly" one)—I like to bend down pages and mark things up, so I ended up buying my own copy. I wrote a letter to you in praise of your work, but à la Kafka's unsent letter to his father, I didn't send it. Some time later, my son interviewed you for his "How I Write" column in *The Daily Beast*, and he passed me your email address. I finally sent you my letter-in-waiting, to which you sent a kind reply, and we have had some nice exchanges. Here is the first of these, which comes with its own bit of preamble:

> **To:** aaciman@xxx
> **Cc:** Diane Charney <diane.charney@xxx>
> **Subject:** a long-delayed fan letter with early birthday wishes
> **Date:** 12/29/2012
>
> Dear André,
>
> This fan letter has taken its time getting to you. Just after I boarded the train today from Rome back to Orvieto, a message popped up from Facebook asking me if I wanted to wish you a happy birthday. As a baby boomer too old to understand Facebook, I am taking this as a sign that I should stop obsessing about whether the time was right to send you a fan letter I wrote last year. It was actually written by my Italian alter-ego, Donatella de Poitiers, who, at her son's suggestion, writes the blog, "In Love with France, At

Home in Italy."

Unlike you, I am not such a fan of big cities like Rome, but I have to admit that reading your essay about it in *Alibis* has made me start to rethink that. And many other things, too, such as my relationship with lavender. The letter, like its writer, is not getting any younger, so I include it below.

I usually find myself writing only during Yale vacations when at home in Umbria, so the two latest blog postings also mention you. I spend the rest of my time helping others to write, and also trying to convince them they can speak French.

Both can be an uphill battle, but very gratifying, *tout de même*. Let me close by wishing you a happy, healthy year, and offering sincere thanks for *Alibis*.

—best, Diane Charney, mother of Noah, to whom you gave a most gracious interview for his *Daily Beast* column

DEAR ANDRÉ ACIMAN

This is the weirdest kind of fan letter, but I know that you will understand. How many times have I read book reviews in *The New York Times* that made me want to run right out and read the book, yet I never follow up on it? Well, this time started out as only a minor exception.

I was cautious. I asked the library to buy the book so I could see if my instinct that we were meant for each other was right. As a so-called writing expert and specialist in French literature, I do not give my writing heart up to just anyone. But the evidence that you might be the one was there.

As I think back to that article I'm trying to recall just what it was that snared me. Was it the lavender? I never actually thought I liked its scent, but now that I have become a newborn in Italy, I have a special relationship with this flower whose relaxing and sleep-inducing properties I have come to appreciate.

166

Or was it all of those references to Marcel Proust? Well he and I have had a thorny relationship ever since as a graduate student, I was forced to swallow every word of his novel.

No, it was the loving references to *La Princesse de Clèves* that nailed it. She and I have had a rocky relationship for a long time. I used to be very angry with her for the way she seemed to allow her cult of self-abnegation to run roughshod over her incomparable suitor. I could see how her 17th century scruples would have led her to refuse the Duke while her husband was still alive. But le Duc was so patient and perfect that it is hard to imagine why she would deny both of their chances for a happy life, once the man she never loved was out of the picture. Over the several decades of our relationship, however, I now see that that was, on my part, a youthful and rash rush to judgment. And now, here you are finding in la Princesse a soulmate.

I had a wild idea about writing a modern love story with her as the inspiration. I am wondering if she, during this age of the Internet, would have eventually reconsidered what she did: run away to a convent in order to preserve her equanimity and fulfill her need to punish herself for having had intense feelings for an irresistible someone other than her aged and then dead husband. Maybe le Duc de Nemours was just one click away on Google.

The way you describe your own imaginary relationship with the gypsy girl at the supermarket—all the elaborate feinting on both sides—have made me rethink the whole thing.

But the clincher was the way you describe your relationship with the feelings expressed by other authors—how you treasure the flash of recognition that comes from meeting in print a kindred spirit. That is the kind of writing I love to read, and that I encourage myself and my students to seek.

I am very excited to have found you.
(http://franceoritaly.blogspot.it/2012_01_01_archive.html)

*

As you can see below, my own first letter to you "incubated" (to quote your great choice of word) for many more moons than your perfect response.

From: aaciman@xxx **Date:** March 16, 2013
To: Diane Charney

Dear Diane,

I have been incubating a response to your fabulous email for months—too many. Now that I'm trying to carve a moment I find that I am speechless. This always happens to me. I plan a fabulous reply, and then, once I find the moment, the reply turns into both an apology and an avowal of an unfulfilled promise to respond in kind.

All I can say is that I totally loved the way you peeled away the various reasons for our spiritual/aesthetic consanguinity. From Proust, to LaFayette, to the gypsy girl and finally to that luminous moment where we discover not only that we "get" other people and are therefore never as lonely or as odd as we feared we were, but that the crossing over to others in that very intimate, bookish manner is not only legitimate but—to use horrible words—mandated by the author and the reading experience. One of the very few things I admire about myself—and I probably don't even admire it as much as writing about it now seems to lay claim to—is my sheer gumption to I assume that I "get" a writer... and then to take an extra step and think that I got them since I was 15. Bold and presumptuous, but in rereading a dissertation on *The Idiot* this week, I suddenly recall that I had already "gotten" the art with which Dostoyevsky framed so many psychological insights into his characters and that, in fact, if there is one thing I learnt from him at 15, it was precisely to admire the craft of insight over any other intellectual/mystical "idea" in his books. I have always thought that Dostoyevsky's ideas were kind of... well, you know what I mean: Weak. How he saw into others, however, was an induction into literature.

For me, Rome was the birthplace of two things: Books and libido. Now, almost a half-century later, I can feel the stirrings of how the two were born, linked, as always. I remember taking a walk by myself to meet a reporter in Rome around 4 years ago; I had just had lunch with my family and had left them at the restaurant to meet a reporter by the Pantheon. This was the first time that I ever walked alone in Rome since 1971. I've been to Rome numberless times since 1971, but never alone. As I walked by myself, eager to meet the reporter who said he was a fan of my work, I was not only back to being 15, 16 or 17, filled with a love for this city that suddenly belonged to me as it had almost 50 years ago, but I was right in my own skin again, myself again, as if all my clocks, scattered throughout the world, were synchronized to a Greenwich Mean Time that was just my own, right for me... and me alone. I knew the feeling wouldn't last, because I belong to NY; still, knowing that I was a "resident" here gave me a tremendous lift. Until, that is, it occurred to me that being a resident might also mean that I might still be living on Via Clelia, that I hated Via Clelia, that I couldn't wait to get out.

I did not mean to bore you with all this.

How I envy you Orvieto. When I think of the cathedral I think of magic. What a joy to walk those streets on an early spring day when crowds of tourists are weeks away still. Just the image of that amazing opera house which I paid to visit told me that a part of me lives in Italy.

And so I envy you spring in Italy, and particularly in Rome. I read so many books sitting on the stairs of the Spanish Steps with April's potted plants all around me, watching the midday sun turn into sluggish afternoons and into early sunsets, books that, as Proust would say, have trapped the light and person I was back then on their pages, so that it's no longer possible to tell the book and the person apart. Which brings me back to Lavender: One day someone will pick up a book I read on those very steps and if they're lucky, really and truly lucky, they'll be able to hear another voice behind the printed words say: Thank God you've heard me!

All my best to you.

André

*

(From Orvieto, August 23, 2016)

Dear André,

I was so dazzled by your response that until now, more than three years later (could it be?), I hadn't noticed many lovely details about it.

First, I admire the confidence you display in that second paragraph, where you are able to talk about the feeling of "getting" what an author has to say. I often feel that way, but then there's the problem of getting others to understand what I instinctively know. What I feel is my brilliant insight can be hard to articulate, which can be frustrating on all sides.

Maybe it's safer to write directly to authors who are long gone? You, of course, are the exception. At this writing, only two of my letter recipients besides you are still with us: Christo who is 81 is no doubt busy at work on his next project; and nonagenarian Roger Grenier, who I hope is well, but who surely has other things on his mind. (When I began writing these letters, there were three besides you, but Michel Butor died at age 89 just as I was writing to him.)

But back to the letter you wrote to me. Your third paragraph is the one! Memory can be so swervy (even *furbo* or *louche*, to use two practically untranslatable words from our favorite languages). Here's the part that is pure "you," but that speaks to the rest of us:

170

As I walked by myself...I was not only back to being 15, 16 or 17, filled with a love for this city that suddenly belonged to me as it had almost 50 years ago, but I was right in my own skin again, myself again, as if all my clocks, scattered throughout the world, were synchronized to a Greenwich Mean Time that was just my own, right for me... and me alone. I knew the feeling wouldn't last, because I belong to NY; still, knowing that I was a "resident" here gave me a tremendous lift.

To write my letters for this book has at times felt uplifting, but often disorienting because, like you and Marcel Proust of whom you are such an adept reader, I have been transported to various iterations of my younger self. I started to write "older self," but as you so eloquently put it, there's a Greenwich Mean Time synchronization effect that makes the distinction between young and old quite irrelevant. I may be nearing 70, but in a flash, I can be that 16-year-old Verlaine-reciting future lover of Camus walking the streets of exotic Montreal. But unlike you, I don't have the comfort of knowing "I belong to New York." Do I belong to New Haven where I've lived since 1976, but that has always felt like a transitory place? Do I belong to France that has been my intellectual home for as long as I can remember? Or do I belong to my adopted country of Italy, which has felt like a rebirth? The best I can answer is "all of the above."

Another purely "Aciman" way of thinking shows up in your remark that as exciting as it might be to be mentally transported back to your youth in Rome, "it occurred to me that being a resident might also mean that I might still be living on Via Clelia, that I hated Via Clelia, that I couldn't wait to get out." I've noticed in so many of your books your impulse to long to be where you are not, and vice versa. This is an area in which we really differ. I abhor transitions: Wherever I am, that's where I want to be. You say that your thing has always been, "how do I get rid of this thing I wanted so badly?" Ever the hoarder, when I get something I wanted badly, my impulse is to hang onto it for dear life. I love the word "plenitude," and feel lucky to have on occasion found it here in Italy. You say, "When you have total plenitude, you don't know what to do with yourself."

I know you take this issue of the ambivalence of desire very seriously, but your sense of humor saves you from driving yourself and your friends crazy. At the end of the New York Public Library event, "Landscapes of Eros and Loss," Colm Toibin interrupted your reference to a place that you never really liked, by saying, "Yes, but it was the rich way of disliking it that really mattered." And everybody laughed along with you both.

As for the last paragraph in your message, I love your allusion to "books that, as Proust would say, have trapped the light and person I was back then on their pages, so that it's no longer possible to tell the book and the person apart...." What you say here so succinctly may be what I've been trying to say throughout the course of this book.

Your last comment raises another issue that has preoccupied me and most of my other letter recipients: The question of audience. From my own notes over the years in connection with writing projects, I see questions like these: Did I just waste precious time? Would I feel more relaxed and satisfied if I had just read for enjoyment and not subjected myself to someone else's deadline and topic? I find intriguing and optimistic your comment that an author's voice might appear from behind the pages of the book you are reading to say, "Thank God you've heard me!" It is very hard not to fall prey to self-doubt. To varying degrees, all of my favorite writers did, and in the course of their writing, many suffered without ever knowing if they would have an audience. In many cases, there was none—at least during their lifetime. Even the often swaggering Nabokov expressed his worries about how his art would be perceived by dolts too ignorant to recognize its worth. But he quickly adds that such doubts are destructive and must be destroyed. According to him, great literature is a comfort that offers wonderful toys that help us transcend the "awful troubles of everyday life."

I have a dear elderly friend who is an exquisite writer and artist in many media, but a very discreet, private person far too modest about her abilities. She asks, "Why try to write something when there are so many brilliant people around? Who ever is going to read it?" Maybe these are legitimate questions since, given the limited time we have, it can be hard to live life and write about it. But something makes us do it. I'm having a JD Salinger-flashback to what big brother Seymour told Franny and Zooey. As a child star on "It's a Wise Child," Zooey refused to shine his shoes because he thought the people running the show didn't deserve any respect. Seymour told him to shine his shoes for the Fat Lady, which made sense to Zooey. Ditto for Franny when Seymour told her the same thing—that she should be funny for the Fat Lady: "I'll tell you a terrible secret—Are you listening to me? There isn't anyone out there who isn't Seymour's Fat Lady."

Maybe today's political correctness police wouldn't even allow a statement like that, but we who write regardless of who may or may not be reading, "get it." With respect to the question of audience, I hope you will believe me when I say that your letter really deserves a wider audience than just myself.

*

I see that another thing I sent you is a birth announcement in April 2013.

To: aaciman@xxx

Subject: From Annunciation to Announcement

As an art history-loving family we've found ourselves over the past nine months shifting our obsession with Annunciation scenes to those of mother and child.

With E's due date on the horizon, Great-Grandma Edith, age 88, and Diane have had bellies on the brain. So when a favorite student invited them to the Yale Belly Dance Society's benefit show, "Hips for Hunger," the two grandmas-in-waiting jumped at the chance to go. In fact they were so jumpy that they arrived at the performance a week early. Did they think that it odd that on Good Friday no one seemed to be around the Medical School auditorium to let them into the show? And weren't they suspicious that the only bellies in evidence that night were their own? Duh... Of course not!

Flash-forward a few days: E made her debut, and Edith and Diane made it to the Yale Belly Dance show. Afterwards they sat in the car admiring all the photos and videos of what came out of a belly in a faraway land at 4:47 AM.

As we hum "For unto us a child is born," we consider ourselves very blessed.

—xxx, Diane

*

My most heartfelt congratulations.
André

*

This next letter, which was actually written and SENT in a timely fashion, still arrived too late for its intended purpose. But it's having another chance now.

From: Diane Charney <diane.charney@xxx>
Date: October 17, 2014 at 3:26:47 PM GMT+2
To: aaciman@xxx
Cc: Diane Charney <diane.charney@xxx
Subject: Disappointed to have missed your talk

Ciao from the Orvieto branch of your Fan Club,

I've been on leave this fall for the first time in decades, and was excited to get the invitation to your Tuesday event, and to realize that you were at the American Academy in

Rome. Unfortunately that was the day we were driving back after a visit to our son, daughter-in-law, and our 1.5 granddaughters.

Although I do not yet understand Facebook, by coincidence, on the very day I saw the post to you about "the Tito-vintage cafe in Ljubljana," we were walking the streets of that beautiful city.

Since it took me quite a while to send you my first letter, I was pleased to think that you might be in Rome all fall, where my husband commutes every Wednesday to teach his "Madness at the Movies" course (or "Psychopathology in Film" as alliteration-deaf Yale forced him to call it: The Psychology Dept. says "You can't say "madness"; the Film Dept. says the word "movie" is *déclassé*; at Yale we teach "film." Jim and I say, OY! Who'd want to take a course with such a pretentious name? Well, as it turned out, everyone did).

I figured that even with my usual foot dragging, there would be time to make contact with you. But then I just saw your photo from your favorite Rome cafe along with the note that in just a few weeks, you would be missing that view. I hope not, but does that mean that you are soon going back to the States? Is your schedule full until then?

I also noticed in the Yale French Dept. Newsletter that you had been at our Proust-a-thon, so that was another missed opportunity to shake your hand.

Please let me know your schedule. With you being so nearby, I would love a chance to say hello in Rome, or for you to visit us in the Orvieto countryside.

We do have a lovely bookstore here that hosts authors, so it could even be a sort-of business trip. My 85-year-young Writing Partner, Erika, was just there telling them about your being in Rome.

BTW, Donatella de Poitiers, my Italian alter-ego, loved your son's NPR piece, and wrote about it on her "In Love

with France, At Home in Italy" blog. (http://franceoritaly.
blogspot.co.uk/2014/09/alex-aciman-on-le-grand-meaulnes-
back.html)

A presto?—best, djc

*

On Mon, Oct 27, 2014 at 6:25 AM, Diane Charney <diane.
charney@xxx> wrote:

**A "mieux-vaut-tard-que-jamais" proposal: Donatella de
Poitiers is trying to get her alter-ego, djc, La Reine de la Pro-
crastination, off her derrière—an uphill battle**

Salve,

On Wednesday, Donatella has to be in Rome for the
day, en route to Firenze via the 6 PM Frecciarossa. She'll
be accompanying djc's husband, biding her time, probably
reading an André Aciman book, while James conducts a
morning consultation at St. Stephen's School and then teaches his afternoon, "Madness at the Movies" class at Arcadia
College. A Country Mouse and no fan of Rome, she might,
if not afraid of getting lost, check out Eataly, which apparently is not too far from either of Dr. Charney's destinations.
Her main task will be to make it back to Termini on time to
catch that train—no easy matter for someone who can't read
a map and has no sense of direction.

Although djc herself would never have had the chutzpah to try to arrange a meeting on short notice, she's trying to reform and carpe one of those diems that her son is
always talking about. Donatella says she should get off her
duff and give it a go.

Ever since we got the invitation from the American

Academy to your talk, Donatella has been fantasizing about a meeting for lunch, tea, or just to say hello. If this Wednesday is not good, the other "D" would gladly make a special trip on another day. It's possible that you are no longer in Rome or are entirely booked, but I am resisting my natural impulse to hide under the covers and behind the written word, in case you are free. Cosa ne pensi? — best, djc

*

From: Andre Aciman
Date: October 27, 2014
To: Diane Charney

What a lovely email! *Purtroppo*, as they say in Rome when Romans wish to prep you for bad news, I am already in NYC. I arrived 2 days ago, totally nostalgic for Rome, craving to be back. We still have to find a way! Best to Noah.

André

*

And now, back to my current Letter to you. Although our paths have not yet crossed in person, I still think we are on the same wave length. If you're one of those courtly writers that Fadiman makes fun of in her essay from *Ex Libris* "Never do that to a book," however, remind me never to show you what I've done to your books. Some, like *Alibis,* have swollen to twice their original size thanks to all the pages whose corners I have turned down. Even if you do think this is a desecration, I'm proud to say that I have only made very discreet check marks alongside favorite passages, so I do have some scruples.

It would take forever and a whole other book to mention all the passages I have marked and that have left their mark on me, so I will limit myself to just a few. Your essay, "Intimacy" contains several.

Here's one: " I learned to read and love books much as I learned to know and to love Rome: Not only by intuiting undisclosed passageways everywhere but also by seeing more of me in books than there probably was, because everything I read seemed more in me already than on the pages themselves..."

I am definitely with you here, especially with respect to the mirroring aspect of what you read and the role of intuition. But the next bit gives me pause: "I was after something intimate and I learned to spot it in the first alley, in the first verse of a poem, on the first glance of a stranger." Here again, I envy your confidence in your first impressions. But you've also said, in the epilogue to *Alibis*, "You write not after you've thought things through; you write to think things through." My approach has always been circumspect. If I don't at first "get" what I suspect I should, I keep at it until I'm more sure that there's "no there," there. I picked up the phrase "rush to judgment" in Shoshana Felman's classes, especially her "Literature, Testimony, and Judgment." For me it's been a good reminder that I'm not that astute in knowing what's at stake in a work of literature, or maybe anything else, for that matter, but I like to observe others to whom this comes more naturally.

My family is full of artists, and I like to watch them as they do not hesitate to draw an unwavering line. I like what you say about the power of artists who can make us feel as if we have seen, felt, or lived through what they have: "The artist converts us; he steals and refashions our past, and like songs from our adolescence, gives us the picture of our youth as we wished it to be back then—never as it really was. He gives us our wish film back. Suddenly, the insights nursed by strangers belong, against all odds, to us as well. We know what an author desires, what he dissembles; we even know why."

OK, maybe I can't claim to know all that, or even to wish consciously that my sheltered youth could have been closer to that of my literary heroes. Yet when you talk about your childhood in Egypt (which is nothing like growing up in Middletown, New York), your love of the beach (for someone who doesn't like to put her head under water), and all the subsequent losses you experienced (to someone who was lucky not to have had to give up everything to go into exile), I am transfixed. And I'm not the only one. The Kirkus reviewer said of *Alibis*, "these essays sing with bracing clarity." Teju Cole of *The New York Times Book Review* calls the book "an extended aria on the sense of smell." Right now on my Orvieto property, the lavender is having its peak moment; the figs and white peaches warming under the cloudless sky and pre-autumn sun are giving plenitude a good name that maybe not even you could resist. But even if you did, I wouldn't love you any less.

Roger GRENIER

September 19, 1919-November 8, 2017

Winner of four of France's most prestigious literary prizes, Roger Grenier is the author of more than forty books. He was also a journalist, television and film writer, radio presenter, and influential board member of the French publisher Gallimard. An intimate of Albert Camus who hired him to work on Combat, *Grenier was a member of the French Resistance who was active in the 1944 Liberation of Paris.*

Cher Monsieur,

I see that you were born in 1919 and remained active until your death just a few months ago at age 98. I know that you were a long-time friend of Antoine Gallimard, but should not be confused with him, a crime of which Diane Charney was guilty (as the following tale will show).

This embarrassing story features my 1988 Paris interaction with you and Gallimard Press which I had believed was interested in publishing my study of André Pieyre de Mandiargues. When I showed up there for what I had thought would be my appointment with Antoine Gallimard, to whom I had originally written about my proposed project, his secretary seemed very surprised to see me. Her boss was out of town and there was no record of an appointment. Oops!

Then, when she called up to your office to try to sort out what had happened, we kind of figured it out. It seems that Gallimard had asked you to call me on his behalf at the home of my host family, the Morinière's on rue de Saint-Pétersbourg, (also formerly known as rue de Pétrograd and then as rue de Leningrad, before reverting back to rue de Saint-Pétersbourg, as the politics in Russia changed: Compliqué!) The phone connection had been poor during our long conversation, in the course of which we had discussed, among other things, Mandiargues' long relationship with the Gallimards, and the new company president's ongoing interest in him. But my appointment was to be with you, not Antoine Gallimard! (In general, I am somewhat allergic to talking on the phone in any language, and here's another example of where a letter would have been a far better way to communicate!)

It certainly wasn't the first time I had goofed in my relations with Men of Letters. As it turned out, you and I did have a nice meeting that day. We reminded ourselves of our mutual love of Pau in southwest France, a city where you had grown up and where I had taught for extended periods. You inscribed and gave me some of your novels, which I enjoyed—especially your 1965 bestseller, *Le Palais d'hiver* set in Pau, a city I loved so much that I expected to retire there. You seemed surprised that anyone would feel that way about your home town—especially an American teacher.

Many years later, by coincidence, while Alice Kaplan was still at my graduate school alma mater, Duke, and not yet French Department Chair at Yale, you and she visited the campus and gave a joint talk at Yale. She had translated your popular *The Difficulty of Being a Dog*, *Palace of Books*, and *A Box of Photographs*, and you had become friends. More than the actual content of your presentation, I enjoyed seeing the close rapport between you and Alice, a wonderful thing that can happen when an author and translator are particularly in tune with each other. Despite our age difference, Alice and I have been on the same traffic pattern a number of times. The world of French letters is not nearly as large as it seems when one is preparing for her doctoral exams. At your reading, I shyly reintroduced myself to you as the dunce to whom in Paris you had spoken and given your books, and you very kindly seemed to have forgotten the particular circumstances of our earlier meeting.

When I wrote my French Writing Partner, Jacqueline Raoul-Duval, that I would be writing you a letter, she had some lovely things to say about you. She said that you, *"un homme d'une douceur exquise"* ("a gentleman of exquisite gentleness") regularly crossed paths with her every morning on Boulevard St.-Germain when she was headed to work. You were always accompanied by your beloved big, blond dog, Ulysse. Neither you nor he ever raised your voice, and you both had the same slightly sad, very kind look, a bit detached from the rest of the world. *"Un homme délicieux qui savait tout sur tout, avec une grande légereté!"* ("A lovely man who knew everything about everything, but who wears his erudition lightly.")

She told me another charming story about you, a dog, and his French-speaking Japanese master, author of *Une langue venue d'ailleurs* and of a magnificent story about his dog, *Mélodie*. This author explains in his preface that one evening he was waiting for you at the Gallimard exit. He spoke to you about your *Les larmes d'Ulysse* and gave you his manuscript about Mélodie. You said to him gently, "But I don't speak Japanese," to which he responded, "Oh, but it's written in French!" You must have liked it, since you went on to publish it. It is a tribute to your keen editorial eye that *Mélodie, chronique d'une passion* by Akira Mizubayashi, which won major literary prizes in 2013 and 2014 was so well received. It's going on my list. I already feel a kinship with the author, a university professor who teaches French to foreigners, who has an acute sensitivity to the presence of music in our lives, and who first came to France at the same age I did. Ensconced in my Ivy League bubble, I had never heard of the book, but already feel moved just from reading the excerpt, where the author focuses in on the lacquer tea box that for 18 years has held some of his father's ashes. He anticipates doing the same for Mélodie whom the reader will come to love as he does. I'm imagining what a pleasure it must be for an author like Mizubayashi to have you shepherd into print a book to which you were instinctively drawn. And kudos to the author for sensing correctly that in you he would find a kindred spirit!

Another author with whom you regularly crossed paths is your neighbor and close friend, Romain Gary, to whom I wrote recently. The June 6, 2014 article "Les femmes et les mythes de Romain Gary" (https://www.lefigaro.fr/livres/2014/06/12/03005-20140612ART-FIG00331-les-femmes-et-les-mythes-de-romain-gary.php) mentions that, at 7:30 AM, you and Gary often found yourselves on the same traffic pattern because you would be out walking Ulysse, and Gary would be out then because he was an insomniac. You loved Gary and were one of the few people in whom he could confide. What an odd couple you were—you so steady and discreet; he so flamboyant and vulnerable! Your preface to his "Le sens de ma vie," the transcription of an interview accorded to Radio Canada just a few months before his suicide is, as is typical of you, a model of discretion.

In doing some belated research about you, I am seeing many other things we could have discussed, so I'm disappointed in myself for not having made the most of the time we spent together. I also wish I had gotten to read more of your books. I feel sure I would like *The Palace of Books (Le palais des livres)* with its questions about why we write that are enriched by your lifetime of engagement with books and authors, as an editor and trusted friend. In fact, you seem to have interesting things to say about several of my letter recipients—Balzac, Proust, and of course Camus on whom you wrote the book, *Camus et moi*. You said you consider him a brother ("to me, the man counts more than his work.")

I admit I was initially uncertain about sending this letter to you, based as it was on an anecdote that highlights my own ignorance. But I'm learning that such self-consciousness is perhaps also a type of self-indulgence—an exaggeration of one's sense of personal importance. (American Writer Josephine Humphrey cites "a quality that serves writers well: Self-doubt so deep it is indistinguishable from vanity..." She says of her grandmother Neta, "she taught me to look at pictures of myself as if the person there were mysterious and significant.") Having known you only in a limited context, I never would have guessed the extent of your connections to so many important literary figures. Although I'm not a fan of John Guare's 1990 prize-winning play *Six Degrees of Separation*, the concept of how closely linked one can be to others is definitely making itself felt in my Letters. Who would have guessed that like Michel Butor, another of my letter recipients, you, too, had studied under Sorbonne philosopher Gaston Bachelard whom I only knew from having used as a reference his *The Psychoanalyis of Fire*? Then I'm reminded that Sartre cites this work in his *Being and Nothingness*. And when I look up Bachelard, I see staring back of me a bearded face that looks incredibly like that of Michel Butor in his later years. For me, this appreciation of interconnectedness has been an unexpected benefit of my letters, giving new meaning to my self-description as one who is comfortable being a small fish in a big pond.

I don't want to tempt fate by saying that in your modest, unassuming way, you managed to maintain a productive life longer than every one of my letter recipients. Although my dream of giving you a copy of this book may not come to pass, I am grateful for this chance to write to you now.

P.S. This is a sad postscript in the very literal sense of that word. I will explain. I wrote the body of this letter to you in time to meet a

1 September 2016 publication deadline. You were then 96. Aware of your advanced age, and that you were one of the very few of my letter recipients still at work, I kept checking to see if you were still with us. As you know, there is often a delay getting things into print, and this letter is a case in point. Yet I took heart from the fact that the last time I checked, you were still on the job at Gallimard. That, however, was until today. So here I sit, reading several obituaries that tell me more about you, and how lucky I was to have met you more than once.

You who believed strongly in the role of chance and coincidence in your life might not think it strange that my late father, who is another of my letter recipients, would have been 98 right now. You died at 98 exactly one month after my father's October 8 birthday. My brother died four years ago on November 8, a day after you. From now on, I will be lighting a candle for you both at the same time.

The Telegraph titled their obituary about you, "Roger Grenier, Wrote *The Difficulty of Being a Dog,*" which they call "a charming meditation on the relationship between man and man's best friend." Never mind all of the prestigious literary prizes you won; somehow, this book that cites the influential role of dogs in the lives of a diverse group of men and women of letters, took precedence over your many other well-founded claims to distinction. As much as I love dogs (mine died just a month before you, and at a similar age), I am more interested in the strong bond between you and Camus. You said you owed him everything, that he made you into the journalist and writer you became.

I liked, however, that the *Telegraph* article reminded me of the importance to you of photography—that your parents were opticians and that you were all keen photographers, that your acquaintance with a young woman who had a Leica camera led to your being recruited by the Resistance, that your having a camera with you during the Liberation of Paris nearly got you executed on the spot, that you once had a job developing photos and being a projectionist in a cinema your parents bought.

The photographic lens also looms large in your 2010 *Dans le secret d'une photo (A Box of Photographs,* translated by Alice

Kaplan); your 2007 *Instantanés* (*Snapshots*); your 2005 contribution to the collection of self-portraits, *Traits et Portraits* that ended up being an insightful portrait of your unforgettable mother, Andrélie; and your close contact with the photographer-writer Brassai. Your 2010 interview with Corinne Amar, "Roger Grenier: Portrait" (https://www.lefigaro.fr/livres/2014/06/12/03005-20140612ARTFIG00331-les-femmes-et-les-mythes-de-romain-gary.php) details many aspects of your fascination with photography.

Most reviews of your *Dans le secret d'une photo* contain this evocative quote:

> Si j'ouvre mes vieux albums, les compagnons d'autrefois, la plupart disparus, me regardent. C'est un plaisir un peu triste et puis, d'autres jours, un face-à-face avec le néant. Certains, certaines étaient jeunes et séduisants, vraiment beaux. Ils n'auront jamais été vieux. Au bout d'un moment, il est intolérable de se dire qu'ils sont dans une tombe, ou réduits en cendres. Je referme l'album. Devant ces photos d'autrefois, j'ai l'impression que le présent est un pays étranger. J'y vis en exil.

I don't have what is surely Alice Kaplan's superior translation at hand, so I will try my hand at it:

> If I open my old albums, companions of times gone by, most of them deceased, gaze back at me. It's a rather sad pleasure and then, on other days, a face-to-face encounter with nothingness. Some male, some female, were young and alluring, truly beautiful. They will never have become old. After a while, it becomes intolerable for me to think that they are in a grave, or reduced to ashes. I shut the album. In the face of these photos of times past, I have the impression that the present is a foreign country. I live there in exile.

Your formative relationship with photography recalls the

reflections on photography by another of my letter recipients, Roland Barthes, in his *La Chambre Claire* (*Camera Lucida*).

Of all the tributes I read about you in the wake of your death, the best is from the France Culture site's "En Suivant Roger Grenier." (https://www.franceculture.fr/emissions/carnet-nomade/en-suivant-roger-grenier)

It includes a series of recorded interviews with you from 1950, 1960, 1992, 2012, and 2015. (https://www.franceculture.fr/littera-ture/mort-de-roger-grenier-incomparable-temoin-de-la-vie-litterai-re-au-xxe-siecle)

The apt headline that announces your death reads, "Roger Grenier, Incomparable témoin de la vie littéraire au XXe siècle" ("Roger Grenier, the Incomparable Witness to Twentieth-Century Literary Life"). Of all the things I heard you say on these precious podcasts, one in particular "spoke" to me. In discussing your affinity for Chekhov, you said, "it's as if I knew him." You call your prize-winning 1992 book about him, *Regardez la neige qui tombe. Impressions de Tchekhov* (*Look at the Falling Snow*), "un tableau pointilliste d'une relation intime" ("a Pointillist painting of an intimate relationship"). In speaking about your choice of the word "impressions" for the title of your book, you remind us that it is derived from the Latin for what is "pressed in" or "imprinted." The etymology of this word conveys the extent to which you felt deeply marked by Chekhov.

What you say next, however, gets at the heart of what I have been trying to do in my *Letters to Men of Letters*: "Some people are often more at ease with the dead. Whether the dead be authors or others, one talks with them." ("On est souvent plus à l'aise avec des morts— qu'ils soient écrivains ou pas—on dialogue avec eux.")

It's as if you read my mind and understood completely what I would be trying to do in this book. Yet when we first met two decades ago, this project wasn't even a gleam in my eye. How did you know? Maybe you're not the only one for whom chance and coincidence are key?

Michel BUTOR

September 14, 1926-August 24, 2016

It can be overwhelming to try to summarize the accomplishments of a polymath like Michel Butor. Although Butor was initially associated with the nouveau roman *("the new novel") movement of the 50s and 60s, in terms of his startlingly experimental literary techniques, he was in a class by himself. The author of a doctoral dissertation in mathematics and the idea of necessity, Butor produced travel essays, art criticism, translations, literary criticism, texts set to music, and five volumes of free-form meditations* (Matières de Rêves, *"Dream Stuff")* on writers, places, and ideas. The title of his 1962 Mobile: Étude pour une représentation des États-Unis (Study for a Representation of the United States) *plays on the multiple meanings of that word: an Alabama city that was the first capital of French Louisiana, a thing that moves freely, the motive or reason behind an action, a Calder-like suspended decoration, a flying squad. Among the many prizes Butor received was the 2013 Grand Prix of the Académie Française for his life's work.*

Dear Michel,

Although the time we spent together many years ago is fresh in my mind, I admit that I have not kept abreast of your accomplishments in several decades. The sheer number and breadth of these is staggering—even to your genuinely modest self. I've often heard your name mentioned with reverence by many varied and hard-to-impress writers and scholars, but even so, until now I had not paid attention to the specifics.

Thanks to a bit of research facilitated by a wonderful web site maintained by the University of Edinburgh's Department of European Languages and Cultures, I see that you have written on and even have had direct relations with many of my other letter recipients. For example, you admire Balzac (whom you call "The Pope of the Nouveau Roman") for his architectural genius in making each of his novels like the single chapter of a monumental construction, but one with mobility and that can be entered through different portals (translations, mine, from your interview with Jean-Louis Kuffer in No.38, October 1998 of "Le Passe Muraille"). Your admiration for Balzac extended to three magisterial volumes that you called *Improvisations sur Balzac*. You also did *Improvisations sur Flaubert,* as well as writing on Proust, Sartre, *La Princesse de Clèves*, Roland Barthes (whom you replaced temporarily at the École Normale Supérieure), John Donne, Kierkegaard, Dostoyevsky, Jules Verne, James Joyce, the collaborative possibilities of Science-Fiction, Ezra Pound, and William Faulkner, to name just a few of your passions. Then there is your extensive writing on travel, art, poetry, philosophy, music, and more. Your complete works currently number nine volumes, but fourteen are planned.

I am feeling as though in trying to get a handle on all that you have done, I may have signed my life away. But if I get to read even a small percentage of your work that intrigues me, it will have been worth it. In the interviews to which the Edinburgh site offers links, while saying the most profound things, you speak so clearly and accessibly that I feel as if we have been having the most extraordinary conversation. Among my favorites are the twenty-minute clip from Sumana Sinha,

Auteurs TV: Michel Butor (2008), and La TVNet citoyenne: Michel Butor "Les choses nouvelles ont du mal à traverser le mur du bruit" (1 June 2012). In the latter, your self-described optimistic self comes across as a beautiful mélange of prophet, humble genius, and the most benevolent Santa Claus. The timeless outdoor setting that appears behind you during the interview looks like a village from a bygone era.

During the course of my googling about you, I stumbled on some interesting things like your having had as your thesis director the legendary Gaston Bachelard who had connections to several of my other letter recipients, and whom, once you grew your long, white beard, you came to resemble. I wonder what it was like to have Bachelard as a mentor. And with respect to the latter interview mentioned above, the reference to "crossing the wall of noise" reminds me of a surprising and telling personal detail that I learned from the telerama.fr site: that your mother became profoundly deaf after her seventh pregnancy. The title of that 12/03/2013 interview with Marine Landrot is: "J'ai besoin de me mettre à l'écart." To hear your thoughts about how your mother's sudden deafness affected you is revealing. You think your other senses became more acute as a result, and that silence has been particularly important for you. You talk about the rich but "silent" conversations you and your siblings could have with your mother via lip reading: Because she was deaf, there was no need to actually voice the words you were articulating. To have had a mother with this disability stopped you from playing the violin (but not from loving Bach and writing an opera), and puts you in the good company of Albert Camus and André Aciman who, in March of 2013, wrote lovingly about his mother in *The New Yorker* article, "Are You Listening?"

I am a lifelong musician who has had some hearing loss, but fortunately for me, it has been correctable. (Come to think of it, my family who had to listen to my early days of viola practice might have welcomed a bit of hearing loss of their own.) Yet I find that to cross the frontier from my more silent world to one that can hear so many of nature's sounds is always startling. The "up" side of this: I definitely think I write better "unplugged," and consider myself lucky to have that choice.

But back to the circumstances of our first contact. Your biographical information lists in only a very general sense your 1973-74 "Trips to America and Vancouver." I want to talk about something more specific. Given your work habits, how did you ever find time to come to my house for lunch and a swim? Maybe I need to refresh your memory about that. While I was living in Seattle in the 1970s, you came to the University of Washington as a visiting lecturer. I have always tried to sit in on courses taught by authors I admired, and the opportunity to spend time with such a distinguished avant-garde intellectual was irresistible. It was a summer when most of the French faculty were away, and I think you felt isolated. Your English was quite limited—you had studied it by reading the Sears Roebuck catalogue! I decided to invite you to our house for lunch. Along with your daughters, your wife brought a "killer" *tarte aux pommes*. You and the family went swimming in Lake Washington off the dock of our lakeside bungalow.

There was only one text for that summer class: Your own *Mobile: Study for a Representation of the United States*, which many consider your most interesting work. You were constantly inventing new forms and genres, which caused many of your books, like *Mobile*, to be termed unclassifiable. Critic Frédéric-Yves Jeannet called it "Une sorte de symphonie spatiale discontinue hommage à Calder" ("A sort of fragmented spatial symphony-homage to Calder"). You dedicated your book to abstract painter Jackson Pollack, and I have read elsewhere your conviction that it is painters who taught you to read, to see, to compose, to write. You also credit photography with teaching you how to look at things.

Even having heard you talk about your own book, *Mobile*, I was curious to see how a site like *Goodreads* would describe this collage/patchwork quilt/travelogue/assemblage of city names like Mobile, Alabama, "road signs, advertising slogans, catalogue listings, newspaper accounts of the 1883 World's Fair, Native American Writings, and the history of the Freedomland theme park" that tries to capture "in both a textual and visual way—the energy and contradictions of American life and history." What a challenge for translator Richard Howard! None of us had ever seen anything like it. You seemed amused by our puzzled reaction. You don't like being considered a difficult author, which you don't think you are. You see the problem as your doing things that are new, and that require that the reader set aside preconceived notions and be open to learning to read nontraditional texts.

Your method for approaching such a text is to read it aloud, and that's what you did in our class. I may have needed convincing then, but now in my work with student writers, I always read out loud what they bring, and encourage them to read aloud to themselves as they write. In a similar vein, in a *French Review* interview from March 1984 with Michelle Rogers, you mention how much benefit you yourself get from reading even a supposedly finished text to an audience, which usually leads to revision. Further, the interaction can also influence what you will write in the future. Well before the advent of books on tape, you cited another persuasive example of how a good reader can make accessible what seems difficult. When there were readings of Proust on the radio, listeners who had been "allergic" to what they thought of his high-brow, long sentences ended up feeling very pleased with themselves for being able to understand and appreciate him. "My goodness! How marvelous! How intelligent I am!"

At the time of our summer class at the University of Washington, I was working on my dissertation on André Pieyre de Mandiargues, and you generously invited me to give a presentation to the class. That kind of kick-in-the-pants is just the thing to get a procrastinator off her *derrière*, and I have always been grateful.

As I recall, it was with an odd mix of pride and embarrassment that you told the class about trying to learn English by studying the pictures in the classically-American Sears Roebuck catalogue. You might be amused to know that I have followed your example: Whenever I try to work on building vocabulary in a foreign language, I reach for publicity flyers such as those from the local superstores like Slovenia's Lidl, and Hoffer. It can be useful to know how to say "Don't miss your chance to buy this week's not-to-be-missed specials: x, y, and the ever-fabulous z!"

On the subject of supermarkets, in the 1984 *French Review* interview cited above, you tell us you encountered your first supermarket, shopping center, and shopping cart when you visited America in 1960. You contend that during the subsequent twenty years, American culture and inventions exercised a very strong influence on France. When this Americanization was under way, the French didn't seem to realize the extent to which the American way of life was pervading Europe on both the urban and suburban scenes. You point out that there were both ugly and beautiful ramifications, but whereas the ugliness is hard to miss, you say it's up to the photographers, painters, artists and writers to point out the beauty. Always passionate about painting, you found it hard to choose between a future in painting and literature. But in seeing yourself as a "book artist, an artist of the book of today that is in the process of transforming itself into something new" ("un artiste du livre en transformation, du livre tel qu'il est en train de changer maintenant"), you have managed to combine your loves.

As an occasional translator myself, I appreciate the value you accord to the profession, and that you have often become friends and working partners with your translators. You say that you learn a lot from their questions and from the interaction which enables you to engage with your own text in productive ways. I am happy to say that I treasure my relationship with French author Jacqueline Raoul-Duval for whom I have done many translations. We regularly exchange ideas on more than the particular translation at hand. I like to think of her as my French Writing Partner.

In her *New York Times* homage to you, one of your own translators, Lydia Davis, cites the moving ending of a 2014 poem you wrote that suggests, optimistically, "the power of the individual to rescue a thing of value, something that could 'galvanize' our lives, from the catastrophe of economic corruption and collapse..."

*

Oh, dear! An uncanny thing has happened in the course of my writing to you. I knew that you were at risk of no longer being one of my three living letter recipients, but at 22:20 I noted that the site I had been looking at to verify some information about you said it had been updated two minutes earlier. I found this surprising since many sites are several years out of date.

And then I saw why: You had died at 22:18. To know that makes me feel extra grateful for the time we spent together today.

*

But you are still here for me. In the interview, "Michel Butor, l'écriture nomade" from the *Chroniques de la BNF* you say how much travel has always opened your eyes:

> To travel is the dream of a writer who is constantly renewing himself and never settling down in one place any more than temporarily, even if he has the intention to return there. It's this impatience with respect to boundaries that fascinates me, but I always feel the need to cross them. I'm not just speaking of frontiers between States, but of those among the arts, sciences, all activities of the mind. It's a question of establishing and maintaining movement as generously as possible.

As much as I like to think about and study liminal spaces, I prefer to stay put and let my mind do the traveling. You, on the other hand, despite naming your liminally-situated home located between France and Switzerland "A l'Écart" ("On the Margins"), have been a fearless lifelong adventurer and barrier buster.

I'm picturing you as a young man in Egypt trying to teach a class of 60 tough, uninterested, unruly boys in a language you don't know. But, of course, you ended up inventing a pictorial method to teach them.

You once wrote, *Every written word is a victory over death.*

In dying last night, you may have just crossed yet another frontier. But thanks to your generous spirit (and 2000 titles!), you have left behind so much for those of us who continue our journey.

André Pieyre de MANDIARGUES

March 14-December 13, 1999

Poet, art critic, and novelist André Pieyre de Mandiargues was affiliated with the Surrealists. He won the Prix Goncourt in 1967 for La Marge (The Margin), *but for a long time, he was perhaps best known as the suspected author of* The Story of O. *The plot of his* Le lis de mer (The Girl Beneath the Lion) *is the heroine's ritualistic plan for her own deflowering. His* La Motocyclette (The Girl on the Motorcycle) *became a film alternately titled* Naked Under Leather. *Photographer Henri Cartier-Bresson was his traveling companion, and he had close ties to André Breton and to the mystical poet and painter, Henri Michaux.*

The two photos of Diane Charney and André Pieyre de Mandiargues were taken by his wife, Bona, during one of Diane's visits to their Paris home.

Cher Monsieur,

I have a story for you. Once upon a time, the fall of 1968 to be precise, a Golden Girl rather dismissive of her own talents thought she should take advantage of the generous doctoral fellowships she received to attend graduate school. In this "decision," as was her wont, she was following a course of (non)action determined by the men to whom she was (semi)voluntarily bound.

The recommendations that got her those fellowships used words like: "Her maturity and judgment are beyond question. Her native talents, her capacity for hard work, the suppleness of her mind, the modesty and enthusiasm that she brings to all her undertakings, all these qualities prepare her eminently for a brilliant career in graduate study. Unlike so many of the applications that will receive favorable action from the readers of my letter, this one will involve no guesswork." But she thought she needed just to bide her time until her brilliant boyfriend of many years felt ready to marry her.

In retrospect I see that she was both like and unlike your sensual but virginal Vanina from *Le lis de mer* who, with great determination and imagination, planned to the last detail her own sexual initiation. Vanina selected her partner and gave the stranger elaborate instructions on just how he should bind her so that in their coupling, she would feel as if she were being penetrated by all of nature. In this pantheistic scenario that has been called a hymn to nature, the lines blur between man and beast, predator and victim, no words will be exchanged, and afterwards, he will comply with her demand that he disappear without even knowing her name.

But Grad School Girl needed to be initiated into the mysteries of the kingdom of academia. In her myopic, astigmatic eyes, her ultimate goal was to become an appendage to a Great Man. She had a modest, well-intentioned father who, watching the accumulation of her academic honors, termed her "an overachiever." She took this to mean that she wasn't as smart as her performance would suggest. Somehow, she was doing better than she deserved.

This was at a time, especially the late 60s in the South, when it was not easy for a woman interested in marriage and family to be taken seriously as a scholar. Her famous undergraduate mentor, Jules Brody, had told her to present herself as going for her doctorate even if her plan was to give it up the moment her "intended" missed her enough to crook his little finger and call her back to his side.

However, once in the very strange, foreign land of Durham, North Carolina where she had gone to study with and be subservient to another Great Man, things did not go according to plan. She started to unravel, imagining that her problem was that she was unable to do the work. Maybe her father had been right? But it was more complicated than that.

It took a lot of hard work and a new Prince Charming to set the unhinged princess on a better track. She and this new man who treated her with kindness and deference spent a blissful summer together in a duchy known as The Big Apple, where he worked in the operating room at a major hospital, while she commuted to NYU downtown to take some courses with other Great Men. One was literature scholar Roger Kempf; the other was Contemporary Literature expert, Thomas Bishop, who had happened to include in his course an electrifying slim novella (or récit, as you liked to call your stories) by an author I had never heard of—André Pieyre de Mandiargues. This was the beginning of our journey.

*

I know you got a kick out of being considered the author of *The Story of O*. In your preface, you lauded it as a sublimely spiritual, not remotely pornographic, work—"the first true novel since Proust." The first time I visited you, as intimidated as I was, I saw the sly smile on your face when you said, "Everyone thinks I did it! I didn't, but I know who did." If that was supposed to be my cue to ask who the real author was, I did not take the bait. But I have to admit that I, too, got a kick out of identifying the author on whom I would be writing my doctoral thesis as the suspected author of *The Story of O*.

Do you remember the day I first showed up at your house when I was just starting my research on you? This was in the spring of 1972, when my husband and I spent all our wedding-gift money on a trip to Europe. Before leaving I wrote you a letter saying that I would be in Paris and asking if I might interview you. If so, you could get in touch with me by leaving me a letter at the American Express office in Paris. That was the way things were done in the pre-internet Mesozoic Era. When I arrived, I felt so unprepared that I was hoping that you had not replied. I had to take a chance, though, because there was no way of knowing when or if I would have another chance to be back in France. But there was the letter, written in your inimitable crimped, spidery handwriting. Not only was your letter waiting for me, but you included your phone number for me to call and make plans for our rendez-vous. I called, desperately hoping no one would be home, but you, yourself answered. Panic was already setting in.

You offered to have me come over that afternoon. When I naively said, "*Formidable!*" I made my first of many missteps. You replied with outrage, explaining that "*formidable*" comes from the Latin and means "to inspire terror," and did I really mean that? Sort of, I thought, but apologetic about having spouted slang to such a purist.

I want to refresh your memory about our first meeting. My husband and I arrive at your house, opposite the Musée Carnavalet. On the landing, there are two doors and two doorbells. We ring one, and the door behind us pops open. We are greeted by a French maid in the type of traditional costume one sees in old French films: white bonnet, frilly apron, black skirt, light on her feet despite the high heels. She looks us over and shushes us with her outstretched finger. I explain that we were invited to see the master of the house. She ushers us in.

I'm stupefied as we walk by walls covered with works of art that I think I recognize (Arcimboldo, Chagall, Ernst, Cartier-Bresson, De Chirico, Dali), many given to you by famous artists about whom you had written. One shocking painting features an open side of beef—surely not the Rembrandt, but maybe the one by Soutine?

In addition to your being a celebrated poet, fabulist, "a realist of the imaginary," and master of a short novel form known as le récit, I knew about your reputation as a distinguished art critic. Our meeting that day felt as if it had the makings of a piece of surrealistic theatre. A slender, frail-looking man with elegant manners and piercing eyes that seem to take in everything, you introduce yourself, kiss my hand, and invite us into your inner sanctum, taking a route through a room filled with dozens of sewing machines. "Ah," I say, idiotically, "your wife is a couturière?" "No," you reply, "not a seamstress, but an artist!" This was not going well.

In only the initial stages of my research on you, I had no clue about how to approach an author on whom I was writing. Not only had I come without a tape recorder; I didn't even have a notepad—just a scrap of paper and a less-than-sharp pencil. Noticing this, you said, "Maybe you would like something to write with?"

I didn't know what to ask you—I was only writing about you for my doctorate at Duke because my supervisor had tried to bully me into a different topic, and I needed to come up with an alternative. Your *Le lis de mer* (published in English by Grove Press with the deliberately inflammatory title, *The Girl Beneath the Lion*) had been a revelation to my naïve self, so I proposed to write a thesis about you. I had originally wanted to write about Buñuel's films, but this topic was nixed by my department. At the time, at Duke, it was considered too avant-garde to write a French Literature PhD thesis on film.

My illustrious supervisor, Wallace Fowlie, was willing to accept my counter-proposal to write about you, and this is how you and I ended up together. But what an unlikely match! I was born in the Midwest and raised in quiet Middletown, NY, the "Big City" in the Catskill Mountains Borscht Belt. You were the suspected pen behind the pseudonym of Pauline Réage's *The Story of O*, the author of a novel *Le lis de mer* whose plot is the heroine's ritualistic plan for her own deflowering, and author of *The Girl on the Motorcycle* (*La Motocyclette)* which became a film alternately titled *Naked Under Leather*. You were well known for your ties with Surrealists like André Breton; with your traveling companion, Henri Cartier-Bresson; with Gallimard editor of your work, Jean Paulhan, whose mistress, Anne Desclos, was revealed in a major *New Yorker* article as the actual Pauline Réage behind *The Story of O*, and with mystical poet and painter Henri Michaux.

You seemed delighted to have your name associated with eroticism and sadomasochism in literature and film. The 1976 film of your Prix Goncourt-winning novel, *La Marge (The Margin,* ably translated by Richard Howard) features soft-core cult actress Sylvia Kristel. I do love that work not for its eroticism, but for the psychologically sophisticated way it portrays the interval between the time one senses that a life-altering tragedy has occurred, and the terrible confirmation of the suspicion. Of course, the news will have come by means of an unread letter that one can carry around while postponing the inevitable. I had a flashback to your masterly evocation of denial in this novel when my friend sent a message about her husband's heart attack. Even if you sense in your heart that something bad has happened, until you read a letter that confirms it, you can (sort of) blissfully go on your merry way.

You did seem to like that I was Jewish, and also that having studied in Mexico, I had some familiarity with the poetry of your friend, Octavio Paz, whose work you had translated and to whom you owe your passion for Mexico. I knew about your love of reptiles and later found out that you kept a python, but I'm happy to say that I did not see it.

In summary, against all odds, you seemed charmed by my naïveté and lack of professionalism. The whole experience of that first visit to your apartment was truly weird, but not so awkward that I was not invited back.

The dissertation topic I ended up choosing was not what you had in mind. You had wanted someone to write a stylistic study of your poetry, but I was more interested in your prose. You surely would have been happy to know there was a recent colloquium centered around that topic at l'Université de Caen. But my title was "Woman as Mediatrix in the Prose Works of André Pieyre de Mandiargues." At least it was on the topic of your particular vision of woman as half-mortal, half-goddess, possessed of special powers.

You had asked me to send you the finished dissertation, which took another three-and-a-half more years to complete. Unlike the official black-bound version I turned in to my doctoral committee, I had yours specially bound in a pure-white cover with a blood-red border that I thought you would like. At first I didn't know if you received it. But when I returned years later to see you, you said you had, and welcomed me back even though you were very ill and infirm at the time.

I visited your apartment once more, after you had died, and met with your wife, Bona Tibertelli de Pisis, (the one who was *not* a seamstress), whom you had married not once, but twice. On that third visit, your widow who had heard of Yale entrusted me with an array of clippings, articles, and files about you, hoping to promote your work through my own.

Years went by, but you appeared on my path again when, by coincidence, we visited Ferrara, home town of Count Filippo Tibertelli de Pisis, the flamboyant artist uncle who had raised your wife, Bona. De Pisis is well represented there in the local art museum named after him, and I found out from the owners of the guest house where we stayed that your filmmaker daughter, Sibylle, whom I had met as a young schoolgirl while visiting you, had spent a lot of time with them while producing a major work on her great-uncle.

Critics have noted the strong influence of Italy on your oeuvre. Of course, I never would have predicted I would have forsaken my beloved France to make my home in Italy, not far from the Monsters of Bomarzo celebrated by you. Perhaps we aren't such an odd couple after all.

I have of course kept the original handwritten letters both to and from you. But now, after all these years, and after several decades as a professor of French Literature, I still have a lot to say to you. I need to admit that I have not yet put to good use the letters or the documents entrusted to me by your wife. This letter is part of my effort to rectify that.

*

But more on the Jewish issue. I should have guessed you had a special interest in Jewish women but needed reminding via a recent article on your affair and ongoing epistolary flirtation with Nelly Kaplan, whom Wikipedia cites as "the only female film maker linked with surrealism." As journalist Benjamin Ivry writes in the publication, *The Forward*, "Kaplan flaunted the attraction of being a bewitchingly seductive, liberated young woman who, to these bookish French poets, incarnated the well-established literary trope of the 'beautiful Jewish woman.'" Your correspondence with her, published in 2009 under the title, *André à Lady N., Lady N. à André, Correspondance Pieyre de Mandiargues/ Nelly Kaplan* features "fervent imaginings owing much to...the Marquis de Sade." According to Ivry, these letters in which you call her your "pantheress" and ask her to write to you about her "lofty deeds and crimes" contain more than a tinge of "acerbic...sadistic wit."

Your letters to me, however, were of an entirely different ilk. In a letter from April 1983, you say you are sending me a book that you hope I will like. But you feel the need to warn me that just before sending it to me, a French critic criticized the book in very harsh terms, calling it "obscene" and even "Nazi." You add that you didn't know what to think, but that you decided to send it anyway, and I can be the judge. You say you are sending me the book in memory of happy days in Paris, and that you hope we will again have the chance to renew our conversations about literature.

While teaching in Paris in 1984, I wrote you full of ambitious ideas for book projects to share my enthusiasm for your work which was not receiving the attention in America that I felt it deserved. Despite being justifiably confused by my rambling, and your suffering from health problems (visible in your barely legible handwriting), you said you would love to see me as soon as possible. Your invitation, "As soon as you arrive, call me," rang some bad bells that still reverberated from the 1972 phone call during which I made one "formidable" faux-pas after the next. But I had learned some things since then and was encouraged by your addressing me as your "Very dear friend" and your affectionate sign-off, "your old friend embraces you."

This was the last letter I have from you, but in June of 1992, I wrote to your widow, Bona, telling her that as delighted as I was to be back in France, "for me everything had changed. Indeed, this would be the first time since 1972 that I would not have the possibility of seeing again the person who had inspired me since 1969, and whose passing had completely overwhelmed me." The most recent French family with whom I lived while teaching in Paris had sent me the sad news of your death. "As much as I had wanted to send condolences, I wanted to wait until I was back in France where I knew I would feel the enormity of the loss." I thanked your wife for taking the photos of you and me together during what, unknown to any of us, turned out to be my last visit. I was glad to have conquered my timidity enough to ask permission to take a photo, and Bona generously volunteered to do it. As I write this, those photos are right here beside me.

*

Cher Monsieur, (despite our years together, I would never feel right addressing you less formally)

Here come a few odd postscripts. Our previous correspondence mentioned above dates from 1972. This next letter to you is far more recent—August 2016. As you can see, you are still very much on my mind.

I'm here at Bomarzo to admire the immense stone "monsters" for the second time in my life. (Maybe the third if you count the time I "visited" by reading your *Les Monstres de Bomarzo*. That was when I was doing research on you for my dissertation.)

Things have changed here since my last visit, and I'm pretty sure you would not find Bomarzo's yuppified new look to your taste. By the way, these days the site is referred to by more than one name: Monsters' Grove, Park of the Monsters (Bosco dei Mostri), Garden of Bomarzo, and Sacred Grove (Bosco Sacro). That last title notwithstanding, plenty of sacrilege has been committed in this place. Here's the story.

The last time we were here, we were free to just roam around the park among the colossal otherworldly statues that have, since the

1500s, defied explanation, and that would make a good Rorschach Test. On our previous visit there were no barriers between us and "les monstres"; no 10-euro admission charge, and definitely no snack bar, cafeteria or vending machines peddling strange stuff. One of the most prominent of these machines, called SEX TEST DELL'AMORE displayed a drawing of a topless man and woman.

From what I could tell, you're supposed to insert your money and then place your hand on the indicated spot to find out if you are sexy. Or to put it more precisely, to find out just how sexy you are. There are six labeled categories each of which corresponds to a particular number of points ranging from 0 ("frigida") to 69 ("bomba sessuale"). Each category has a light bulb next to it to reveal the truth about you. I presume that the cartoon drawing of a cavorting apple with a bite out of it, a lascivious smile on its face, and its tongue hanging out is supposed to be a further stimulant to the experience.

The human hand of the visitor/patron also figures prominently in the imposing box-shaped machine located just to the right of the Sex Test machine. This one is a replica of the Bocca della verità statue. The insertion of one euro and of your hand into the mouth will allegedly get you an answer to any burning question you ask. A germaphobe might be thinking of how many unwashed hands had gone into that mouth. A cinephile might flash to Audrey Hepburn and Gregory Peck in *Roman Holiday*. Me? I'm reflecting on you (the once-suspected author of *The Story of O* and the actual author of a number of kinky works) and on what might be your response to all this.

But perhaps there is something here for everyone. Directly across from the two aforementioned machines are glass cases filled with multilingual books inspired by Bomarzo. I looked in vain for yours. Shame on them!

An essential feature of Bomarzo is the ongoing mystery of the place. These so-called truth-seeking machines that populate the visitors' pavilion that now offers the only entrance to the park seem to have come from a planet different from that of its contents. The statues themselves which have remained fascinating after centuries are in no danger of losing their mystique. I have my doubts, however, about how long the SEX TEST DELL'AMORE will last.

Closer to the window where one pays the entrance fee are a number of striking black-and-white photos of the statues from many years ago. One that I'm sure would have caught your eye is that of a young woman lying in the mouth of the whale statue, arms and legs akimbo, skirt raised in a way that highlights the whiteness of her long legs. Her face is not visible, but her long, dark hair flows every which way with abandon. Her sultry, supine pose evokes erotic mystery. She made me think of your virginal heroine, Vanina, from *Le lis de mer*, whose self-orchestrated, ritualized deflowering in an outdoor setting might resemble that shown in the photo.

I mention this by way of consolation for both of us that the sacred spirit of Bomarzo has not been completely despoiled.

*

Cher Monsieur,

Since my return to Bomarzo a few days ago, in recollecting my thoughts about you I've been doing some research on the internet, something I believe that you would have seen as a worse sacrilege than the Sex Test Machine. As one who was dragged kicking and screaming into the computer generation, I now see the extent to which I have dropped the ball on keeping up with current interest about you. At the time I wrote on you for my dissertation (completed in 1975), although you were well known in France, you were much less so in the States. I had been hoping to help remedy that, but did not have the necessary persistence to follow through, and I apologize for that.

So, I was thrilled to find an appreciation of you from 2011 in an article by Edward Gauvin, "An Introduction to a Great Mid-Century Weird Fabulist," in, of all places, *the Weird Fiction Review*. Gauvin had contributed his prize-winning translation of your story, "The Red Loaf" to Words Without Borders, an online magazine of international literature that had run an issue whose theme was "The Fantastic."

Gauvin admits how difficult it was to translate you, and mentions that Jean Genet introduced you to Sartre, with whom you were not impressed. Gauvin rightly cites your conscious cultivation of "artifice and excess...rituals of initiation and sacrifice, impossible encounters, pervasive malaise, ingenious cruelty, abrupt doom, and the arduous extremes of ecstasy." He finds that your "intricately wrought" stories arrest "with the power of their horror or strangeness, the dazzle at the mad edges of extravagance." Although you have been called by critic André Gascht "a realist of the imaginary," your own daughter who now presides over colloquia in your honor said of photographs you took that many would consider failures, "He does not know how to frame what is real" ("Il ne sait pas cadrer le réel"). She added that you were taught to "see" by your lifelong friend, Henri Cartier-Bresson, observing that your extensive travels with him marked for both of you your passage from adolescence to adulthood.

Gauvin's remarks were a welcome reminder of the excitement I felt when I discovered you. I also liked his appreciation of your style as elegant and exact: "Its classical cadence, its glories and labors of language could be mannered and forbidding, but it imposed on his chaotic imaginings...a sort of order, a degree of absolute coherence. He explored the impossible with maniacal precision and implacable rigor... He was scrupulous in describing, even itemizing, the props and settings of his worlds, no matter how bizarre those worlds become. However exuberant, violent, or frenetic his tales, they staked claim to plausibility through minute detail."

This description of your style could well apply to that of another of my letter recipients, Gustave Flaubert, someone whom you, too, admired. And on the theme of admiration, I see that you received plenty of it in 2009, the year of the hundredth anniversary of your birth. Among the celebrations was an exhibit at the Paris Maison de L'Amérique Latine organized by your daughter Sibylle and Mexican author and filmmaker, Alain-Paul Mallard, titled *André Pieyre de Mandiargues Pages Mexicaines*. The cover of the accompanying book shows you as a young man seated next to a giant sculpted face that recalls the statues of Bomarzo that so fascinated you. More about that in a moment.

Where was I during all of this? How could I have been so oblivious? I was busily teaching at Yale, where I had already been ensconced in my ivory tower since 1984. That, however, is no excuse. But you know what? I've decided to stop beating myself over the head about what I didn't do. In looking over my collection of letters to and about you, I see one from Hélène de Saint Hippolyte, attachée de Presse at Gallimard, whose card Bona gave me along with the articles Mme. de Saint Hippolyte had sent her about you. It contains a handwritten note that says,

Dear Madame,

Here at last are some articles published after the death of your husband.
In remembrance, Hélène de SH

I see that after I visited Bona on July 6, 1992, I followed up immediately with efforts to gain support for a writing project about you. This was at the suggestion of Bona. I have already talked more about the humorous outcome of those efforts in my letter to author and editor Roger Grenier whom you know from Gallimard, and with whom I found out that I share some unexpected connections.

In writing about you to a friend in the French publishing business, I berated myself about not trying to do more to publish my work about you. Here were my plans. First, I wanted to seek publication in France of my own dissertation on you. Another goal was to publish in America and in France a critical edition with excerpts of your oeuvre chosen around the theme of "woman as mediatrix." I also proposed to translate and publish in America a selection of your work aimed at a larger, non-scholarly audience that would emphasize the erotic and out–of-the-ordinary elements in your writings. In thinking about marketing issues, I would seek to have one of your stories placed in a publication that has demonstrated interest in good literature, such as the *New Yorker, Harpers, Atlantic Monthly*, or perhaps even *Playboy*.

What was different about my proposed projects? As marvelous as the translations into English by Pulitzer Prize-winning poet, Richard Howard are, they were of single works, whereas I wanted to select your most fascinating pieces from different collections. You and I discussed this, but although you liked the idea, because of the question of publisher's rights, you thought it would be difficult. I was thinking that now that you are gone, your publishers might consider such a collection that would have the added advantage of offering an overview of your work. But enough about my good intentions.

I apologize for boring you with all these details. As someone who was never driven to have a large audience, and who had little interest in being a "hit" in academia, you listened politely and patiently, but probably took my ambitions with a grain of salt. It's probably more than time for me to do the same. I see that in recent years, many of your works have been reissued along the lines of what I had proposed to do, and that is the important thing.

I want to say a few things about a recent discovery. I learned some things about you by watching an interview of your now-adult daughter Sibylle speaking about the short film she made of your apartment, and about the *Pages Mexicaines* exhibit. When the interviewer asks about her father, she refers to you as "André," and talks with indulgence and understanding about your attraction to the violence in Mexican art and culture. She specifies, however, that you are interested in the violence of desire, as opposed to a violence that destroys.

The only violence I observed while living and studying in Saltillo, Mexico during the summer of 1969 was the "pistola" and bullet belt that the father of the family, Señor Alfredo Valdes de la Fuente would strap on when we'd go out on our Sunday afternoon rides in the countryside to show off his car. When asked about this, he explained as he raised his pistol with a grand flourish: *BANDITOS!* Indeed, if there were banditos lurking about, we were not very well camouflaged in our gargantuan, arrest-me-red Chevy.

Although I'm leaving the love of violence to you, as a wordsmith and passionate teacher of writing, I share your love of the comma, and also, as we discovered, of outdoor food markets. As Sibylle says, some people like to live close to danger and excess. Others, myself included, just like to hear about it, and prefer to lead a much more measured life. Maybe you demonstrate a bit of both attitudes. Of course, given your imagination, you were always able to "travel" wherever you wanted. In your "Dangerous Liaisons"-style correspondence with daring beautiful women like artist Leonor Fini and Nelly Kaplan, you seemed to love hearing about their wild escapades.

The synopsis of your daughter Sibylle's 2005 film as stated on the Unifrance site is: "The passage of a young woman through her childhood home after the death of her parents becomes transformed into a voyage into memory. The child in her rises to the surface and brings back those she has lost until the moment when she accepts that it is time to definitively bid them adieu." (translation mine, with apologies because it sounds so much better in French).

In her film, your daughter has made an homage to you and Bona that I feel pretty sure would please you. Sibylle's evocatively titled 19-minute *Demeure* contains a double meaning that works well in French: It can be both a noun that signifies a longtime home, and the imperative of the verb "stay" or "remain." Sibylle speaks of the now-empty family apartment as a place of voyage for both you and Bona. This was true for her as she was growing up, but especially true for you when your scoliosis and other physical problems made it difficult for you to leave home.

I who have always loved to fill my house and spaces with touchstones can truly relate to what she is saying and showing by making this film.

It is a nice coincidence that I am learning about it during my own period of divestment and separation from my home of thirty-five-and-a-half years. Not a filmmaker, I only had my iPhone camera to ease the transition, but it helped.

Time for a weird association. I don't know why, but I am thinking about the stutter that plagued you during your youth. Did it have psychological origins? Were you just neurologically wired differently? A bit of both? I recall your referring to it during our first meeting.

In addition to the exhibition photographs of your and Bona's Mexican idyll, Sibylle included in *Pages Mexicaines* some written memorabilia: Two letters you had atypically written in French to Bona. I was surprised to learn that you who took such pride in your mastery of your native French, had always written to her in Italian.

À propos of language issues, among the articles published at your death that Bona entrusted to me were several in Italian. The time has proven ripe for me to be looking at these now when, having lived in Italy for the past nine years, I am able to read them.

People who know me well but who have not read you say some version of "I can't help but ask myself how in the world Diane got involved with this author who makes me think of the poorly written bestseller *Fifty Shades of Gray*." I never would have thought to compare your work to that, and wonder what you would make of that novel. Your own stories are dreamlike, often very strange and otherworldly, but are told in very precise, elegant, refined language. To quote Pierre Bourgeade in *Les Lettres Françaises*, "André Pieyre de Mandiarges, with his aristocratic reserve and disdain for what is in style, reminds us with each of his books that he is one of the greatest writers of our time." Guy Dupré of *Le Figaro Littéraire* says "Mandiargues' aphrodisiac style is the most captivating of our literature." Italian critic, Elena Guicciardi of *La Républicca* titled her article about you "The Metaphysical Eros of Mandiargues." Would critics be making comments like these about the author of the *Fifty Shades* series?

As for you and I being an unlikely match, I've thought about that. Why at a certain point in our lives do we become "attached" to certain authors? I don't have an answer, but in telling my long story, I think I was hoping to show something of interest about scholarship on the margins, and the mysterious process of attachment.

I'd like to close with a few facts. It's the 49th anniversary of my first contact with you; the 46th since our first meeting when you, at 63, were younger than I, at 71, am now. You and Bona married twice.

You and I, too, were separated for a number of years. But I am so pleased that we have once again found each other.

*

I confess that the above was just another false coda. It's hard for me to ever feel I am saying adieu to you. So I want to close with some excerpts from *Le lis de mer*, which is where our relationship began in the summer of 1969. I'm thinking you wouldn't mind if others were seduced by them, too. These are from page 132 of Richard Howard's translation from the Grove Press edition of 1958, titled *The Girl Beneath the Lion*.

> Then Vanina abandoned herself body and soul to the pain and the pleasure of knowing herself a helpless creature, conquered, seized, bound, thrown to the ground, handled without indulgence, her every intimacy rifled, every secret exposed, and she realized she was "in love's power" (as the expression has it), and she imagined the soft muzzles of cows, the majestic trees all leaning over her together at the consummation of this inhuman and splendid sacrifice. The moonlight flooded the sand, its whiteness blinding at the level of the girl's eyes. The sea lilies had another whiteness, aureoled with fire, on their pointed foliage that also gleamed in the moonlight over the tops of the dunes, and their perfume rolled to the floor of the area in a wave heavier and more powerful than ever. Vanina's breasts were offered to the moon, magnificently high and naked...she saw them swollen as if they had fed on the nectar of lilies, or floated in their fragrance as on a heavy liquid, and she delighted in the unexpected revelation, not of a resemblance, but of a kind of essential analogy, a relation between her breast and these waxen flowers and the moon itself....
>
> Vanina's hair had worked into the sand like roots, a mouth, fishlike, grazed her thighs, her naked belly, a hard knee knocked against her forehead. "There is nothing so marvelous as love, she thought, as the limits of her selfhood dropped away, naively overwhelmed, intoxicated with pleasure, filled with a presence so enormous and superhuman that at last she felt, as she had so desired to feel, "in communication with all of nature."

Roland BARTHES

November 12, 1915-March 26, 1980

Roland Barthes (1915-1980) was a ten years younger contemporary of Sartre, but the two died within days of each other. Although Barthes was identified with the structuralist movement, his restlessness of thought makes him, according to critic Peter Brooks, "the most nourishing intellectual of his time... Barthes liked the moment where—stuck between two radio signals, for example—messages overlapped in uncertainty. He compared writing to the work of the spider spinning its web...out of itself... dissolving in the secretions constructing its web." Later in his life, he became "the acute analyst of human desire." These Peter Brooks quotes are from material connected with the December 8-9, 2000 symposium, "Roland Barthes Twenty Years After," an event that brought together many of the biggest names in comparative literature.

Dear Roland,

Where were you when I was in graduate school? As I check the dates 1968-72, I see that you were busy and famously doing your thing, but somehow, at Duke, you passed under my radar. At the time, Durham, North Carolina, or at least the parts I frequented, was Hushpuppy-Barbecue & Brunswick Stew Country, but with a too heavy "side" of the Great God of Criticism Northrop Frye, to whom I never took a cotton. I eventually "got" his ideas about apocalyptic and demonic imagery, but the other machinations of his literary theory left me cold. I loved reading and thinking about French literature, but not in the way our very own example of demonic imagery, Professor X, went about it. We all sat in terror as he would proceed to call on us with his trick questions while we cowered in our chairs. Example: "What is the action of every comedy?" Hint: The answer is NOT to amuse and entertain. After lots of flailing about on our part, he would give the one and only correct answer (according to him and critic Francis Ferguson): "To unite two lovers." Okay. But I'm sure there could have been a less painful way to arrive at that answer.

Once in graduate school, I had longed to reread and delve more deeply into the eighteenth-century classics I adored, like Beaumarchais's *Le Barbier de Seville,* Voltaire's "Candide," Marivaux's *Le Jeu de l'amour et du hasard (A Game of Love and Chance),* even some Diderot, but not the esoteric and (to me) justly obscure plays by him and my hero Voltaire. Not only were we not a match made in heaven, but this professor made most of us wonder what had ever possessed us to come to grad school in the first place.

I recall that there was only one person in the class who could politely stand up to the bullying: the thoroughly charming Scotsman, James McNab, already a mature, seasoned young French professor from of all places, Virginia Tech. Older than the rest of us and way less plagued with self-doubt, Jim managed to earn the respect of our hard-to-please professor, but even he agreed that the air in that class-room was nasty.

I was able to drop that course, which is how I happily ended up taking two more at NYU the following summer, where I studied with Professors Thomas Bishop and Roger Kempf, and found my dissertation topic in the process. But getting permission to do so required a sit-down chat with Professor X.

Without having the nerve or stature to criticize his teaching methods, personality, or choice of curriculum, I tried to explain that none of these were what I expected. When I told him about what I had hoped we would be studying (instead of memorizing Frye's *The Anatomy of Criticism*), what I felt as his disdain filled the office. But for once, I didn't care. Whatever I had to say or do to be free of that course was going to be worth it to me.

Even so, during the time we were together, I admit I learned a lot from this professor, especially that how to get the best from my students would not be to create a poisonous, intimidating ambiance in the class. To be fair, perhaps my antipathy to him was due to my shaky psychological state at the time, which probably had little to do with him. But even so, I know I am remembering correctly the effect he had on my classmates who were not in the midst of a personal crisis. When I subsequently discussed this experience with my equally distinguished undergraduate mentor, seventeenth-century scholar Jules Brody, he seemed to understand what I was talking about. But in retrospect, maybe part of the motivation for Professor X's behavior was to toughen us up for the dog-eat-dog professional jousting that can be an unavoidable part of academia. And maybe that's why I have put all my energies into my teaching, where I go out of my way to make my students feel they have come to the right place—one where there is no such thing as a stupid question if it is genuinely well motivated. I thought hard about what to put on the blurb that goes under my French Department photo, and after nearly fifty years of teaching, it still holds: "Diane Charney teaches advanced language courses in which she tries to cultivate in her students a sense of confidence and a lifelong passion for France. Interests include inter-relations among the arts, psychoanalytic approaches to literature, and literature as lessons for life."

How did you, dear Roland, and I meet? I finally found you when brilliant Visiting Professor, Evelyne Ender, came to Yale to teach a seminar called "Writing and Memory." Although thoroughly modest, she had a compelling psychoanalytic approach to literature.

That year my photographer friends Judy and Phil Rosenthal were cleaning out their old photos of us and asked us subjects to comment on them. I really liked the piece that I wrote, very much inspired by you, on the topic of writing and memory which was displayed along with the photos as part of Phil and Judy's exhibit.

A key text of the Writing and Memory seminar was your *Camera Lucida* (*La Chambre Claire*), a slender book that I found mesmerizing. I just stood there in the Yale Bookstore and read the whole thing. It made me think completely differently about everything, especially photography. Much of your musing in your classic book about photography emerged from your looking at a picture of your then deceased mother, with whom you had been totally involved. In the book, you explain the "punctum," that which pierces, the point at which the camera focuses—a concept that pierced me, too, but in a good way.

I'm thinking of two favorite photos that have an aura comparable to the one with your mother. Both show my beloved grandfather at different times of his life. One from Russia pictures him in uniform as a handsome young soldier in the Czar's army. The other shows him sitting with me when he came to visit me and my new husband in Seattle, Washington, having traveled from my parents' home in Middletown, New York.

What makes these photos so precious? In the first one, I'm not yet even a twinkling in anybody's eye. My young grandfather is pictured alone but does not appear lonely. Independence is not the same as isolation. Yet I still feel a part of this picture. I often imagine what my life would have been had he not had the courage to leave Russia. And then I think about all that that decision cost him—a lifetime of struggle to earn a living, the loss of his mother tongue and of the ambitions he must have had at the time of that photo.

And yet in that other photo, the one of us sitting together in Seattle in 1973, the connection between the two of us is palpable. Long before I had ever heard of the term, "unqualified positive regard," the type of unreserved adoration babies need from their caregiver, I knew I had it from him. Despite the difference in our age and experience, in this photo of the two of us, his blue eyes and mine are twins. My quiet happiness at being reunited with him shines through, recorded forever. Because I am now in the midst of moving from my New Haven, Connecticut home of thirty-six years, one that he never lived to see, that photo is currently packed and waiting to live in a new space. But my brimming eyes prove that it has not moved from my heart.

Right now, at this moment, my love for my grandfather, Louis Londer "of blessed memory" as one says in the tradition of the Jewish faith (for which he had not much regard), is sending me back to your *Camera Lucida, Reflections on Photography*. This involves a different type of love affair, but maybe not quite as different as it seems.

In *Camera Lucida*, you say,

> A photograph can be the object of three practices (or of three emotions, or of three intentions): To do, to undergo, to look. The operator is the Photographer. The Spectator is ourselves, all of us who glance through collections of photographs—in magazines and newspapers, and books, albums, archives... And the person or thing photographed is the target, the referent... which I should like to call the Spectrum of the Photograph, because this word retains, through its root, a relation to "spectacle" and adds to it that rather terrible thing which is there in every photograph: The return of the dead.

Spectator, spectrum, spectral. To a lover of words, despite its intimations of mortality, your way of thinking is even better than chocolate!

But there's more. I find intriguing what you have to say about the artful pose:

> It can happen that I am observed without knowing it... But very often...I have been photographed and knew it. Now, once I feel myself observed by the lens, everything changes:

I constitute myself in the process of "posing," I instanta-neously make another body for myself, I transform myself in advance into an image. This transformation is an active one: I feel that the Photograph creates my body or mortifies it, according to its caprice...

Here again is that reference to death, but there is another step in the process necessary to produce the ideal photo.

I lend myself to the social game, I pose, I know I am posing, I want you to know that I am posing, but (to square the circle) this additional message must in no way alter the precious essence of my individuality: what I am apart from any effigy. What I want, in short, is that my (mobile) image, buffeted among a thousand shifting photographs, altering with situ-ation and age, should always coincide with my (profound) "self..."

Let's talk more about your punctum—

the Element which rises from the (photographed) scene, shoots out of it like an arrow, and pierces... A Latin word exists to designate this wound, this prick, this mark made by a pointed instrument: The word suits me all the better in that it also refers to the notion of punctuation, and because the photographs I am speaking of are in effect punctuated, sometimes even speckled with these sensitive points; precise-ly, these marks, these wounds are so many points... Punctum is also: Sting, speck, cut, little hole—and also a cast of the dice.

A photograph's punctum "is that accident which pricks me (but also bruises me, is poignant to me)." To summarize, the punctum re-fers to what touches and moves us profoundly.

From what I can tell, you both lost and found yourself (and her) while caring for your dying mother: "During her illness, I nursed her, held a bowl of tea she liked because it was easier to drink from than from a cup; she had become my little girl, uniting for me with that essential child she was in her first photograph." Once she died, however, you felt truly lost, but then had the sense of being back in touch with her essence thanks to what you call "the Winter Garden photo" of her as a child. It is understandable that you find in Proust's evocation of his lost grandmother a kindred spirit. With my own nonagenarian mother having suddenly taken a turn for the worse, your and Proust's comments are "speaking" to me more urgently than ever.

Here are a few more striking statements from your book, some of which at first seem counterintuitive, that I want to keep in mind:

The Photograph does not necessarily *say* what is no longer, but only for *certain* what has been. This distinction is decisive... (To paraphrase that assertion, you present the photo as defining, but not as a definitive, closed, lost forever record of a moment.)

In front of a photograph, our consciousness does not necessarily take that nostalgic path of memory... But the path of certainty: The Photograph's essence is to ratify what it represents...

Every photograph is a certificate of presence...

Not only is the Photograph never, in essence, a memory... but it actually blocks memory, quickly becomes a counter-memory...

The photograph is violent: Not because it shows violent things, but because on each occasion it fills the sight by force, and because in it nothing can be refused or transformed... (I am thinking that like me, you would be no fan of Photoshop, and would shun it as dishonest.)

Each photograph always contains this imperious sign of my future death...

Another quote of yours is ringing a bell for me: "The only photograph which has given me the splendor of (my mother's) truth is precisely a lost, remote photograph, one which does not look "like" her, the photograph of a child I never knew." This thought recalls Nabokov's complex emotions in the face of an image of his own future baby carriage purchased prior to his existence, and that to him, "had the smug encroaching air of a coffin." From his autobiography, *Speak, Memory*: "He caught a glimpse of his mother waving from an upstairs window, and that unfamiliar gesture disturbed him, as if it were some mysterious farewell..."

Early in your career you famously wrote about "the death of the author" which was widely interpreted as meaning that only the text mattered, not anything about the author himself. Even if taken literally, however, the so-called death of the author leaves all interpretation up to the reader. Well, this particular reader is exercising her freedom to suggest that nothing about *Camera Lucida* is irrelevant to your life.

This book inspired by your overwhelming grief at the loss of your mother turned out to be your last, and despite its beauty, there are some sad ironies connected with it. It is plausible that your depression over her death adversely affected your ability to recover from the accident that occurred when you were hit by a laundry van after having lunch with philosopher Michel Foucault and François Mitterand, soon to be elected president of France.

Your mother's death may have been the point of departure for *Camera Lucida*, but I am selfishly going to say that it has become a touchstone for my own aging self as the daughter of a wonderful mother born in 1924 who on August 1, 2017 celebrated her 93rd birthday.

Jacques GUICHARNAUD

July 7, 1924-March 5, 2005

From 1950 to his retirement in 1997, Guicharnaud, a specialist in 17th, 18th, and 20th century French literature and theatre, brought grace, elegance, eloquence, and verve to the Yale campus. A student during the German Occupation of France, he was part of a circle that included Albert Camus, Jean-Paul Sartre, and Simone de Beauvoir. Known for his authoritative Modern French Theatre from Giraudoux to Beckett, *Guicharnaud produced highly regarded translations of Tennessee Williams and Ring Lardner, short stories, and a novel. An accomplished actor himself, he wrote and directed plays for stage and television. His imitation of James Dean as Hamlet may have been legendary, but Jacques Guicharnaud was perhaps best known as "a human being of immense decency"—a justly deserved homage from a former student.*

Dear Jacques,

When I was in graduate school at Duke, I used your classic book on modern French theater as a constant reference for my own work. You were the go-to source for information on the field and its authors.

When I came to Yale to teach, you were suddenly a colleague. I could go to your courses, chat with you, and follow you around like the groupie I was. One day, I was formally introduced to you in my office, along with several more-established colleagues. I said, "I am so excited to meet you!" "How do you know me?" you asked. "*Par réputation*!" I replied. You didn't quite know what to make of this, but we hit it off. I audited all of your courses that I could, though I was also teaching. You subsequently sent me a card that I treasure. On it you wrote how honored you felt by my regular attendance in your classes, and how my coming gave you heart. ("Votre présence assidue dans mes cours m'a honoré et m'a donné du courage.") What a precious thing to say! Of course, the honor was mine.

The last course you taught prior to retiring was about the adolescent in literature. It was a beautiful thing—you went back to the books you had loved as an adolescent, as a way to reconnect with your youth, and then to reconsider them from the perspective of a seasoned scholar esteemed for his expertise in the entirely different specialty of French theatre. In that course I got to revisit some of the books I, too, had loved as an adolescent, some like *Le diable au corps* that I had taught, and others like *Le Grand Meaulnes (The Lost Estate)* and Colette's *Le blé en herbe (Green Wheat)* that I had always wanted to read. You had never taught anything like this before, and I really admired you for taking on something new as your swan song. I lobbied to teach that very course at Yale after you had retired, as an homage to you, but they never let me—Yale can be like that.

After you retired in 1997, one year I taught an intensive, advanced French Composition and Conversation class, and I invited you to come to discuss the novel *Bonjour Tristesse* that you had included in your Adolescent Literature class. The class met at 9:30AM. You wanted to come, but had trouble explaining why you couldn't—that

a nice touch to include on the program's back cover one of your whimsical illustrations for *Spot Luck, A Novelette for Children,* a 1957 collaboration with Olga Scherer-Virsky.

I want to close with a tribute to you that I wrote at the time of your retirement dinner, a little something, but only the statements by the most famous of your admirers were chosen to be read that evening. I still think you liked mine, in which I briefly explain why you are my "madeleine." Here it is as originally written, and then in translation (mine):

Jacques Guicharnaud est ma madeleine. Comment est-ce que je le sais? Au son de sa voix éloquente je me trouve transportée jusqu'à mes premiers jours d'étudiante à Paris: Mon demi-siècle d'années se fond, et je redeviens jeune fille naïve, émerveillée, et éblouie devant le grand amour de sa vie—la France

—*Diane Joy Charney, New Haven 1997*

Jacques Guicharnaud is my madeleine. How do I know this? At the sound of his eloquent voice, I find myself transported back to my first days as a student in Paris: My half-century of years melts away, and I become once again that naive young woman, dazzled and filled with wonder, in the face of the great love of her life—France.

It's true that as a former professional actor, you have a wonderful reading voice. When the Yale Language Laboratory was being closed, I noticed a pile of audio tapes that the staff was about to discard. Naturally my hoarding instinct kicked in, and I am glad it did. Among them I saw a cassette tape labeled "Jacques Guicharnaud reading from Marcel Proust's *Combray.*" You offer a brilliant reading that makes Proust accessible and fully alive. That one is definitely a keeper.

In your will, you generously established the Guicharnaud Fund that sponsored our Proust Marathon (where one hundred students, scholars, and guests read favorite passages from Swann's Way in a replica of the author's cork-lined room) and that will enrich the French Department's theatrical and cultural offerings for years to come.

In a reluctant effort to say goodbye, I've been looking over a lot of comments about you and have been disappointed at their failure to capture you.

I'm going to the dictionary for help and I'm looking up the word "charisma," which is always elusive and mysterious:

Compelling attractiveness or charm that can inspire devotion in others
a divinely conferred power or talent
a personal magic

Yes! You were all of the above.

Louis GILLMAN, MD

October 9, 1920-December 21, 1983

Louis Gillman was the eldest son of immigrants from Ukraine and Romania who settled in St. Paul, Minnesota. Revered by his patients from a tri-state area, he graduated from the University of Minnesota and trained at New York Skin and Cancer. The father of four children—Diane, Leigh, Cherni and Jackson—and husband of Edith (1924-2018), Dr. Gillman practiced dermatology in Middletown, New York where he was associate attending dermatologist at the Horton Memorial Hospital. Highly knowledgeable about Judaism, he was devoted to the synagogue of whose congregation he was a longtime leader.

Dear Dad,

In undertaking this project, I had been planning to save my letter to you for last. But as my deadline looms, and with several more letters to go, I find myself needing to start now.

In explaining to a friend why I was including you in my book to men of letters, I described you as a dermatologist to whom letters and stories were always important. A big part of our family tradition has been our willingness to go miles out of our way to avoid a confrontation. I'm sure you had our best interests at heart when you taught us not to make waves, rock the boat, or assert ourselves. Although the contrary can be true, I always wondered if this were a Jewish thing. This lesson has been a mixed blessing. To try to blend in, be a good girl, and never cause any trouble can end up causing trouble for one who attempts this. It has always been hard for me to ask in person for something I want and feel I deserve. My life trajectory reflects this, and my naïveté that a benevolent authority figure (a dad, a thesis director, an administrator who knows the quality of my work) will always go to bat for me. But you also taught us that a letter was different. If you choose your words carefully enough, you can control the situation, minimize the risk of offense, and perhaps succeed.

When a mistake was made on my high school class ranking—a mathematical error that could have cost me entrance to the college of my choice, as well as the scholarships I might receive, some parents would have picked up the phone and demanded to speak to the person in charge. You, however, took a break from seeing your typical fifty patients a day, picked up your pen, and wrote a letter to a family friend who you thought might be able to help. You didn't say that it didn't make any sense that the numbers that had been used to compute my grades bore no relation to the facts. How could the average of my marks be lower than any mark I had ever received? You very politely pointed this out and asked them if they would recalculate the figures. Sure enough, an error had been made: In calculating the average on which class ranks would be determined, someone had miscounted and divided by the wrong number. The correction was made in time for me to be ranked correctly near the top of my class.

When you knew it was likely that your ailing heart could give out at any moment, you wrote each of us a letter to be opened at the time of your passing. In it, you expressed how you had always tried to say to me "yes, my darling daughter," and you also acknowledged how often I tried to say to your requests, some version of "yes, my darling daddy." You were one of the most respected people in the community—be it the religious community of the synagogue, or the medical community who knew you as a master diagnostician of the skin woes of a tri-state area. Your patients revered you for the patience and kindness with which you healed them and listened to their stories. I remember your explaining how you chose to be a dermatologist. Never a fan of what you called the "cut-out-the-offending-part" mentality of the surgeon, you said you realized that to be able to cure a person suffering from a terrible itch was a true "mitzvah." Of course, you often had to do more than that, but I understood what you meant.

With you as my model, I became quite the letter writer. While living abroad in France from 1966 to 1967, I used my carefully crafted letters home as journals to record what I sensed was the formative experience of my life.

In terms of important business-related letters, I don't think I ever sent one without asking you to look it over beforehand. You were my personal editor, proofreader, and sounding board, and maybe that's part of why I became a writing teacher. Further, I have an image of you sitting at your desk, dictating notes on your patients onto the blood-red plastic Dictaphone belts that were the height of technology in the fifties. I think we had the Dictaphone Time-Master model of 1958, the ads for which show smiling secretaries happy not to have to decipher their boss's handwriting (and yours was a doozy!)

There's even a photo of a relaxed-and-in-control Don Draper from *Mad Men* leaning back while dictating into his machine.

The ad copy for this machine is priceless: "For the price of a hat check, you can save $6 a day with the new Dictaphone Time-Master!"

In 1972-76 when I lived far away in Seattle and missed our Passover seders, I remember asking you to record our home service for me. I was conscious of the need to preserve our family tunes and chants from The Old Country which were unique to us, and likely to die out if I did not pass them on. By this time, however, audio cassettes had been invented, and I still have those that you made for me. When I listen to them every year, it feels as if you are right in the room. But there's an unintentionally funny aspect to them: When you add commentary to introduce or discuss a section of the seder, you automatically say, "period" at the end of most sentences—a remnant of your Dictaphone days.

Despite being a technodunce, I marvel at the way I can just dictate into my iPhone in English, French, or Italian, and have it magically write more or less what I am saying. I'm sure that you who loved gadgets would have gotten a kick out of that.

Indeed, language was always a source of fascination for you. You loved listening to the accents of your patients, and it took you no time at all to guess their country of origin. Although the languages in the air of your parents' household were a mixture of Russian and Yiddish, I was surprised to learn about another linguistic legacy that relates to my own love of *le mot juste,* a phrase associated with Flaubert's relentless search for the most precise word. Your father, Jacob Gillman, who ran a tiny corner grocery store in Minneapolis, had come to America through Mongolia and Manchuria, working on freighters and arriving in San Francisco. You, who always had a prodigious memory and a keen ear for languages, used to tell with great pride how your father, the shy grocer, was a fluent speaker of many languages. His hobby was translating Shakespeare into Yiddish. Grandpa Gillman, because of his intelligence, was the only Jewish child in town allowed to attend the best school, the gymnasium, in his native Ukraine. This background which I only learned about as an adult sheds light on your and my love of language.

I have one other memory related to your office. Earlier, I wrote to Vladimir Nabokov about his and my mutual love of notecards, and of how, against all logic, I found it impossible to discard the ones from my dissertation. And then in one of those free associations that Nabokov would have disdained as having nothing to do with Freud,

I had a flashback to the yellow-lined notecards that you kept with information about each of your patients. I sometimes used to help with filing those, and am thinking that even if you had lived long enough to contemplate retirement, you would never have given them up. As sick as the angiograms indicated that you were, you continued dedicating yourself to your patients. Did you unconsciously choose to die with your boots on to save yourself from having to decide whether to part with those cards?

And what about Mom's box of the letters your twentyish self wrote her? She just turned 92 and recently went through a rough patch that would have felled a lesser woman. I'm thinking about that gray square box full of the letters you sent her while stationed at Fort Meade in Maryland, and she at twenty-one was living with her parents on Pleasant Avenue in St. Paul while pregnant with me. For a while, at my sister's request, I had stored that box of letters at my house. At some point, however, mom asked about them, and I returned them to her. But whenever I ask from time to time if she has looked at the letters, she says she will get to it someday, but that it was not yet time.

I've never been good with numbers, but what is it about 63? That's how far three of the men in my life—Grandpa Gillman, you, your number one son my brother Leigh, and an ex-boyfriend made it.

You died at 63 in December of 1983, just a few days before my 37th Christmas birthday, so you never lived to see me hired by Yale, where I began teaching French in 1984, something that might have surprised you. Part of the reason I got there was by being at the right place at the right time and having a dear friend, Liliane Greene, on the faculty to advise me about how to get a foot in the door. But perhaps my skill at writing the right letters played a major role in making it happen.

I once wrote a piece about how fresh in my mind your 1983 death has remained. I would like to show a version of it to you now.

To be the lone dissenter in a "do not resuscitate" order—that's one place where one's voice counts. That was the situation when you were in the hospital after what seemed to be a terminal event.

My ever-kind baby brother disagreed with my position of lone dissenter who was not ready to give up on you. I understood where he was coming from when he said, "Would you want your last memory to be of someone frantically pounding on your chest?" No, but if it turned out not to be my last memory—that I would live to have a few more—I might be grateful for that.

In your case, the cardiac arrest situation did not present itself, and we did get an important two-and-a-half more months of vital memories.

Was the disagreement over whether to resuscitate part of the drama of the eldest child—which tends to include certain reservations about sharing?

As I continue to try to focus, develop, and print this "picture" that is autobiography, what I see is the need to stand back from it, to gain perspective. I learned about this from Roland Barthes. The apparent dilemma between living and writing about life may be an illusion. An ill-focused shot. It's a question of knowing where to put the focal point.

*

The Autopsy Report Versus "Don't you want to see him?"

These recollections remind me of the day we all knew would come: One of the private duty nurses calls from the hospital to say that you are gone. She, upset that this happened on her watch, has taken great care to arrange things, including you, for our final visit. We hear further dismay in her voice as we say, "No, we won't be coming today." "But don't you want to see him?" she says, incredulously, not realizing that you are not there.

I do, however, want to see the autopsy report, even though I know that you are not there, either. I write a poem about you. That's where I think you are.

*

(Flash forward 33 years)

In wondering why I am writing about this now, it occurs to me that my mom has made it to 92 relatively wrinkle-free and with her sense of humor, independence, and marbles intact. I am hoping that if there are hard decisions ahead, they will be far in the future, and that we will all be in agreement.

*

This will be my 33rd year at Yale, where I have been happily teaching French, helping students write better papers in all subjects as college Writing Tutor, and being part of the English Department's teaching team for a unique creative writing experience called Daily Themes, which has a long, storied history of producing famous writers. I find it thrilling to have the chance to work with such talented students.

Although I am on leave this fall, I know that today is Move-In day for the new freshman. I never lose sight of how important these milestones are, and of the hard work and sacrifice that led to these parents producing a child who would be welcomed to Yale. Similarly, at the other end of their journey, as I watch students with whom I've often had the privilege of working during the four years of their under-graduate career, I love to watch from the sidelines their family's pride and joy as they receive their diploma. So, I'm sure you would be proud and pleased that I, too, have found great happiness and satisfaction in my work, as I saw you do.

And I know that you would be tickled to see that your grandson Noah who was only four when you died has enjoyed so much success with his writing. Unlike the rest of us in the family who are missing the marketing gene, he understands the art of the query letter, which allows him to manage many projects at once. Of course, you required no time at all to point out that he was a genius. You loved to quote, to anyone who would listen, all the big words that used to come out of his little mouth. Maybe you could sense another wordsmith-in-the-making?

Although my writer son is definitely his own person, I see some fundamental characteristics we share. The first verbal snapshot of me, at 22 months the youngest little "adult" ever accepted in the history of my nursery school, proved prescient:

> When Diane first came to school, she was quite unhappy and homesick. She has since made a fine adjustment and is very cheerful in school. She has accepted routine activities such as washing, eating, and resting, and is very self-sufficient.
>
> Diane is very alert and has a very long attention span for one so young. She uses all play equipment and participates in all group activities. The music and storytelling interest her most. She listens intently and absorbs quickly. She also derives much satisfaction from painting.
>
> Diane is not too steady on her feet, but this bright little girl manages to get along very well. She can make herself clearly understood, as her speech is very well developed. She often intrigues adults with her well-organized sentences, which are almost as big as she is.

I looked at other key moments in my private writing past. When I had to decide what would be inscribed on your gravestone, the poem, "Writers Block" emerged. In a more public vein, at your funeral, I found myself quoting Emily Dickinson and alluding to a type of language I had made up in order to communicate with you in the Intensive Care Unit once you could no longer speak. During the two months that you were dying, although it was hard to manage the demands of teaching and my own husband and four-year-old, I am grateful for the extra time we got to spend together, and I think the feeling was mutual. I thought of all the final questions I wanted to ask you, and you were able to answer clearly by blinking for "yes" or sticking out your tongue for "no." This worked well, and I like to think that it gave both of us comfort.

Another piece I'm thinking about in the context of autobiography of a place is one that I wrote on the occasion of my 25th Middletown high school reunion. It is in harmony with author Barry Lopez's admission that to be a writer one has to "get out of town." In considering the phenomenon of the madeleine as described by Marcel Proust, I see how all of France has been my personal touchstone—how my engagement with words has allowed me to feel that I am on the way to internalizing the other key precept (from Lopez) of being a writer: "Become Someone!"

Here's what American author James Alan McPherson says about finding one's niche, which he observed in his father's expertise with electricity: "I think that a certain kind of creative man finds one thing he likes to do and then does it for the rest of his life. I think that if he's really good at what he does, he masters the basics and then begins to play with the conventions of the thing." Maybe that's what I've been doing all these years of frequently teaching the same material, but without ever finding it boring. As a professor, I like to think out-of-the-box. I find that easier to do when I am already so familiar with the subject matter at hand.

When we read Kafka's "Letter to his Father" I felt a shock of recognition. This was not because you bore any actual resemblance to the terrifying father in question. Rather, I think it was due to my discomfort with all authority figures—especially ones with the serious type of health concerns that plagued you for such a large part of your life.

(OOPS! A very BIG snake just slithered up and came to call at my partially open kitchen door. Ah, life in the Italian countryside! After I closed that door and ran around to the front one, I found him enjoying a bit of shade in an outside corner of our stone house. As I snapped some photos of him, he hissed at me. His way of saying hello? Or of warding off a nutty writer with a camera?)

Never mind. Where was I? I was talking about how hard it was for any of us in the family to NOT do what would please you, or even to disagree forcefully for fear of causing a heart attack. Self-assertion can be a healthy rite of passage and an important life skill. I missed that lesson and accept the consequences for my complicity in that. Be that as it may, it is also a key life skill to be able to express oneself via the written word, which has been my refuge and salvation. You helped teach me that.

I see that without realizing it, a number of pieces I've written use the phrase, "Catching up with myself." You used to say admiringly about little me, and then about your grandson, "s/he's so ahead of himself!" It's clear that you thought this was a good thing. To catch up with myself has been a lifelong task—Camus' Sisyphus could tell us a thing or two about that—but to be able to write about it helps. On that theme, there's one other piece I would have liked you to see called "Still Getting Ready to Write," in which I muse about my main job of helping others to write. Although what I wrote in it in 1995 still very much applies, I am pleased to be able to say that after putting so much of myself into writing these letters to men of letters, I have done more than get ready to write.

"Ripeness is all." I have always loved that quote and I even used to think I understood it. But now, as I near the age of 70, I see that I am just beginning to get the picture. Part of the excitement of writing this book that I am sorry you did not live to see has been the role of serendipity and propinquity—such musical words—as I have noted how often what I read and encounter in everyday life seems startlingly in synch with the particular author on whom I am focusing my attention. I have felt alternately absorbed and disoriented as I waver among now, then, and now, as my current self writes these letters that include so much of my past self. Ever a musician, I tend to think in musical terms. Am I trying to avoid cacophony? Am I in search of harmony? So far, synchronicity is what's turning up, and I have no quibble with that. "One is always at home in one's past," says Nabokov. Fellow exile André Aciman said, "All we have in the end is ourselves, our loneliness—not even our memories but how they've lied to us...I, too, one day would have to learn to be alone again, but in the end the work of memory is the work of loneliness."

I frequently walk by New Haven's historic Grove Street Cemetery, and it looks like a nice place to be. Further, that it's populated by so many honchos suggests that they are less likely ever to be disturbed. And I've always said that sooner or later everyone who is anyone comes to Yale, so chances are that this might be a good final resting place. I am going to look into it. To be there would also be in keeping with my life choice to enjoy being a small fish in a big pond. I once wrote,

It's fall, and death is in the air. But then again, it always was. From Day One. Life is what we do to keep ourselves from noticing.

Perhaps what I should have said is "To write is what we do to keep ourselves from noticing"?

Even after 40 years, New Haven feels more like a transient place than like home. But as a lover of words, I like the sound of residing quite permanently in a new haven. I was raised in a place called Middletown. Is that why I'm so attracted to the idea of the liminal zone? After all, what is a letter, if not the attempt to bridge a gap between a certain "here" and elsewhere—a way of encapsulating and holding in one's hand something that has been in both places? A way of marking and capturing lost time? Maybe the letter has always been my madeleine.

Leonard COHEN

September 1, 1934-November 7, 2016

A *native of Montreal, Leonard Cohen initially received recognition as an exciting new voice in Canadian poetry. Before becoming what many, including Bob Dylan, consider "the number one song writer of his time," Cohen was also a novelist who, despite winning literary awards, realized that he could not support himself through literature. He did not write his first song until age thirty-three and was at first a paralyzingly shy performer who preferred to have others sing his music. This changed in 1967 when he was coaxed onto the stage by Judy Collins.*

Cohen's 1984 "Hallelujah," which the New York Times *called "a majestic, meditative ballad infused with both religiosity and earthiness," has been the subject of a book, sung by hundreds of artists, and featured in many film and tv soundtracks. Cohen's visionary songs that reflect the influence of the Hebrew bible and Zen writings have as themes love sacred and profane, war and peace, ecstasy and depression. An ordained Buddhist monk who spent five years in a monastery, septuagenarian Cohen found himself "driven by financial necessity" to embark on epic world tours from 2008-2013 after his business manager was discovered to have misappropriated his savings. These tours, however, definitively revitalized him and his career.*

Dear Leonard,

Last year I wrote you something I called a valedictory valentine on the first Valentine's Day since you left us. But as happens with some regularity, when I say goodbye to the men of letters to whom I write, I don't really mean it. As I sit here on this gorgeous fall day trying to salvage the good parts of my aging peaches, I realize that because we are in this for the long-haul, I may very well be writing you a valentine every year of the rest of my days.

I knew that I was on to something when I saw the reaction to my first valentine to you which was published in *Versopolis*: It made nearly everyone, myself included, cry.

This preamble is just to explain why this letter to you looks nothing like the others in this book. I'm going to show you what I mean.

November of 2016 started out badly with the confirmation that this year you were not inscribed in the Book of Life. You may no longer be with us in a physical sense, but you will always be here with me.

*

The first time I wrote you was from my home in Italy in 2012 when I said:

Leonard Cohen under the Umbrian sun?

While puttering around in the kitchen, I often have music in the background, usually of the soothing classical variety. But when I came in from outside on this brilliantly sunny day in the Umbrian countryside, I was met by your unmistakable raspy voice singing "Suzanne." What could you be doing here? Fish out of water?

My awareness of you came late in life. One day your "Hallelujah" sent me reeling. I found myself trying to sort out the words amid the mystery: the danger of David gazing at Bathsheba and going for broke. In fact, that last is a key word:

It's not a cry you can hear at night
It's not somebody who has seen the light

It's a cold and it's a broken Hallelujah

Our place here in Umbria was a total ruin, broken beyond belief, but we fixed it, and it seems to have had a similar effect on us. I usually only turn on your music when I'm in a particularly sensitive mood, and I would not have guessed that today would be a day when you would "speak" to me. Yet I love the Italian way of saying that I am *molto* wrong, something that comes up frequently in my life here: "Ho sbagliato." As I think about it, though, you are right for all places and seasons. Yet you don't appear to be someone who feels at home, except perhaps while singing about what it means to be human.

*

I wrote that four years ago, but now I feel I know you better. Popular culture has never been my strong point. It's true that during the sixties, I raised my teenage head from my books long enough to notice the Pat Boone and Elvis wars, but the squeaky-clean, soothing Brothers Four were more my speed. They sang so sweetly that I never even noticed the dark side of my favorite song, "The Green Leaves of Summer:"

A time to be reaping.
A time to be sowing.
A time to be living.
A place for to die.
'Twas so good to be young then
in the season of plenty
when the catfish were jumping
as high as the sky.

I never focused on the dying and "the green leaves of summer are calling me home" part. But isn't that the way with things that sneak under your skin?

Let's get back to the day I caught a few bars of a song that talked about King David getting his hair cut by a woman he had observed bathing on a roof who later tied him to a kitchen chair, and I was hooked. What could it all mean? Why did I feel you were speaking directly to me?

Like the baffled King knocked off his throne, I became obsessed with wanting to figure it out. This was nothing like what they'd taught us in Sunday School. Could this be the same kid with a slingshot? The guy who wrote the most perfect psalms? Whose Lord was his shepherd and whose cup runneth over? And wasn't it Delilah, not Bathsheba, who gave Sampson the buzz cut that destroyed his powers and left him so enchained that all he could do was pull down the temple pillars on his own bald pate? What lessons were we supposed to take away from that?

Here's what can happen to a bookish woman with an obsession. First I need to seek out all the versions I can of "Hallelujah." Then I must listen to everything else by this Leonard Cohen guy. This leads me to all kinds of crazy flashbacks and connections. And to what seem like odd coincidences: our families that spent a lot of time in the synagogue. Montreal—your birth-place and the city where a number of my immigrant relatives ended up. And where I, as a 16-year-old student at the French university, learned to be alone. My flirtation with Buddhism and integration of yoga into my life. My conviction (and I'm guessing yours) that music is the least disappointing thing in life. My recent rediscovery of what the spirit feels like under the sun of a wild Greek island—a place where in the arms of Marianne, you seem to have found yourself and your voice. Thanks to my husband, like you, I got to see Janis Joplin, but not in the way you describe in your Chelsea Hotel song.

Here's a bit more about where my obsession with you has taken me. Since first hearing the line in "Hallelujah" about knowing "how to shoot somebody who outdrew ya," I wondered what it could mean. But to watch your admirable patience with intrusive interviewers whom you manage to outmaneuver with your charm may shed light on that. This, in itself, is an art! I would have wanted to shoot or at least punch some of them.

Some interviewers of both sexes like to imply that you use your facility with words to ensnare women. A line from your poem in *Let Us Compare Mythologies* reads:

I heard of a man
who says words so beautifully
that if he only speaks their name
women give themselves to him.

You laughed at the idea that that could refer to you. You said you feel it's the other way around—that it's woman who possesses the true intimate connection to poetic mystery.

I wrote my doctoral dissertation on "Woman as Mediatrix in the Prose Works of André Pieyre de Mandiargues," another of my letter recipients who viewed woman as being charged with special goddess-like powers. Now I have to wonder why I'd be so taken with two men who have this idea.

And while I'm thinking about men who have marked me, let's talk about fathers. We both had fathers we wanted to please. You lost yours when you were nine; mine was busy and unwell for the latter part of his life. I read that as a twenty-two-year-old, you dedicated your first book of poems to your father. Later, you dedicated your first album to him. I dedicated my doctoral dissertation to my father, and here I am now, as I write my first book, writing a letter to each of you.

Can we talk about translation? I read how long it took you to translate the Garcia Lorca poem, "Little Viennese Waltz" and what a labor of love it was to transform it into your own haunting "Take this Waltz." As someone who does translations, I'm interested in the psychology of the translator who willingly devotes so much to the art of someone else. I'm also thinking here about the delight you took in hearing others, even four amateur Norwegian guys, sing your songs, and I don't think that pleasure necessarily has to do with the royalties.

Then there was your initial terror at performing in public—you seemed fine with having others, professional or not, sing your creations. This reminds me of the odd mixture of self-effacement and creativity of the dedicated translator. As outraged as I was at the "out-ing" of the author behind the mesmerizing Elena Ferrante books, I took some pleasure and satisfaction from seeing that she had been previously known mostly for her translations.

I'm still wondering what the Nobel Prize Committee was thinking when they decided who would win this year's prize for literature. Dylan instead of you?

Huh? I haven't yet read your books of poetry or your novels, but I know that all your life you have been a serious writer. And that even among my well-educated friends, as was the case with me, your writing had somehow passed under their radar. Yet how many song writers have named their only daughter after Federico Garcia Lorca, the poet who knocked your youthful socks off? And who went on to write in 1986 an intoxicating song, "Take This Waltz," that was his free translation of Lorca's "Little Viennese Waltz"?

In calling this a "valedictory valentine" and trying to process how you ended up salutatorian to Dylan's valedictorian, I went back to find a precise definition of that word.

The chosen valedictorian is often the student with the highest ranking in the graduating class who delivers the farewell valedictory at a graduation ceremony.

A salutatorian is a graduate who finished with the second highest rank in his or her class.

I would have liked to be a fly on the wall at those Nobel literary prize committee discussions: *Let's do something really surprising— give it to a musician. But which one? Between Cohen and Dylan, who should be the valedictorian?*

With respect to a book I've been writing, I thought my letter to my father would be the last of my *Letters to Men of Letters*. Not so. What do he and you have in common besides Judaism, periods of major depression, the same Hebrew name, and some relatives in Montreal?

He and I prided ourselves on our memory; you proudly profess total amnesia. In one of your songs, you wrote,

I don't remember
lighting this cigarette
and I don't remember
if I'm here alone
or waiting for someone.

Separately from your music, I've heard you say things of similar ilk about your total lack of recall about people and places. But then there's this:

People change and their bodies change and their hair grows gray and falls out and their bodies decay and die... but there is something that doesn't change about love and about the feelings we have for people. Marianne, the woman of "So Long, Marianne," when I hear her voice on the telephone, I know something is completely intact even though our lives have separated and we've gone our very different paths. I feel that love never dies, and that when there is an emotion strong enough to gather a song around it, that there is something about that emotion that is indestructible...

And this:

I'm not a very nostalgic person. I don't really look at the past and summon up regrets, or self-congratulations, it just is not a mechanism that operates very strongly in me. So, I neither have regrets nor occasions for self-congratulations.

Maybe, however, these are examples of different types of memory, and my original definition of the sort of acute memory my father and I shared was too narrow.

You had been deeply depressed for much of your life. Precisely how that depression eventually lifted remains a mystery, and like so many of the mysteries to which you give voice, one best left alone.

As I watch videos of you at various points in your life, I feel as if you are always teaching me something.

You got me to ask myself, "Why would someone with a memory like mine need to be a hoarder?" You seem to have instinctively understood when to let go, and that to do so does not necessarily imply waste:

> Before I can discard the verse, I have to write it... I can't discard a verse before it is written because it is the writing of the verse that produces whatever delights or interests or facets that are going to catch the light. The cutting of the gem has to be finished before you can see whether it shines.

When words are so hard won, the idea of throwing them away can be painful to a serious writer. But what you say here shows how well you understand the lesson of the sweeping away of the mandala and the need to remove attachment. Maybe it helps to be a Buddhist monk?

I used to think I wanted to be a muse in service to a great man. Your Marianne, a pure, generous soul, convinced herself to be satisfied with the good seven years you had together. But the regret is palpable in her reminiscences of that time when as a young mother abandoned by her husband and totally devoted to you, she admits to having felt lost and eclipsed by the artistic people around her. I think you had a sense that this was happening when you wrote,

> We sold ourselves for love but now we are free
> I'm so sorry for that ghost I made you be
> Only one of us was real and that was me.

As much as you like to tout your amnesia and lack of nostalgia, your poignant final message to her as she was dying belies that:

> ...our bodies are falling apart and I think I will follow you very soon. Know that I am so close behind you that if you stretch out your hand, I think you can reach mine.

And you know that I've always loved you for your beauty and your wisdom… But now, I just want to wish you a very good journey. Goodbye old friend. Endless love, see you down the road.

I think my favorite article about you is from your friend of twenty-five years, Leon Wieselthier. (https://www.nytimes.com/2016/11/14/opinion/my-friend-leonard-cohen-darkness-and-praise.html)

In referring to you as "the most beautiful man I have ever known," he says:

He lived in a weather of wisdom, which he created by seeking it rather than by finding it. He swam in beauty, because in its transience he aspired to discern a glimpse of eternity: There was always a trace of philosophy in his sensuality. He managed to combine a sense of absurdity with a sense of significance, a genuine feat. He was hospitable and strict, sweet and deep, humble and grand, probing and tender, a friend of melancholy but an enemy of gloom, a voluptuary with religion, a renegade enamored of religion.

According to this source, you "had a supremely unsanctimonious temperament." I'm thinking that my dad could have matched you for Talmudic knowledge, but not in the "unsanctimonious temperament" department.

In terms of journeys, there is something beautifully valiant about the way you accepted your own lack of perfection and vulnerability to crippling depression. Your manager, Robert Kory, used the word "crippling" not in the context of your depressions, but in praise of your "crippling candor." Like a bird on a wire, you tried in your way to be free. And as Janis Joplin said to you in the Chelsea Hotel, we may be ugly, "but we have the music."

In your *Book of Mercy* you wrote,

Blessed are you who has given each man a shield of loneliness so that he cannot forget you.

You understood that brokenness is our lot, but that we are not entitled to whine about that. Even at our lowest point, you remind us to:

> Ring the bells that still can ring
> Forget your perfect offering
> There is a crack in everything
> That's how the light gets in.

I've decided that on this Valentine's Day, it's time to say au revoir. I recognize the imperfection of this letter to you, and I am still unsure about whether to keep it. But you taught me that like the rest of what I write, I shouldn't rush to discard it. It has to be finished before I can see "whether it shines.

Something you said in your *Book of Longing* reminds me of the way another man of letters, Vladimir Nabokov, thought about his works as having been already written—that he was just the agent of their crystallization:

> You should go from place to place
> Recovering the poems
> That have been written for you
> To which you can affix your
> Signature
> Don't discuss these matters with anyone.
> Retrieve. Retrieve.
> When the basket is full
> Someone will appear
> to whom you can present it.

You presented this to me. And I am offering it back "to ya" with eternal gratitude on this first Valentine's Day since you left us.

—yours in music, Diane Joy Charney

POST SCRIPTS TO MYSELF:
MY BOOK IS NEVER OVER

NO, THIS IS NOT ANTOHER LETTER TO A MAN OF LETTERS

Post Script (P.S.) One

Although I only wrote my letters to one author at a time, in rereading them I find striking the amount of overlap and internal references among them. After I believed my book was finished, I found myself writing a joint letter to three of my letter recipients.

Dear Ionesco, Sartre, et Marcel,

How naive of me to think that my Letters project might be over! After all, the whole point of my book is that you three and the other fifteen authors to whom I have written are my lifetime companions. To quote another man of letters whom you probably don't know, catcher Yogi Berra from the New York Yankees baseball team, "It ain't over till it's over." And when will that be? Never!

Pardon me for making another weird association. Yogi's name reminds me of something I learned from being a practitioner of yoga for the past 50 years. I see that in some circles, yoga has become a bit of a fad that requires aficionados to buy special clothing and attend crowded classes with famous teachers. My teacher, Alan Bitker, may not be famous, but he is wonderful, and there's always plenty of room in our six-person class where nobody cares what you wear. I've learned that it's not enough to practice yoga in a once-a-week class.

One needs to integrate yoga into every aspect of life. Even though he may be 3000 miles away, I carry Alan's voice around with me at all times. As I follow Voltaire's exhortation to cultivate my garden, I can hear Alan saying, "Shine the heart forward."

Similarly, I should have known to expect to continue hearing the voices of you three and my other men of letters, and I thank you all for that gift.

P.S. Two

I recently came across a one-sentence description I had written of my *Letters to Men of Letters* project: "A scholar who advocates the study of literature as lessons for life writes letters to the authors living and dead who continue to keep her company." But although accurate, that synopsis does not really convey the power of literature and letters to offer a unique stimulus to memory and to self-understanding.

I have mentioned before how many times during the course of writing these Letters to Men of Letters fate seems to have placed something uncannily relevant on my path. Here are a few examples:

My French writing partner Jacqueline sends me her three great pieces for *Versopolis* on Flaubert and Kafka, two of the authors to whom I write. Of course, this should not have come as a surprise since we seem to be so "in synch" with each other on so many levels. This fortuitous situation has led to a collaboration that has greatly improved my translations of her work.

*

The Meursault Investigation

A book by the Goncourt-winning author of a new work inspired by Camus's *The Stranger* adds food for thought to my lifelong conversations with Camus. In what looks like a case of bad timing, while I am on leave from my Yale teaching and living in Italy, the very author of that book, Kamel Daoud, comes to Yale to give a lecture. But before I can lament too much having missed a chance to hear him, my chairman, Alice Kaplan, sends a message to say that his Yale lecture is now available on line.

*

Further, I never expected to be able, thanks to the Internet, to study videotapes of my correspondents such as Nabokov, Christo, and André Aciman, but I had the good fortune to stumble on these during my research.

*

In a charity used bookstore in London, while thinking about Roland Barthes, I came across a brilliant explanation of Roland Barthes' theories in the form of a sort of comic book (Philip Thody's *Introducing Barthes: A Graphic Guide)*.

*

Just as I was rereading my letter to Romain Gary, a message from maRATP, the French metro company, urges me to give my adored novels a second life by donating them to a good cause that encourages reading. And which book do they picture in their come-on? My favorite book by Romain Gary, *La promesse de l'aube!* I'm sorry, but no way am I giving away that one!

P.S. Three

My Ionesco connection keeps returning, and Eugène brings along with him hints of Proust and Nabokov's *Speak, Memory.*

What follows is from my 1966-67 Paris Junior Year Abroad roommate, Karen, who had the good sense to maintain a journal of her experiences of our year in France. She recently sent photographs of some of the journal pages, and although I remember much of what she describes, it is fascinating to see our life in the former Sartre apartment through someone else's eyes. In searching for a dramatic way to title what she wrote, I came up with, "She was there: Eyewitness Account of the Bloody Events of January 5."

Of course, I can't speak as an observer about what it was like to find me collapsed on the bathroom floor in a sea of blood after returning sick from Christmas vacation.

With two friends from the Hamilton program, I had gone to London, Frankfurt, and Amsterdam. But at the end, I had taken off on my own for Amersfoort, Holland, to visit my 6'6" Dutch friend, Joop. There, I got a warm reception, but passed the coldest night of my life sleeping in an unheated guest room where, despite having covered myself with every huge woolen suit jacket of Joop's that I found in the closet, I could still see my own breath.

I had had a bad cold even before that, for which I had taken some unfamiliar remedies. And I must have been run down from all the traveling. While in England, we three travel mates had stayed in a cheap place that had its own version of central heating: Located in the center of the room was a radiator into which you had to keep inserting coins in order to get any heat. Even with three of us, we ran out of change pretty quickly.

The night I got back to Paris, I had a massive GI hemorrhage that was thought to have been a reaction to the larger amount of aspirin in European over-the-counter cold remedies. I was told to beware of aspirin for the rest of my life. I was just lucky that this happened in my French home, and not the previous night when I was all alone sleeping in a cheap garret hotel room in London prior to my return to Paris.

Poor Karen! And my worried French family! My own parents weren't quite as concerned since they got a reassuring letter from the head of the American Hospital, once the situation was in hand.

What Karen doesn't recall is that the emergency doctor who came to the house in the middle of the night to decide what to do with me was a gentle, young Vietnamese. And there he was, ministering to me, citizen of a country that was in the process of bombing the bejeezus out of his native land. Sick as I was, the irony of that did not escape me. His decision to pack me off to the American Hospital by ambulance that very night turned out to be the right one. But I don't think Karen has correct the date of my return. I think that my scrapbook (now in shreds but carefully packed up back in America) would corroborate that I was in the hospital for 11 days, after which I emerged, transfused and strong, to enjoy the rest of my junior year abroad.

The American Hospital was a posh place that took care of bigwigs like Aristotle Onassis, as well as of "little wigs" like Diane Joy Gillman of Middletown, New York. I recall that my hospital roommate, Eve, had flown in from South Africa for an elective operation. We hit it off, and she gifted me with an ivory bangle bracelet that I still have.

I also remember my French mother, Mme. Peguillan, dressed in her finest (kid gloves included) coming to visit me. This required quite a number of metro trains, since the hospital was at the other end of Paris from our fifth arrondissement home. The Hamilton Program head, Professor Marcel Moraud, sent assistant director of the program, Mme. Alice Triantafilou, to see me, too. I felt very important, a bit like one of the characters from the French nineteenth-century novels I loved.

I remember well the young residents who took good care of me, especially the cute red-headed one who missed his fiancée. The other well-meaning one was sweet but clumsy. After his many messy attempts to find a vein to draw my blood, a distinguished surgeon took only a painless second to insert a fine needle into the back of my hand. That was an unforgettable first for healthy me, who had never needed to know I had tricky little collapsible veins that could be outsmarted like that. I've kept that tactic filed in the back of my mind for future reference.

Anyway, although a madeleine dipped in linden tea might have tasted better, I am very grateful to Karen for sharing her version of this particular memory, and her offering some other snapshots of our French family life.

December 2: We just got the word that Jean-Philippe has scarlet fever, which is terrible for him. Meanwhile, Bertrand, Diane and I have to take 9 pills a day (6 penicillin) as a preventative measure.

January 17: Oh yes - the big news of today is that after 4 months of not seeing a barber, Bertrand got his hair cut. It really looks different. He went to a photo machine and took "before" and "after" pictures, so he could show everyone how much better (?) it looked longer."

February 1: Today was the day of the grève. It was crazy because the metros were running but the people who sell and punch tickets were on strike, so you could ride the metro free. (Note from Diane: This was the year just before the time of the 1968 student riots that shut down the Sorbonne and resulted in much destruction in the streets, not to mention no academic credit for students who had come to Paris to study abroad that year.)

March 2: After supper we* all...played Monopoly in French. Instead of Atlantic City, it was Paris streets... It was really fun and weird because the exact same rules were used. (* "we" was Bertrand and his friends Thierry and Michel, you, me and Jean-Philippe)

Karen adds, "I notice the journal entries got fewer and fewer as time passed. Ah well, at least I have something to help me jog my memory.

Hope you're enjoying your time in Italy!—love, Karen"

P.S. Four

Will I ever stop writing to Marcel Proust? Obviously not!

Dear Marcel,

It's 2016 and a dear friend is being treated for a rare cancer. She misses France, and I wanted her to have a little souvenir from our recent trip there—my first return since teaching in Paris in 2008.

My husband was heading to Rome today for work, and I knew he was going to be visiting Shirley. I wrapped up a little gift package, French-style (but not anywhere near as prettily as they would have done it). It contained a few mini-madeleines. I cut out a little heart that I attached to the box and wrote, "Are you ready for your Proustian moment?"

Shirley is not much of a tea drinker, but in an attempt to seduce her, I included a sensual teabag of a favorite flavor, Thé des Alizés (Tea of the Trade Winds) from Le Palais des Thés: *A green tea enlivened by flower petals and delicately scented with pieces of white peach, kiwi and watermelon. The green tea and the juicy freshness of the fruit are wonderfully balanced. Can be drunk hot or iced.*

Who could resist their description? Maybe Shirley can. She is doing an amazing job of resisting discouragement in the face of the threats to her health. But I can also count on her not to mince words. We'll see if she takes the bait and downs those madeleines with my luscious tea or insists on accompanying them with a decadent cappuccino.

P.S. Five

Dear Diane Joy Gillman Charney,

Aren't you the kid who, when asked in sixth grade what you wanted to be when grew up said, "I'm going to be a writer?"

And is this not the year in which you will celebrate your 70th birthday?

Never mind all those better-late-than-never clichés. Aren't you a little slow on the uptake?

I'm just sayin'.

—xxx, you-know-who

P.S. Six

More from the Weird Connections Department—

As I look out at the Umbrian countryside from our renovated ruin in Italy, it strikes me that the motif we chose for the wrought iron that outlines every window looks like a butterfly. Was my connection with Nabokov subconsciously pushing me in that direction?

Next, I recall a link to the Yale colleague and now friend who really taught me about patterning in Nabokov, Vladimir Alexandov. I once saw his young daughter perform a ballet dance dressed in a butterfly costume. Then, he tells me recently that he enjoyed meeting my letter recipient André Aciman at a Writers' Retreat where both were working on projects.

This reminded me of the days when Aciman was less well known outside academic circles, and I used to have to explain who he was, before going on about my passion for his writing. But since he knocked the ball out of the park with the film of his *Call Me By Your Name*, that is no longer necessary.

Right now, I can see my father, who always loved such "small world" moments, smiling about these serendipitous interconnections.

P.S. Seven

I'm so busy writing to my favorite men of letters that I don't usually pay too much attention to what's going on in the life of Hollywood stars. An exception is when I'm getting a haircut, and I think this is how I came across a July 15, 2016 *NYTimes T Style Magazine* article about the longstanding correspondence between film star Natalie Portman and writer Jonathan Safran Foer. I did not know that they had been exchanging emails "about family, creativity and angry koalas" until earlier this year, when their epistolary archive mysteriously disappeared. On the eve of Portman's ambitious directorial debut, the old friends start anew, reconnecting online to reflect on how the times have changed, and how they themselves have changed over time.

I'm no beautiful, intelligent actress like Natalie Portman posing in high-fashion bikinis. Or a hugely appealing famous author like Jonathan Safran Foer. But these letters of mine to the men of letters I have been carrying around with me appear to be serving a purpose similar to theirs. And I'm thinking that my letters and theirs might be something to which other passionate readers can relate. I have always loved portraits in most any medium. I can happily lose (and find?) myself in the Yale British Art Center and the British Portrait Gallery. All those human faces that have transcended time and place, and permitted me to look them in the eye. I don't necessarily know much about them, but nevertheless I feel a connection. This is happening as I read about Portman's and Foer's emails.

Portman talks about her changing response over the years to Amos Oz's memoir, "A Tale of Love and Darkness," the film version of which she will direct. Portman considers what her reaction to this and other books reveals about her own evolution. Her words rang bells for me as I thought about my ever-changing but ongoing relationship to my men of letters.

Furthermore, as a downsizing hoarder who recently had to make some painful decisions about what to do with a lifetime of "treasures," I was identifying with what it would be like to have everything just disappear in one fell swoop. Would I feel bereft? Liberated? I found

Portman's attitude toward her vanished letter exchange instructive: "I was happy to think of the lost correspondence being somehow replenished with, or redeemed by, a new exchange."

Another of Portman's and Foer's comments on the subject of Wonder resonated for me. He talked about a dinner game his family plays called the Wonder Line:

> If one of the kids can tell me something that generates the experience of wonder — the cocked head, slight nod, raised eyebrow and muttered "hmmm ..." — we call it "clearing the Wonder Line." If they can clear it five times, they get to decide how we end the night, i.e., have ice cream, or watch a "Pirates of the Caribbean" iteration.

I like to think of my "In Love with France, At Home in Italy" blog as the place where I record my moments of Wonder (and also plenty of things that my ignorant self wonders about) as I try to learn a new culture.

Portman also considers the difficulty of living one's life and working, versus writing about it. She says, "I like weekends better when I'm working because then they truly feel like I'm regenerating energy, whereas when I'm not working, time blends into one continuous, undifferentiated stream." Like Portman, I've noticed that my own best ideas often come when I'm too busy to do much about them. Is it the contrast between busyness and work that makes time so precious? And if I retire, as I am poised to do, how will I feel?

I also feel in synch with Foer's sensitivity to the aura of a place. About the idea of touring Gettysburg, he notes,

> I never have followed through on my threats of a tour, but Gettysburg's presence is constantly felt while in the area: the innumerable signs commemorating battles, the ammunition in the antiques shops, the memorials. It also exudes a ghostly aura. I feel silly writing that, but there's nothing silly or ignorable about the feeling. And it isn't just the proximity to

history. It's something else—something in the air, and in the ground. Are there places where you feel a "something else"?

This question of aura is something to which I find it easy to relate. I want to mention two examples.

My brother and his family live in the lovely Cape Cod house that his wife inherited from her maiden aunts—two elementary school teachers revered in their little town of Onset whom I had never met. But the minute I set foot in that simple house, with its burnished wood that shines with the patina of age, I feel a special aura. I could give a number of examples of the places and spaces where I have had formative experiences that seem to have retained an aura.

My other example concerns the male half of our architect team. We became very close to the architect couple who helped us find and completely renovate the former ruin in the Italian countryside where we now live. I fervently wish that "live," the verb I just used, could apply to Daniele, whom we lost last year to pancreatic cancer.

Although their own renovated ruin in another part of the countryside could not be more beautiful, we learned that years ago, Gabriella and Daniele had first tried to buy a property near ours in a deal that fell through at the last moment. That very "Italian" situation also happened to us several times before, on the fourth try, we succeeded in getting the right property.

In all of their work, our architects Gabriella and Daniele regularly brought their expertise and creative genius to bear. But perhaps as a result of their special attachment to the area where their youthful selves had hoped to set down roots, they put their collective heart and soul into our project.

I don't think I have ever known a couple so joined at the hip. Gabriella even went so far as to develop a more treatable form of the same disease that killed him. Their work skills were diverse but entirely complementary, and in their very different temperaments, they also seemed to complete each other.

Now that Daniele is gone, despite her pride at having collaborated to make something as beautiful as our home, it is emotionally hard for Gabriella to be in either their house or mine.

I have a special memory of an early spring moment before our project got under way. There were wild daffodils growing on our un-tamed hillside, and Daniele rushed down to scoop up a bouquet for me. His smile as he extended it is etched in my memory. I haven't dis-cussed this with Gabriella, but I think I sensed then the shared aura of death and daffodils that this place has for all of us.

After our renovation was completed, I looked anxiously toward the site of those wild daffodils. Could they have survived all the up-heaval of construction?

I shouldn't have worried. Who knows how many generations they have witnessed? Like Daniele's spirit, and that of the Men of Letters to whom I write, they are still here.

P.S. Eight

Dear Camus,

While we are on the subject of spirits that are always with me, I want to say a word about mothers. I know that you were very at-tached to yours.

While teaching your *L'Étranger,* one of the Yale grad student in-structors who was a member of our teaching team lost her mother, giv-ing extra poignancy to the opening lines of your novel, "Aujourd'hui maman est morte. Ou peut-être hier. Je ne sais pas." ("Mother died today. Or maybe yesterday. I can't be sure.") Ever since reading those words for the first time in 1962, I knew that one day I might be saying their equivalent. That moment has come.

In my earlier letter to your Meursault, instead of the too-facile interpretation of him as a strange, unfeeling monster worthy of the guillotine, I talked about understanding how an only son could have been so disoriented by his mother's death that he lost all sense of time.

I empathize with his disorientation even more acutely now, hav-ing lost my own mother very recently. Let's see. Exactly when was it? Yesterday? A week ago Wednesday? I would have to look at the calendar to be sure.

Since this is a book titled *Letters to Men of Letters* I won't be writing my mom a letter here, but I am dedicating this book to her. She was 93.5 years young when she died while I was in the final stages of readying this book for publication.

I have always been moved by another affecting line from your book that comes out of the mouth of Meursault's kindly, guileless neighbor Émile from whom he asks to borrow a black armband that shows he is in mourning. The plain-speaking Émile gives it to him and says, compassionately, "On n'a qu'une mère." ("One only has one mother"). Simply put, and true.

Thank you, Albert Camus, for giving me, fifty-six years ago, the words I needed today.

This book is for Edith Elaine Gillman, beloved by all, and a gentle force for good. August 1, 1924-March 7, 2018.

P.S. Nine

Mirella and Me

By standard measures of time, Mirella and I may seem like relatively new friends. But in our case, that feels like an illusion. When it comes to literary soulmates, time follows an arc of its own. In fact, the previous observation is what drives my *Letters to Men of Letters*.

The friendship between Mirella and me blossomed this year in the wake of the loss of a dear mutual friend who, although a fellow forever Francophile, was very different from us. Even so, I like to think that Shirley is smiling down on our collaboration.

Yet when I first decided to call the last chapter of my book "Post Scripts to Myself, My Book is Never Over," Shirley was still with us. In "P.S. Four" of that chapter, I wrote about trying to persuade Shirley to become infatuated with the sensual tea I had gifted her to accompany some buttery mini-madeleines. I had hoped the combination would offer her a Proustian moment while she appeared to be holding her own against an insidious blood cancer. But it was a "no go" on all counts. Ever a woman of strong opinions, no way was Shirley going to be seduced into forsaking her beloved cappuccino by some flowery language, even if it was in French. And no way was that cancer going to let go.

But here we still are, Mirella and me. I have never met anyone like her. Although Mirella has had much sadness in her life, her deep sensitivity to beauty sustains her. At times the strength of her passions can overwhelm her, but always in a good way. In her artistry, Mirella incarnates Baudelaire's poem, "Enivrez-vous" in which he exhorts us all to intoxicate ourselves with the passion of our choice. He declaims that such a stance can be the only bulwark against the curveballs that will inevitably come our way. Mirella has understood this approach to life in a highly visceral manner. Thanks to her total engagement in her art, whatever the obstacle, Mirella quietly forges ahead.

Mirella invited us to her recent exhibit at the French Institute Bookstore in Rome. She and Shirley had met and become friends in the French classes they attended at the Institute. A very private person, Mirella does not often have house guests, and we were honored to be

invited to stay overnight at her place. My husband and I, former restaurant critics, remain obsessed foodies, whereas vegan Mirella lives on a tight budget and eats like a bird. That difference did not stop her from planning perfect meals for us, and being an ideal hostess. To our mutual delight, as we roamed the city together over the course of a day and half, we found ourselves on the same wave length.

Superficial differences

be damned! What are the chances that Mirella and I would end up wearing nearly identically-colored outfits during the visit to her exhibit? As the photos we took that day demonstrate, the answer is 100 percent.

It was a privilege to see so many of my favorite authors adorning the walls of Mirella's combination home-studio. And of course these did not include the many portraits already on exhibit.

With respect to the official exhibit, in her characteristically modest, non-materialistic fashion, Mirella had been shy about making it clear to visitors that her displayed art work was for sale. A savvy friend had made a price list on Mirella's behalf, but I had to ask the bookstore staff to see it. It took two people a while to locate it behind one of the portraits.

It was not easy to decide which painting to buy. But then the answer became clear. I have been writing to and about Albert Camus forever, and I doubt that will change. But now, thanks to the talents of my colleague and fellow Francophile, artist Mirella Daniel, I will always have him nearby.

In noticing how many favorite authors we share whom she had serendipitously already painted, Mirella generously offered to allow me to use her portraits in the print edition of my Letters to Men of Letters. After seeing the author photographs in the ebook version, Mirella found herself inspired to portray twelve of them with whom she feels a particular affinity. I feel very fortunate to have such a unique, talented friend whose art so wonderfully complements my vision for this book.

Acknowledgements

Where would a certified technodunce like me be without my husband, James Charney, who helped keep my hysteria under control and rescued me from computer jams that no one could imagine how I got into. His good editorial eye is another talent that he has shared with me.

And where would a mother who has had lifelong quirky relationships with authors living and dead be without a son who thought she ought to write about them? Thanks to my proudest production, Noah, for inspiring and shepherding this project from beginning to end.

My brilliant Italian "writing partner," Erika Bizzarri, read and reread every word of this book, offering insightful comments every step of the way.

Jacqueline Raoul-Duval, my French writing partner, gave ongoing support and inspiration for many of these Letters.

Among my colleagues and friends who read parts of this work are André Aciman, Vladimir Alexandrov, Constance Sherak, Lauren Pinzka, Ruth Koizim, Martha Crockett Lancaster, Susan Roe Gravina, Ian Morley, Michael Jacobs of Abrams Books, and Karen George Watson.

My thanks to Frank Juska for suggesting the letterbox image.

The author is grateful to the Christo Foundation for their interest in my Letter to Christo and for their kind permission to use the accompanying photo.

Credit for the beauty of the original ebook goes to patient and masterful designer Uroš de Gleria.

The print version of this book owes its existence to the talents, support, and encouragement of my wonderful daughter-in-law, Urška Charney.